Otaku Trash

Adelaide Newton

For Carmelle-chan for introducing me to anime and manga.

For Alice for the company through the experience that is growing up in #villagelife.

For Stinky-dog for the countryside walks - miss you.

And for my parents for the continued support.

Chapter 1

Rose

Trampled to death by cows while trapped inside a Ford Focus is not the way I expected to go, but life makes fools of us all.

And over the last few weeks I've felt the Universe has been having a good laugh at me.

"Jesus," Mum swears, as one black and white tank runs down the side of the road, kicking up its back legs. Ahead of us, at least a dozen others surge along the tarmac like a bovine tsunami, their tails swishing, heads bobbing, while that weird bit of skin swings between their front legs. I swear they look at us through the windscreen as they charge the car. Mum's knuckles glow white on the steering wheel and suddenly it's a lot harder to breathe.

Dear Universe. Is this your way of punishing me for not heeding the call of veganism? I tried, I really did, but the creamy temptation of cheese and the saltiness of bacon is just too much. I mean, I've been a good flexitarian, haven't I? Think of all those times I opted for the veggie option, all that falafel and humus I've eaten, and that nut milk I've started buying. So, please, don't let this be the way I go.

Although, the Universe is not at fault for putting me in this situation. That award goes to Mum and her stupid but awesome new job in Dubai. If she hadn't taken it, I'd still be in London, with all my stuff in its allotted place, not squashed into boxes in the back of the car. I wouldn't be in the middle of nowhere, busting for the loo, and would only be at risk from a normal death like being mowed down by a rickshaw driver looking at his phone.

A quadbike zips along the outside of the cows. A guy, who I can only describe as a hipster farmer, sits on it with a brown and black dog perched on the back. He zips to the front of the tsunami, while another man rushes down the outside and stands in front of our stalled car. For a dumb moment I think he's going to do some Chris Pratt velociraptor shit, but instead of trying to calm the walking beef burgers, he shouts at them and claps his hands. He must be some sort of cow whisperer, because the cows move off the road and onto the verge. A short woman herds the last of the cows past us. The cow whisperer pats the car bonnet.

"No need to look so worried," he says, "they won't hurt you."

Mum gives him a nervous smile in reply, but as he walks away, she whispers, “Jesus,” and restarts the engine.

“I thought you said Helen and Clover lived in a safe and secluded village,” I say, watching the cows retreat into the distance in the wing mirror.

“It’s as safe as any village,” Mum replies.

The Focus trundles down the road and bounces over a pothole. My head brushes the car ceiling from the force of it. If the cows don’t get me, these crater-studded deathtraps of roads will. Mum leans forward, peering closely at every house we pass.

“Now which one is it...” she mutters.

Since seeing the Harboury village sign, we’ve only passed seven houses and a church, and now with another ten ahead of us the other village sign is visible at the end of the road. Mum wasn’t kidding when she said this place was *small*. Like, there’s fewer houses here than on my street in London. And there’s so much space. Endless fields in every direction with glimpses of other villages in the distance. The thought of what could be lurking in those fields, inside those hedges, ready to grab me as I walk by makes my skin prickle. I mean, I haven’t even seen a village shop. Dark ages central. Bet they still get cases of the black death here.

And I’m going to be living here for two years with an aunt and cousin I haven’t - apparently - seen in thirteen years, while Mum and Dad live it large in Dubai. They’ll be dining at Michelin-star restaurants and going on luxury yacht rides while I attend pagan sacrifices.

Although, I guess I made my choice. Because that life

could have been mine, but I chose this instead of living in a country where I a) don't know anyone apart from my parents, and b) would have to start my first year of A levels not only in a new school, but also in a new country. And, "No, Rose, you are too young to live on your own, so it's either come with us, or live with your estranged aunt and cousin in the middle of the Shire." Now I have to live with my choice. My stomach twists into a knot and the air in the car suddenly feels even stuffier.

"Ah, damn!" Mum mutters as we drive past another cottage. "I think that was it. Need to find somewhere to turn around..."

"What are Helen and Clover like?" I ask, for what must be the dozenth time. But I need to talk – I need to reassure myself that I am not about to make the worst mistake of my life stranding myself here.

"Oh," Mum says. She pulls the car into a field entrance and turns us around. "Helen's nice. She's chill. She's all into spiritual energy and tarot card readings and stuff. Grows her own fruit and veg, you know. Lives her best country life. From what Helen tells me, Clover's very arty." She sighs and the weight of that sigh settles on my shoulders. "I'm sorry I can't tell you much more – that this is the first time you're really meeting them. But this is your time to really get to know them. Here we are." Mum flicks on the indicator and pulls into a brick driveway. We rattle over a cattle grid—

And nearly run over a cat sitting on the drive.

Mum slams on the brakes and we jerk forward in our seats. "Jesus!" she says again.

By now the poor man's ears must be burning like

freshly fried doughnuts.

The cat stares at us in contempt for a moment before sauntering off. I can almost hear Mum's heart pounding in her chest as she pulls up behind a small car parked in front of the house, her eyes scanning the last few metres to ensure no other animals are going to get in our path.

We both sigh with relief as she kills the engine.

"There," she says, undoing her seat belt.

"And we only died nearly, what, like, five times?"

"There was no danger of death when I overtook that tractor."

"There was a dip in the road. You had no idea what was coming."

"Well, there are dips in the road everywhere here. We'd never have arrived if I hadn't taken the chance." Mum rests her hand on the door handle. "Rose, you know if things don't work out, we can sort something out. Helen assures me the school is great, but if you really hate it let me know. And you can come visit us every school holiday if you want to – not just in February half-term. OK?"

I nod. There's a wetness behind my eyes. "OK."

Mum gives me another smile and pops the door handle. "Come on. Let's meet the family."

The cottage is painted white with a brown roof. It *looks* old, with its slightly lean-to structure and lots of plants creeping up the outside, although the windows are plastic. It's nice, though in a cute way – the sort of house you would see in an influencers' Insta post about their long weekend in the country.

As I pop the boot and start assessing the damage on

my boxes, the front door opens and a white woman dressed in a long floaty skirt and top, adorned with lots of jewellery, with a thick hairband pushing back her bushy hair hurries towards us, her face alight with joy. I guess that this is my spiritual Aunt Helen.

"Hello!" she says.

"Hi," Mum replies, mirroring my aunt's smile.

The two women step up to each other and pause. Their arms strain at their sides, reaching to hug each other, but for a few seconds neither of them move. I can sense the barrier between them that the thirteen years of separation has built. There's a hesitation in Mum's eyes that I'm not used to seeing, like she's considering turning away, but then my aunt's arms wrap around her and the look disappears. Mum returns her hug with the same ferocity. They rock on the spot, going back and forth with the usual "How are you?" and "It's so lovely to see you". I watch them from the back of the car, my mum and aunt together for the first time in my memory. It's strange, seeing this woman who obviously means so much to my mum but means nothing to me but should.

They break apart and I step around the side of the car where Helen greets me. "Hello, Rose."

"Hi," I say. I should add a noun, but she doesn't feel like an auntie, or an Aunt Helen, and it's too soon to call her Helen.

Helen doesn't care, because she opens her arms and says, "Do you do hugs?" I nod and her bangles jangle as she envelops me into her arms. It's a short hug, but the love radiates from her.

"You're all grown up," she says, her voice now tight.

“The last time I saw you, you were this tall—” she puts a hand to her hip, “—and *obsessed* with *Angelina Ballerina*.”

“Wasn’t everyone obsessed with that show?” I ask and Helen laughs.

“Clover was as well, although she’ll never admit to it now. How was the drive?”

“Fine,” Mum says, “although we were nearly mowed down by a herd of cows as we entered the village.”

“That would have been the Dales. They asked me to help out, but I said I had some very important guests to wait at home for.”

“Are you still working over there?” Mum asks.

“When they need me and I haven’t got clients to see. Right, come on inside. I bet you’re both busting for the loo.”

But as we turn towards the front door, a white girl dressed in a pair of tatty jeans, an over-sized black hoodie and a pair of chunky worn boots comes around the side of the house. Her electric blue hair falls to her shoulders, thick and straight. A chocolate Labrador trots beside her on a short lead. The dog’s ears perk up and its tail starts whirling like a helicopter blade. My heart melts. Finally, after suicidal cats and death-homing cows, here is an animal I can love.

I want to crouch down and spread my arms wide, ready to receive the slobbering puppy affection, but the girl tugs on the lead and whispers, “Come on,” and quickens her pace. She doesn’t even glance at us.

An awful feeling sinks to the pit of my stomach.

Dear Universe. Please don’t let this surly girl be my cousin.

"Hi, Clover," Mum calls and waves.

Goddammit, Universe.

"Clo!" Helen calls. "Come say hello."

But Clover is already out the gate and has disappeared behind a hedge.

"Sorry," Helen says. "She's still getting used to the change." She puts an arm around my shoulders and steers me towards the house. "She'll come around, don't worry. Tea?"

"Coffee would be amazing," Mum says.

The chance to rewind my life a few months would be amazing, I think but say, "Either's great."

Chapter 2

Clover

The sound of the car engine running in the driveway makes my stomach drop. My hands still on the sketchpad, in the middle of an arc, as a vehicle pulls into the driveway.

Throwing my sketchpad onto my desk, I dash out of my bedroom, across the sunken landing and into the spare room that overlooks the front of the house. Slowly, trying not to let too much of my face show in the window in case someone looks up, I peer outside, wanting to see this mysterious cousin that is invading my house and my life for two years.

I hope she changes her mind.

I hope she turns around and leaves.

I hope she wants to be here as little as I want her to be here.

“Please,” I whisper. “Please.”

The silver car door opens. A Black lady with a head of dark short curls gets out of the driver’s side. With her jeans, jacket and suede boots combo, she looks like she’s stepped right off the page of a fashion magazine. Aunt Claire, I’m guessing. Then the passenger door opens, and a girl in a floaty summer dress and sandals, who looks her mum’s spitting image, except with faded sides to her short dark curls and wearing round thick-framed glasses, climbs out. Like she’s stepped out of a taxi onto Oxford Street.

Yup. This isn’t going to work.

Because there is no way she and I will see eye to eye. This is gearing up to be a massive train wreck.

I withdraw my phone from my pocket as I dash back to my room. Downstairs, Mum shouts, “Clo! They’re here!”, but the words

Ko-chan
Where are you?

are already typed on the screen. I smash the send button as I grab a clean pair of walking socks.

I reach the bottom of the stairs. The front door is wide open and Mum has her sister wrapped in her arms. I hurry past, ducking low for all the good it will do me, and scuttle into the kitchen. In the utility room, Bonnie looks up from her bed. As soon as she sees the walking socks, her tail starts to thump against the floor and her tongue lolls out of her mouth.

"Walkies?" I whisper, which makes her ears go up. I smile and grab my walking boots from the shoe rack, just as Leon's text comes through.

Lee-kun
In the field down the road
Finished herding the cows

Ko-chan
Be right there
Aunt and cousin have just arrived
I NEED TO ESCAPE!

I shove my phone into my pocket, not wanting to see Leon's inevitable reply telling me to make an effort to get to know my cousin before I start rejecting them. But I know - I just know that it's pointless. There is no way a girl like her in her catwalk outfit and a girl like me will ever get on.

Eleven years of school have taught me that much.

Faster than I've ever dressed, I pull my boots on and lace them up like a pro. Now Bonnie is whining at the back door, dancing around like the floor is made of lava. So she doesn't shoot off the moment I crack it open, I clip her lead onto her collar.

"Stealth mode today, Bonnie," I say, but she still strains at her lead when we step outside. The abnormally hot August sun strikes my pale skin with a blazing vengeance. I could double back and grab my sun cream, but no. If I do, there's no way I'll be able to escape the incoming awkward first meeting. This is the coward's way out - the awkward first meeting is going to happen sooner rather than later – but I can't deal now. My anger at this whole situation is bubbling under my skin and I might lose control of it if I have to pretend to be happy that my home is no longer my one safe space.

I'm taking the flight option, so I can live to fight another day.

My mistake becomes clear as I step around the side of the house. I thought by now Mum would have dragged them inside, but they're still talking on the driveway.

I could duck back around the side of the house, but Rose has already seen us. Well, she's seen Bonnie and her eyes are wide and sappy. In response, Bonnie's tail becomes a blur.

"Come on," I whisper and tug on her lead. Eyes ahead, Clover. Perhaps you can still get away with this. Perhaps Mum and Aunt Claire won't—

"Hi, Clover," Aunt Claire says.

Holy cow balls. Code red. Upthrust the boosters. Increase velocity. Abort! Abort!

"Clo!" Mum calls. "Come say hello."

But my trusty legs have already carried me out the gate and around the side of the hedge. Out of sight and onto safety. I take a deep breath and the tension in my shoulders slides away, even though there is a small voice in the back of my head telling me that was a very rude thing to do. That small voice can go to hell.

I find Leon and his dad, Robert, behind the gate, watching the cows spread out across the field. Alexander – Leon's black and tan huntaway – spots us before they do. He starts barking as I let Bonnie off the lead and push the gate back, allowing her through. Robert calms him down as I slip into the field.

"Silly dog," Robert says. "You know who that is."

Alexander stops barking when Bonnie wanders over to him for a sniff.

"Hey," Leon says.

"Squidge," I reply. Leon shuffles forward on the quadbike and I squeeze on behind him, the side of my shoulder against his back. Bonnie and Alexander have finished sniffing each other's butts and are snuffling some fresh cowpats away from the herd.

"Think we saw your aunt and cousin arrive," Leon says.

Robert chuckles. "They looked frozen in fear at the sight of the herd coming down the road."

"Well, they are from London," I point out. "Don't suppose they get cows being herded down Oxford Street."

Leon's elbows me in the side. "And why are you here, rather than greeting them?"

A lump of mud stuck on the side of the quadbike suddenly needs my undivided attention. I pick at it with my stubby nails, feeling Leon's judging stare on me. Robert has wandered off across the field to check a piece of fence. The cows are now munching on the grass. Looking out across the expanse of patchwork fields, I find inner peace and forget everything that's going on at home.

That is until Leon says, "Clo, you need to try to get to know her. She might be really nice."

The mud comes off the side of the bike and lands on the ground with a soft thud. I think of Rose's make-uped face and flowing summer dress, and a lump of dread weighs down my chest. "We're not going to get along."

"Why not?"

"She's just... one of those girls."

Leon twists in his seat. "What does that even mean?"

I shrug, although I know very well what it means, but Leon doesn't get it. It's easy for him at an all-boys school. No one there has given him any grief for what he likes. I've taken hell for it, mostly given by girls who make nasty comments about other girls who don't look like they've come off an assembly line.

The little voice starts to murmur again, but I squash it before it gets too loud. Bonnie comes over to me, nose to the ground, with Alexander beside her. I run my hand along her wiry coat as she passes, and end up brushing out a handful of hair. Most of it drifts away on the thin wind – I wipe the rest of it off onto my walking trousers.

"You won't know until you talk to her," Leon says. "Give her a chance."

I pull a face. "No promises. You up for a binge session before we go back to school?"

"Sure thing, as long as you don't make me watch the newest season of *Free!*"

I gasp and press my hand to my chest. "I'm insulted you thought I would have waited for you to watch it." I've been hopping on each episode the moment they're released. No one keeps me from my swimming boys. I've waited four years for them to dive back into my life. Even though there hasn't been enough MakoHaru fanservice to satisfy me this season.

"Have you watched *Megalobox* yet?" I ask.

"Nope, and don't give me that look."

"You've got your back to me. You can't see what look I'm giving you."

"That 'I-can't-believe-you-haven't-watched-this-anime-yet-because-it's-been-out-for-a-whole-year' look. I can't watch anime as fast as you."

"It only finished airing in June, and I've accepted that your love for anime isn't as all-consuming as mine. But if you haven't watched it, then we can watch it together."

"Alright. Why don't you invite the cousin along?"

I snort. "I don't think she's into anime."

"Have you asked her?"

"No. And I'm not going to. Because she isn't. And—" I pull on my hoodie sleeves, "—I don't want the risk of her telling anyone at school."

Leon's voice softens. "Alright." And the tightness inside me uncoils. He might not have to keep his interests hidden like I do, but after the last couple of years at least he understands why I do. "Where are you and Bonnie going for a walk?"

I shrug. "I just wanted to get out the house."

"Want to come back to the farm? There's a shit tonne of mucking out to do. I can lend you Genny's overalls."

I laugh. "Who could resist such an offer?"

Chapter 3

Rose

The inside of Aunt Helen's house looks like the interior of a vegan café and smells like a Yankee Candle shop. The floors are all wooden and the walls all off white, but she's brightened the place up with some funky wall hangings, rugs and blankets. Every piece of furniture looks upcycled. There are candles, incense burners and diffusers on most surfaces. And any space that isn't taken up by fragrance, or tiny statues, or crystals, is taken up by plants. The living room is a jungle of tall spiky foliage, hanging terrariums and broad-leaf monsters.

The Universe is strong with this one.

And I'm sort of loving it. It's completely different to

the polished dark wood feel of my house. Although as we enter the hallway I notice a really ugly Victorian-looking vase on a table by the door. It's brown with frilly handles, top and base, with a small vignette painting in the middle of a man and woman standing in a field, kissing. It looks so out of place – like a telephone box in an Apple store.

"Oh, god," Mum says. "You don't still have that old thing, do you?"

Helen sighs. "I can't very well put it away when she comes over all the time. She'll *comment* if it's not there."

I take a guess that they're talking about Grandma.

We have coffee and cake – lemon and blueberry, made by Clover – in the jungle, and Helen shows me to my room. The upstairs is sort of trippy. The staircase goes up from the hallway, reaching a pinnacle, and drops a few steps down into a large sunken landing with four doors off it, which are accessible up short flights of steps. The doors to the rooms are all wooden with iron latches – instead of shiny chrome door handles. Inside, there's a double bed, a small wardrobe, a chest of draws, and a desk and chair. A huge wall tapestry of a sunset mountain range and forest, strung along the top with fairy lights, hangs above the bed. The window looks out at the side of the house into the wide strip of garden and the fence between next door.

It's nice.

But it's not *mine*.

"Clover's room is opposite yours," Helen says, nodding at the door across the sunken landing. "The door to the right leads to the bathroom. I'm just there, near the stairs. I have my own bathroom, so you don't have to worry about sharing with me. There's also another toilet and shower room by the kitchen. We mostly use that for hosing down Bonnie after a walk but feel free to use it in an emergency."

I nod, too choked to speak.

Helen understands, because she squeezes my shoulder and leaves me to catch my breath. Once I'm no longer on the verge of tears, I go back downstairs and help unload the car. Too soon my new bedroom is full of boxes. The moment I've been dreading has finally arrived.

I cling to Mum tight as we hug in the hallway. And I'm sure she hugs me back with the same intensity.

"Call me anytime you want," she tells me. "All the time. I won't care. Well, perhaps not when I'm flying or in a meeting."

"You're flying on Saturday, right?" I ask.

"Right. I'll let you know when I've arrived at the house."

She kisses my forehead and hugs her sister goodbye.

"I'll take good care of her," Helen says.

"I know you will," Mum replies. Then we're waving goodbye to her from the house doorway, watching the Ford zoom out of sight, leaving me with a hollowness in my stomach and questioning whether I've just made the biggest mistake of my life.

"Do you want any company while you unpack?" Helen asks.

I should, probably, use the time to get to know my new aunt, but right now I want to be alone, so I push my glasses up my face and say, "I'm OK, thank you."

"Alright. Dinner's at six thirty, normally. Shout if you

need anything, and don't be afraid to rummage in the cupboards if you want a snack or drink. There's plenty more of that cake."

She disappears into the kitchen while I go upstairs and look at the mess of boxes and suitcases. I take a moment to stand with my hands on hips and blow my cheeks out. "Right," I say and rip open the first box.

I have half my clothes put away and half scattered over the bed when my phone starts buzzing. Maryam's photo shows up on the screen. I smile.

"Sorry," I say, flopping down onto the bed, "I can't take your call right now. Mobile phones weren't around in the dark ages, therefore this phone call is impossible."

Maryam chuckles. "Goddammit, Rose Simmons, I miss you already. I assume you made it to the village alright, then?"

"Yes. Almost got trampled by a herd of cows, but we made it OK."

"What? Really?"

"I might be exaggerating a little, but a whole herd of them did come charging down the road towards us."

"What's it like, apart from riddled with cows?"

I shrug, and then remember Maryam can't see me. "Small. Not sure, otherwise. We passed a church on the way in. I might have seen a phone box. Didn't notice anything else, really."

"So, no shops?"

"None."

"Cash point?"

"Nope."

"Girl, that really does sound like the arse end of nowhere. Are the mysterious family at least decent?"

"My aunt's really nice. She's definitely a child of the Universe – the décor in this house is super cute. Hang on. I'll show you." I switch us to a video call and sweep my camera across my room and out into the sunken landing, showing Maryam the rugs, wall hangings, fairy lights, hanging seat and ribbon tent. And plants.

I turn the camera back to myself. "OK, that's pretty cute," Maryam admits. We prop our phones on our desks and sit in our chairs. Maryam's got some wicked wings on her eyes today as well as gold eyeshadow. It hits me hard that I can no longer rely on her expert eye skills at short notice when I need to dress to impress. My skills with eyeliner end up with me looking like I've been punched in the face. "Have you met the cousin yet?"

"Only glimpsed her as she escaped out the front the moment I arrived."

"Oh, shit. Well, it's her loss. But if she turns out to be a massive bitch, tell me—," Maryam cracks her knuckles on the screen, "—and I'll come down to take care of her."

"Buckinghamshire is north of London."

"Whatever. Tell me. I'll be there."

My heart aches with longing to wrap her up in a hug, but there's a glass screen and fifty miles between us.

Dear Universe. Why do you have to be so cruel? Why couldn't you have given some scientists a kick up the arse to get them to create teleportation faster? Or parents who don't get jobs on the other side of the world?

"But, seriously, Rose," Maryam says, "you're so brave going to live with family you've never met before."

"Well, technically I have met them before – it's just that the last time I saw them I was super into *Angelina Ballerina*."

"Which means you've basically never met them." She leans forward, resting her face in her hands and her elbows on the table. "How are you feeling otherwise, about the whole move thing?"

I blow out my cheeks and let the air out slowly as I try to make sense of the cocktail of emotions jumbled up inside me. Talking to Maryam has filled in the hollowness but seeing her face and hearing her voice, which I would usually only have to ride the overground one stop to experience IRL, has left me feeling heavier than I was before.

"Strange," I say in the end. "Sad, perhaps. I'm missing everyone already – you, Mum – even though she left like an hour ago – Dad, my house, Sienne, Zoe, the waffle house and just... my life. Eugh." I rest my forehead on the desk as my stomach clenches. "And I've only been away from it for a few hours."

"But you're not stuck there for a solid two years," Maryam points out. "It's like a half-hour train ride from Euston to the nearest train station to you. You can pop back anytime you want. Like now, if you really wanted to."

I take a deep breath and lift my head. Maryam's expression is worried. So I give her my best smile. "You're right. I've just got to find a way of getting to the train station from here." I frown. "I don't remember seeing a bus stop on the way through the village."

"Well, when you do finally get here, I'm going to give you the biggest hug. I can't wait to see your face again."

I didn't think my heart could get any heavier, but when I say goodbye to Maryam and cut the call, the weight of it drags me back down to the desk. I sprawl on it, arms outstretched, fingers gripping the edge on the other side.

Dear Universe. Give me strength.

But the Universe don't give a shit, so I stuff my headphones in my ears and put on my get-up-and-go song – Taylor Swift's "Shake it Off". The lyrics have me up and dancing in a few moments, which continues when the song changes to WALK THE MOON's "Shut Up and Dance". Soon I'm shuffling around my room, back to unpacking, mouthing along to the lyrics as my playlist wears itself out.

I'm taking a break to scroll through social media – Zoe and Sienna are at Westfield, picking outfits for each other and doing photoshoots in the changing rooms, and I'm laughing myself to the point of feeling sick at their stories and captions – when I hear voices downstairs.

"... stink. Both of you."

"I'll wash Bonnie off before taking a shower."

"Both of you should go in the shower together, but I'll clean Bonnie while you go upstairs. Leave your clothes in the downstairs shower room."

"*Hai hai.*"

There's the sound of claws on hard floor, the clanking and whoosh of a shower and then the creaking of feet on the stairs. I sit frozen on my bed, caught between staying where I am and going out there to greet Clover. But as her footsteps grow louder, I realise if she's going to take a shower, she likely won't want me jumping on her. Especially if she's left her clothes downstairs.

By the time Helen calls us for dinner, Clover hasn't emerged from the bathroom. I head into the kitchen, which now smells like pork. Bonnie looks up at me as I enter the room. For one gut-clenching moment I think she's going to bark at me – Dear Universe. Don't let me blow this – but I let her sniff my hand and her tail starts thumping against the ground.

"Good girl," I coo and pet her.

"Watch out," Helen says, coming in from the back of the kitchen with a bowlful of courgettes, "she's moulting at the moment. How's unpacking going?"

"Mostly done," I say. "Just got a few things to find a place for."

"You're doing better than me. I still have a few sealed boxes in the loft left over from when we moved here."

"When was that?"

"Ooohhh..." A great cloud of steam rises into the air as Helen drains the potatoes. "Eleven years ago."

I stand up. There's dog hair all over me. I brush myself down, but the hair sticks into my dress.

"Don't bother," Helen says. "You'll need a roller to get that stuff out. There's one in the utility room."

"A roller?" I ask.

"Sticky paper on a roller. It's on the side – had to brush myself down after washing Bonnie."

I go into the long thin tiled room at the back of the kitchen. There's a washing machine, a tumble dryer, a big sink with a counter, and a small shower cubicle and toilet in a separate room off the back. The roller's beside the sink. It gets rid of most of the hair, but I have to pick off the remaining ones.

I return to the kitchen. Clover is sat at the kitchen table, tapping on her phone. She doesn't look at me as I sit opposite her. Coldness radiates off her. I don't want to stare at her like a creep, but at the same time it might be the only way to get her to look at me. Or should I talk to her? Perhaps if I do, she'll acknowledge that I'm here.

I push my glasses up my face as I take a seat. "Hey, Clover," I say.

Nothing.

She doesn't even look at me.

For a moment, I'm too stunned to feel anything. A flash of irritation passes through me. I mean, this girl is literally ghosting me when I'm sat *right here*. What the hell is her problem?

Helen places my dinner plate before me; balsamic vinegar drenched pork chop, buttered boiled potatoes with courgettes and peas. She places another in front of Clover, who puts her phone away. Hearing her say, "Thank you," calms me down. I remember that she's in the same situation as I am. It might be worse for her, having someone she's never met before coming to invade her personal space.

I need to be patient and give her time. I'm sure she'll warm up eventually.

"Dig in," Helen says, and we do. It's good. Simple but delicious. We have a lot of takeaways at home, or ready meals, as Mum and Dad often work late.

"This is great," I say.

"Thanks. Potatoes are from down the road. The pork's from Dale's Farm," Helen explains. "That's the same farm whose cows you had an encounter with on the road here."

"Shame it's not beef, then," I say, and Helen laughs.

"Courgettes are from the garden. It's likely the last of them for the year."

"Thank god," Clover says, sawing into her chop. "If I see another courgette in this lifetime it will be too soon."

"We've been a bit overwhelmed this year," Helen explains. "I might have planted too many."

"Do you grow your own vegetables?" I ask, even though it's completely obvious that, yes, Helen does that, because I am literally eating a vegetable she grew, and I'm pretty sure Mum told me she did in the car. But it's a good conversation starter.

"Courgettes, carrots, broccoli, beans—"

"So many beans," Clover mutters. I smile, liking her dry humour, but she has her eyes on her plate and doesn't notice.

"—tomatoes, pumpkins and chard. I've tried growing sprouts, but they never work. We also have a plum tree, a cherry tree, an apple and a couple of pears. Oh, and a fig, and a gooseberry bush."

"That's a lot," I say. a little stunned that someone could grow so much in their back garden. Our back garden consists of a patio, some bushes and flower beds, which are all tended by a gardener who comes around once a week. On the rare occasions we get out into it, we sit around on the patio, or lie on the sun loungers and sleep. I've never seen Mum with a pair of gardening gloves on and probably never will. What was the wedge that drove Mum and Helen away from each other for thirteen years? They really are like oil and water.

"I'll show you around the garden after dinner," Helen says, "and perhaps Clover can give you a tour of the village tomorrow."

"There's enough to see in this place for a tour?" I joke. Clover shoots me the evil eye and I realise my mistake. Helen laughs, though. It seems my cousin is very protective about her home. But, hey, at least she finally looked at me.

"There are a few things that might surprise you," Helen says.

We have dessert - apple crumble and home-made custard, which Clover made because apparently Helen is no good at making sweet stuff - and Helen takes me out into the garden while Clover feeds Bonnie. The garden stretches out long and thin at the back and curves around one side of the house. Beyond, there's a field and the fences of other back gardens. She points out the different fruit trees and vegetables in the borders along the sides, encouraging me to help myself when I want something. Around the bottom of the apple tree some of the fruit has already fallen. Helen tuts and mutters something about windfalls.

Back in the house, Bonnie is licking out the inside of her food bowl. Clover scoops it off the floor, flicking soap suds everywhere, while Helen points to a calendar on the wall.

"That's the family calendar. Any plans you make, stick them on there, then everyone knows where everyone is."

Clover's plans are written in purple. Helen's in green. And there's a blue pen tied next to the purple and green pen, with a sticker with my name on it on the side. The sight chokes me. I scan the calendar. There's very little purple and a lot of green, most of which read yoga, mindfulness, meditation, crystal and tarot.

"You do a lot of yoga and mindfulness classes," I say.

"Those are my classes."

"You teach?"

"In Littleton village hall."

"That's where Grandma lives?"

"And where your mum and I grew up. And where Clover's dad and I got married. I can take you there one day if you want."

I nod. "I'd like that."

"You might run into Grandma, though," Clover says.

I smirk at the comment, while Helen grimaces. "Yes, there's always that risk. Do you..." She pauses, and when she continues there is pain in her voice. "Do you see her often?"

"She visits every so often – she always comes to London. I've never been to her house."

Helen sighs. "Claire never likes coming back here."

My ears prick up. Is Helen going to reveal the reason for the thirteen-year feud? But she grabs a tea towel and starts on the drying up. Clover's turned slightly in our direction, listening in. I guess she knows as little about the situation as I do.

It's always felt like a family secret to me, why I never got to see my mum's side of the family, apart from my grandma. I knew Mum was adopted and that she had a sister, who had a daughter. There's a photo of the four of us in one of my parents' photo albums – Mum and Helen sat next to each other on a bench somewhere. Clover and I are babies, yet old enough to sit upright on our mums' knees. They're smiling in that photo – so happy that it seems impossible they would spend over a decade not talking to each other.

I grab a tea towel and offer to help, but Helen tells me to chill.

"Perhaps we can watch a film tonight," she suggests.

"Sure," I say, although Clover doesn't make any sound of enthusiasm.

I go back to my room, lay out the last bits and pieces and check my phone.

"Tea?" Helen calls from downstairs.

"Yes, please!" I call back.

As I hear footsteps on the stairs I step into the sunken landing. Clover scales the rise. She pauses. There's no openness in her expression. In fact, everything about her screams, "Fuck off."

I straighten my spine and force my best smile.

"Hi," I say. "Um, I, um, wanted to say hi. Properly. I know this whole situation must be as hard for you as it is for me, but I wanted to say that—"

And Clover walks right by me.

Literally, with her eyes straight ahead, she glides past me while I'm mid-sentence talking to her and walks up the steps to her room.

"I don't want you here as much as you don't want to be here," she says with her back to me. "So keep out of my room and I'll keep out of yours. Let's just get through this."

She slips into her room and shuts the door behind her.

If this was a nineties cartoon, my jaw would be on the floor.

Instead, I blink. My irritation turns into a torrent of anger. But I take a deep breath.

It's fine.

It's *fine.*

If she doesn't want to be friends, then we won't be friends.

Dear Universe. Look, I tried, so if you could not make the next two years of my life what I fear they're going to be, that would be much appreciated.

Chapter 4

Rose

There's a moment of confusion when I wake up the next morning.

In the little light coming around the side of the curtained window, I can see a wardrobe where my bedside table should be. It's only when I roll over and see the desk and chair that I remember.

My stomach sinks a little.

Dear Universe. Why couldn't you have made it all a dream?

But everything around me is very real, and it's not going away for another two years. So I might as well make the most of it. I reach for my glasses and fling the covers aside and roll out of bed.

I relieve the pressure in my bladder and rummage through the chest of drawers until I find my running kit. Clover's bedroom door is still shut. I remember her all but slamming it in my face the night before and feel a tad sick. But Helen's cheerful face at the kitchen table lessens the anxiety. She has some tarot cards spread out in front of her in a complex pattern, a green tea, a crumb-scattered plate and open notebook beside her. Bonnie looks up from her bed when I enter the kitchen. I smile when she walks over for a sniff, her claws clicking on the tiles.

I stroke her head as I say, "Morning."

"Morning," Helen sings, scribbling something down in her notebook. "Tea?"

"No, thank you." Bonnie trots back to her bed and I wipe my hands on my leggings. "I'm going for a run. Is there anywhere I shouldn't go?"

"Most people jog down the road – you can run to the next village down a track. It's normally pretty quiet along there." She makes a face as she turns a card over. I guess that one isn't a good one. "But you should go cross-country. There are some lovely routes round here."

A nervous laugh escapes me. "I'm not sure I would know where to go."

"Stick to the marked footpaths and you'll be fine. They're all signposted. You can turn off at most points and end up coming back in a circle."

"Alright," I say, but when I stand at the top of a field and see all that open space, and the roaming cows, I turn back to find the road. It's a nice path down to the next village – mostly flat with a few inclines that make me push myself. The next village over is even smaller than Harboury. They have half the number of houses which sit along a winding single track road. It's cute. I touch the iron gates at the front of their church and turn and jog back.

I return to the house and find Helen's car is gone. My stomach sinks as I remember I didn't pick up any keys. But I find a set hanging in the front door. They have a tag on them that reads *Rose* in scratchy handwriting.

What sort of person leaves their keys hanging in the front door?

Although what sort of moron am I for going out without a set of keys?

I shower and find a note on the kitchen table in the same handwriting: *Hopefully you found the keys in the front door. Thought you should have your own set :)*

Clover's bedroom door is still shut, but Bonnie is gone from her bed, so I guess they are out for a walk. I grab some muesli and a banana for breakfast, make a tea and head back upstairs. When I set my mug down on my desk, it hits me.

What am I meant to do now?

I fall down an Instagram hole as I sip my tea, watching random videos, some of which make me laugh and some of which leave me feeling empty, but I don't stop scrolling until my mug is dry. By which time it's 9.35 a.m. I throw my phone face down on my bed and sigh. I'm restless – the sort of restless where I want to text Maryam, Zoe, Sienna or Kai to see if they want to hang out.

But there's no way for us to do that now.

So what do I do?

Have a wander around the village, I guess. I put my sandals on and head out back out the door.

I walk from one end of the village to the other in fifteen minutes. I find twenty houses, a farm, a noticeboard, a post-box, a church and a red telephone box, which has been turned into a library and food bank. The most exciting thing in this village is an old water pump, which doesn't produce any water when I work the handle. Seriously? If this place is going to be dark ages central, can't their cool dark age stuff at least work?

I come across a few people on my wanders – some of them say good morning and others give me suspicious looks. I can practically hear their, "She's not from around here," thoughts. I smile and wave to them, and try not to worry that someone might call the police to report a Black girl hanging around the village. Everyone I see is white and most are in their fifties or sixties.

It makes me feel even more isolated.

During the three days leading up to the start of school, I fall into a routine of running in the morning and then lounging around the house for the rest of the day, spamming Maryam, Zoe, Sienna and Kai on WhatsApp to let them know how bored I am.

I only see Clover in passing when she walks Bonnie or goes down to the kitchen. Otherwise I stare at her shut bedroom door across the sunken landing. I spend some of my afternoons with Bonnie, chilling in the garden when it's warm enough with a book. She sits in the shade beside me and I fall in love with her. Just having her there stops me from feeling like I'm adrift in a rowing boat on a large sea. Although I don't miss the jealous looks Clover shoots me when she's in the kitchen. I'm tempted to stick my tongue out at her, but I tell myself not to be so petty.

Helen is out most days, her calendar jam-packed full of client calls and classes. She's always home in the evening for dinner. Clover and Helen take it in turns to cook and wash up, although I ask for the chance to help with the washing up – just for something else to do, and to stop myself from feeling so guilty about being the only one who doesn't do anything to help. Although I hoovered my bedroom and the sunken landing one day – yes, I was *that* bored.

At dinner on the second evening, I asked Helen where the nearest bus stop is and where I could find the timetable, as I wanted a day in town.

"I've looked online, but I can't find anything for the village."

Clover's laugh makes my stomach drop.

Are you fucking kidding me?

"Sorry," Helen says, "there isn't a bus service in the village. One used to come through on a Friday, but you had to ring ahead to make it stop for you. If you want to head into Aylesbury, you'll need to walk over to the next village. There's a bus stop there. It's about an hour across the fields. Or you can walk in the opposite direction to Littleton and get the bus to MK from there – that's about an hour and a half walk."

"OK," I say, deflated. "I'll give it a miss."

"Sorry," Helen says again. "But, hey, during the next weekend I have off, you can come into Leighton with me. They have some cool independent shops there – lots of nice places to have a mosey around or have a coffee."

"That would be nice, thanks," I say, although I want to scream.

I get a call from Mum the night she arrives in Dubai at 8 p.m., even though it's 11 p.m. UAE time. She looks tired but sounds happy. Dad spends the call hanging around in the background, waiting for his chance to talk to me while Mum tells me about the journey and asks me how I am settling in. I lie through my teeth and pretend I'm not going mad with cabin fever and loneliness. I don't want them to worry about me. I made the decision to stay behind.

"Has Clover prepared you for tomorrow?" Mum asks.

"Em," I say, "I'll be OK, but I'll check with her if I need anything."

"I'm sure you'll knock their socks off," Dad says, pushing his face closer to the camera. "They'll be super impressed by you."

I give him a weak smile. "Thanks, Dad," I say, feeling like a primary school kid.

"Text us tomorrow evening to let us know how your first day at your new school was," Mum adds. "And remember: we're always here if you need to call."

My throat's thick as I nod. "Alright."

We chat a little more, then Mum hands the phone to Dad, who talks my ear off about the latest case he's working on, and then about a really boring corporate golf day he had to go to for networking reasons.

By the time we say goodbye, I'm pinching myself to stop the tears from spilling over. I manage to hold them back until I hang up the call. Then I put my phone face down on my bed, lie on my back and let them out.

Fucking hell. I never thought I would miss my parents so much.

As ever, I'm awake before my phone alarm goes off. I'm never sure why I bother setting one as I always wake up before it, but I still feel compelled to set one. Just in case. I lie in bed, focusing on my breathing and not the nervousness swelling in my stomach, until my phone starts to buzz.

7 a.m.

Up and at 'em.

When I'm in the bathroom, I hear Clover's alarm sound several times. By the time I've washed, styled my hair and done my makeup, she's snoozed the thing five times. It finally falls silent as I step out of the bathroom.

For my new school, the dress code for Year Twelve is 'office attire'. So because my parents are lawyers, my mum bought me a wardrobe of suits, plain skirts, jackets and shirts, and my shoes are so shiny I can see my face in them. I bought a few more colourful and personal pieces that I could get away with. All my classmates won't be in business suits. Will they?

Downstairs, there's a spread of food on the kitchen table – cereal, bread for toasting, a dozen different spreads, croissants, waffles, cooked sausages, bacon, boiled eggs, a bowl of fresh fruit, a pot of coffee, a pot of tea and a carton of juice. Helen sits in her usual seat with a cup of green tea, and a bowl of muesli and fruit, a spread of tarot cards in front of her. Without looking up she gestures at ALL THE FOOD laid out on the table.

"Help yourself. First day back at school, you're going to need all the energy you can get."

Because it's a special occasion – or perhaps just an excuse – I pile sausages, bacon and waffles onto one plate, and also get a bowl of fruit. By the time I have finished and given Bonnie a fuss, the nerves that have been building all morning reduce to little twinges. I'm nervous, but not as nervous as I thought I might be. I'm going to a school where I imagine most people will be like Clover – staying on for sixth form in the same place they started at in Year Seven – but there will likely be other newbies like me there. I'm sure I'll find someone to talk to, and I've sort of missed school – I like the routine and, for the most part, I find the lessons interesting. Zoe's forever calling me out for being a nerd, but you can't help what you like.

Sipping my coffee, I'm very content, until I see the time. I have ten minutes to brush my teeth and grab my stuff. As I head upstairs, Clover comes hurtling down them. She's dyed her hair what looks like a natural shade of brown. I press myself against the wall as she practically flies past me.

"Sorry!" she says, which catches me by surprise. But before I can respond she's disappeared into the kitchen.

"Getting up this early should be illegal," I hear her say to Helen as I head upstairs. When we're in the car together – because we have to drive to the next village for the school bus to pick us up, because *of course* we do – I notice what Clover is wearing; linen trousers that are clinched at the ankles, a loose white shirt decorated with little candy skulls, a black linen jacket, and Toms. Now I feel exceedingly overdressed.

Dear Universe. Please don't let me be the only person who looks like they've stumbled out of the City.

"You both look so grown-up in your business wear," Helen says when we're waiting for the bus to show up. There are a couple of other people waiting at the stop, all of them dressed in grey jackets and grey trousers, with white shirts, and navy and pale blue striped ties. I guess that's the set school uniform.

A bus appears in the rear-view mirror, and I assume from the "Have a good day," comment from Helen, and the way that Clover jumps out the car, that it's our bus. I climb aboard behind Clover, who heads straight to the back. As I follow her, the hierarchy in the seating arrangement becomes clear – the seats at the front are filled with the younger students and then they get older the further back we go. Clover slumps in the right corner seat at the back of the bus and immediately plugs in her headphones. I claim the seat in the left corner, take out my phone and prepare myself for the forty-minute bus ride to school.

Back home, I had a thirty-minute walk to my school. It was a tradition with Maryam that after the first day of school we would go to the waffle house around the corner for the biggest stack we could get our hands on. Maryam sent me a photo yesterday of her, Zoe and Sienna sitting in the waffle house, towers of waffles decked in cream, syrup and fruit in front of them, but they are all giving the camera their best sad faces.

It was captioned: Miss you.

That photo did little to improve my mood.

Although I felt a little smug that I got an extra day of

holiday because of #privateschoolperks.

The bus winds its way through some backwater country roads, haring around tight corners and stopping in obscure places to pick up more children in grey uniforms. Then in a village where I swear to God we passed a bona fide windmill, a tanned white guy dressed in a slim black suit and tie steps onto the bus. Like everyone else, his eyes are glazed with morning sleep, but when they sweep over the back seat and alight on mine something changes in his face. Something that makes me narrow my eyes and feel very aware I am wedged into a corner. But when he sits down, he leaves a seat between us and there's a warmth to his smile that relaxes me. He has a nice face as well, and dark hair that's styled into a nice quiff. He too looks like he's stepped out of a City firm. Still, the attention of a boy is not what I am looking for.

"Morning," he says.

"Hi," I reply.

"I'm Ari."

"Rose."

"I'm going to assume by the fact I haven't seen you before that you're new this year."

"And your assumption would be correct."

"Cool. You from London?"

"Yeah." I grin. "What gave it away?"

Ari laughs. "It was just a guess."

With Ari to chat to, the rest of the bus journey goes past very quickly. I don't notice as the countryside outside the window changes to a townscape and then back to countryside again. By the time the bus turns into a drive with fields on either side, I know that Ari is studying business, computer science, economics and media with the view of doing something in tech. His parents own a house in Cyprus, where he spent most of his summer holiday, working at a little beach bar waiting tables getting a tan, swimming in the sea and climbing hills. He speaks a smattering of Greek and Turkish, which he tries to impress me with, but I tell him it all sounds Greek to me, and then get a lecture about the differences between the languages. He learns that I'm studying history, English, politics and French, why I moved from London to Buckinghamshire, and that I spent a week during the summer in Devon with my parents before my dad had to fly back to Dubai. I don't tell him that my parents spent most of that holiday answering work calls and typing away on their laptops.

When I tell Ari that Clover and I are cousins, he's very taken aback.

"It's just, you're very unlike each other," he says, glancing at Clover sitting behind him, who's gazing out the window with her headphones in. I can't help but agree.

"We're not related by blood – our mums are adopted sisters," I say and for some reason feel very guilty for admitting it. It sort of feels like a betrayal, although Clover has done nothing to earn my loyalty.

The school is an old country estate – a black and white house and a stable, I repeat, a *stable*, that have been converted into classrooms. The rest of the rooms are less impressive Terrapin buildings – the sort that look like they might fold like cardboard boxes if they get rained on. The science block, where the sixth-form common room is located, is a new red brick building. There's also a massive field out the back, a double set of tennis courts, and an old gym. It's not the all singing and all dancing state-of-the-art private school I imagined when I came to see it for the first time. In the video on their website, they very conveniently cut out the terrapin buildings when the camera pans across the school.

When we get off the bus, Clover sweeps off towards the science block, but Ari waits for me on the gravel drive and shows me the way. On such a small campus I could have found the way on my own, but it's a such a nice gesture I don't complain.

As we push our way through the hordes of grey uniformed students, Ari waves at a few people who fight their way towards him through the throngs of younger students. He hugs a few and fist bumps a few others, and introduces me to all of them. There's Rachel, Rory, Henry and Natasha, and I'm glad they too look like they've stepped out of the City. Henry's even carrying a briefcase, which the others tease him mercilessly for. Rachel doesn't look up from her phone as Ari bumps his fist to hers. I smile and say hi to them all, trying to sound relaxed when I am quaking inside from nerves, and also from the growing sense of panic as I keep scanning the crowd of students, seeking out a face like mine. But I might as well have stayed in Harboury for the handful of Black and brown faces I'm able to pick out. I dig my nails into my palm and push away the growing sense of loneliness.

It's fine. I'm going to be fine.

The sixth-form common room is on the third floor of the science block. It has a small kitchen with tea- and toast-making facilities, lots of comfy waiting room style chairs and low tables, and a few high desks against the wall, on which stand a handful of computers. The room is already pretty full of sixth formers, chatting and laughing. Clover's sat with a group of people. Relief washes over me. I was so worried she would be sat on her own.

I follow Ari and his group to a cluster of comfy chairs, where we all sprawl and the conversation keeps flowing, all of them catching up on what they did over the summer. I listen in and can't help but feel a tinge of resentment that this is what I would be doing if I was back at my school. Then I notice that Henry is talking to me and I completely missed what he just said.

Dear Universe. Help me get over myself.

"Sorry," I say to him. "I missed that."

"What subjects are you taking?" Henry repeats.

"History, English, politics and French."

"Ooff," Rory says, pressing a hand to his gut like he's been punched. "Heavy. What do you want to do after school?"

"Study law at uni," I say.

"Fair play," Rachel says, her thumbs a blur over her phone screen.

"Like your parents?" Ari asks.

I nod, swallowing down the strange taste that comes into my mouth.

"You from London?" Rory asks.

I smile while Ari laughs. I have a feeling I'm going to be repeating myself a lot today. "What gave it away?"

"Lucky," Natasha says. She's been pretty quiet this

whole time, scrolling through her phone instead, long manicured nails tapping on the screen. "I can't wait to get out of this shit hole and move to London."

"Why is everyone so obsessed with moving to London?" Rory asks. "It's expensive. It's overcrowded. It's dirty."

"It's got life," Natasha says. "This whole county is boring. There's nothing here except fucking cows. Isn't that right, Rose?"

"There is a lot less to do here," I say.

"Tactful," Ari whispers to me.

"There's plenty to do," Rory objects. "There's the chair-making museum, the model village, the Roald Dahl museum, Bletchley Park, the national history museum in Tring—"

Natasha holds up her hand. "Oh my God, just stop."

"And Milton Keynes," Rachel adds. "You can spend a whole day there going round and round the roundabouts."

"Basically," Natasha says to me, "this place is a dump."

"Dark ages central," I tell her, which makes Natasha raise her eyebrows and hold up her hand for a high five. I slap it.

"This county has *charm*." Rory sniffs.

"I can't wait to start driving," Rachel says wistfully. A couple of cars containing sixth formers pull into the small car park beside the science block. "I'm so done with taking the bus every day."

"Not long now," Ari says.

"For you," Rachel says. "Your birthday's in October. I have to wait until June."

Ari sighs with exaggerated loudness, leans back in his chair, kicks out his feet and puts his hands behind his head. “Three more weeks, baby.” He cries out when Rachel throws a book at him.

Chapter 5

Clover

I'm so fucking done with school already.

It's only the end of day one and I'm ready to set the place on fire. The thought of having to go back every day – having to dress in stupid uncomfortable "office wear", to listen to the endless pointless chatter around me, and to teachers drone on about stuff I really couldn't give a shit about – is making my stomach hurt. I wish I could stay home and draw. At least I can now spend my break and lunch times in the sixth-form common room, or art or photography rooms, rather than wandering around on my own outside.

But when Mum asks me how my first day back was

when we're doing the washing up with Rose upstairs, I pick up the next saucepan to dry and say, "Fine. My timetable's half decent – got lots of free afternoons I can spend in the art or the dark room."

"What about media studies and religious studies?"

I shrug. "I'll squeeze them in."

With her hands deep in washing up suds, Mum bumps me with her hip and I bump her back. In the corner of the kitchen, Bonnie starts licking out her food bowl. The metal rattles against the hard floor. As I retrieve it, Bonnie gives me a hopeful look.

"When have you ever been given seconds?" I point out, fussing her ears.

"Always hopeful," Mum says. I grab the frying pan off the drying rack.

"They told us today that we need to start thinking about what subject we want to study at uni." I stick out my tongue and make a farting noise. "I've just chosen my A level subjects. I have no idea what I want to study at uni... If I even want to go to uni..."

Out the corner of my eye, I glance at Mum, whose eyes are on the sink. She doesn't even look like she's listening.

"You'll work it out," Mum says. "You've got loads of time to decide what you want to do."

I nod, despite the pain in my chest.

"Help me!" I want to scream, but I keep drying everything she washes.

"Have you spoken to Rose, yet?" Mum asks.

For a moment I stop moving, then I renew my drying. When the silence has dragged on for a minute, Mum bumps me with her hip again.

"Come on, Clo. At least give her a chance?"

I put the frying pan down on the counter with more force than necessary. "We won't get on. I can tell how much Rose hates it here."

"Well, think about what it would be like if you were in her shoes. What if I had to jet off to another country and sent you to live in London?" The look of disgust on my face makes Mum laugh. "Exactly. Just be nice to her, Clo. A kind word here and there never cost anyone anything. And, who knows, you might get on more than you think you will. You never know until you try."

"You sound just like Leon," I mutter.

"Leon is very wise for his age. You should listen to him more. Perhaps you could take Rose for a walk with Bonnie? Show her some of the local sights and what a beautiful part of the country we live in. It might help Rose feel more at home here, and it will give you a chance to talk to her."

I make another farting noise and roll my eyes. I'm being childish, but why can't Mum see what a hopeless situation this all is? How Rose and I are never going to get on? How we obviously don't have anything in common, and how there's no way I can be myself around her? Girls like her belittle girls like me as part of their morning routine.

I know, because I've spent the last five years on the receiving end of their comments.

But when Mum wraps a soapy gloved hand around my waist and kisses the top of my head, my heart leaps. Mum really is serious about this whole thing. She really wants us to get on, and I feel awful for letting her down.

"Fine," I say. "I'll take her on a walk with Bonnie." I hear Bonnie's tail thumping on the tiled floor at the "w" word. I raise myself on my tiptoes and stare at her over the kitchen counter. "You've had yours today."

We finish the washing and drying. As Mum waits for the kettle to boil, I ask, "Why did you and Auntie Claire not talk to each other for so long?"

There's a long silence, in which I have to focus on my breathing to stop myself from going into full panic mode for asking the wrong question, but then Mum says, "We had a stupid argument that went on for far too long."

And that is all I am going to get out of her on the subject. For tonight at least. She'll tell me one day. It's only since the beginning of this year that she's started talking to her sister again – and since something clicked into place that made me realise that there was a divide between Mum and my aunt. (I mean, Grandma's been making comments for years about how Mum and Claire needed to talk more, but I don't tend to listen to anything that Grandma says. She talks a lot of bullshit.) I knew Mum was adopted and that she had a sister, and that I had a cousin, but I thought the distance between us was something that just... was. I didn't twig that there was something off about it until I overheard Mum talking to my aunt on the phone. Hearing them speak, the lack of communication taking place between them before became clear, as well as how I had a whole side of the family I didn't know.

A side of the family I still don't know.

It's a tradition that I spend the first weekend after the first week back at school in bed, recovering. And the first weekend after my first week as a sixth former is no exception.

I roll out of bed and into the bathroom. I'm about to head down to the kitchen for a drink, when I see Rose's bedroom door is open. A glance at the shoe rack confirms my suspicions – that Rose is already out for a run. How the hell can someone get up so early even at the weekend? Doesn't she understand what weekends are for?

Back in bed, I pull my laptop from the bedside table onto my lap. I boot up the latest episode of *Free!* and wriggle back under the covers with my laptop propped up on my thighs.

I'm shouting Haru on as he races towards the finish line, when I hear the front door open and shut. Like a soldier under fire, I grab my headphones and shove them in the headphone socket. Mum's out at work, so that could have only been Rose coming in and I do not want her to hear that I'm watching *Free!* Not that she would know what *Free!* was, but she'll overhear the characters talking in Japanese and will make assumptions. Assumptions that are very much correct, but ones I don't want her to have as arsenal.

While she's in the shower I finish watching the episode and scroll through my phone. There's some new trailers for the Autumn 2018 season. I send the one for *That Time I Got Reincarnated as a Slime* onto Leon – it looks like something he would be interested in. I listen out for Rose's door latch to click, and when it does I yawn and roll back out of bed, into some clothes, down the stairs and into the kitchen. Not literally. Although I am tempted. I'm so sluggish today. I'd forgotten how much energy school drains out of me.

I finish breakfast and find Bonnie looking expectedly at me. She knows what we do after I've had my breakfast.

"OK," I tell her. "Just give me a sec? Got to do something before we set off. Something I really, *really* don't want to do, but..." I sigh and push a hand through my hair. "But it's something I probably should do... Ugh. OK."

I stand outside Rose's bedroom door before I can change my mind. My heart's thundering in my chest so loud I'm surprised it doesn't echo around the landing as I raise my hand to knock.

I really don't want to do this.

It's going to be a disaster.

She's going to say no and it'll be super awkward.

Or she'll say yes and it'll be super awkward anyway. We're going to spend the whole walk in silence, because we have nothing to talk about.

IT'S GOING TO BE AWFUL!

So I turn away and head back to my room, but halfway across the sunken landing, I stop and take a deep breath. A thought, clearer than any I've had all week, passes through my brain.

Fuck it.

My knuckles make a satisfying rapping noise on the door.

The look of surprise on Rose's face must mirror the one on my own, because I can't believe I just did that. We stare at each other. I try to speak, but the words have turned to peanut butter in my throat. This is while Rose stares at me like I've got three heads.

At last she pushes her glasses up her face - even though they look like they're as high as they can go - and asks, "Err... do you need anything?"

I clear my throat. "Ahem. Yeah, I... er... I—"

Oh my god, Clo. Just spit it out already.

She's already looking at you like you're a freak, so you might as well say it.

"Walk," I blurt out. "I... I mean, I'm going to take Bonnie for a walk. I was wondering if you wanted to come."

Rose blinks and says, "Sure."

I blink back at her. "Cool. Meet you downstairs."

And I hurry away.

I sit outside the kitchen sliding doors with my head and arms between my knees, while Bonnie sniffs around the garden. I can practically hear Mum saying, "Now that wasn't so awful, was it?"

And I wish I could tell her that it really was.

But I did it.

Now I just have to survive the next hour of awkwardness.

I hear a rustling of leaves and look up to check Bonnie isn't trampling on Mum's vegetables, but she's just sniffing under the gooseberry. The wind picks up and I breathe in the fresh cool air. My shoulders drop and everything loosens up. A stray leaf detaches itself from somewhere and settles in the middle of the lawn. Its edges are tinged with orange. In the corner of the garden, the pear tree is dripping with fruit. Next to it, the apple is groaning under the weight of its crop, while the plum tree is starting to spring back from its hard summer. I look forward to the autumn every year – to the open fires, the hot drinks, oversized fluffy hoodies, fruit crumbles and stews – even if it means having to go back to school.

Rose takes so long that I start throwing Bonnie's ring Frisbee for her to chase. Just as I start to get irritated, Rose appears.

And holy cow balls. She's wearing denim shorts and tights, a nice turtleneck jumper and *trainers*. And a fresh face of make-up. So that's what took her so bloody long.

Seeing the look of despair on my face, Rose asks, "What?"

"Why are you dressed like that?" I ask.

Rose's forehead crinkles. "We're going for a walk."

I roll my eyes. "Yeah, and it's rained for four days straight. The fields are going to be muddy. You'll trash those clothes if you wear them."

You would think I had told her to wear black tie for our walk from the look of bewilderment on her face.

"But what am I meant to wear?" she asks.

Is this girl for REAL?

I am seriously, *seriously* regretting my decision to ask her to come with me. Bonnie and I could have been halfway to Penton by now.

"Something you don't mind getting covered in mud."

"How bad is it going to be?"

I sigh. "You'll find out when you have mud smeared

around your trouser cuffs."

The penny drops and Rose takes a deep breath. "OK. Give me a sec."

I almost tell her not to bother, that she can stay behind because I can tell she doesn't really want to come and I just want to go, but I hold my tongue and hurl the Frisbee as far as I can. I curse as it sails over the fence and into the field. Bonnie chases it as far as she can, then stops at the fence and gives me a look.

"Alright, alright. I'll go get it."

By the time I clamber back over the fence, with the slobbery piece of plastic in my hand, Rose is back dressed in her running gear. It looks too nice to get muddy, but I'm not going to tell her that.

"Have you got any waterproof shoes I can borrow?" she asks.

Another sigh escapes me. How can someone not own a pair of waterproof shoes?

"Mum's wellies are by the backdoor. They're a size six."

"They'll do," Rose says.

Then finally, *finally*, we're on the footpath heading down the grass field at the back of the village. Bonnie trots ahead of us, holding the Frisbee in her mouth. I wrestle it away from her and throw it. She goes haring off across the field, bounding through the plastic-wrapped bales, leaving behind Rose, me and a silence I don't know how to break.

By the time we get to the bottom of the first field, I'm simmering. The usual peace I feel striding across the fields isn't there – instead I've got a knot of anxiety and stress in my stomach. I've never felt lonely walking Bonnie by myself, but now I do.

The awkwardness between us is so strong I can almost see the ellipsis written in the air between us.

The second field has already been ploughed and the footpath hasn't been put back in, meaning we have to pick our way across the waves of soil. By the time we're halfway across the field, the mud is sticking to the bottom of my boots in a thin layer. Bonnie trips over the waves of ploughed earth, her Frisbee held protectively in her mouth, mud squidging between her toes. Halfway across the field, I turn back to check Rose is still behind me. She's there, shaking her feet every few steps to dislodge the mud. If she thinks this is bad, just wait until she sees the mud that will be caking the fields by Christmas – in October the mud sticks to your shoes so thickly they end up looking like snowshoes. I kick my foot out in front of me, sending a clump of mud flying. Bonnie chases after it but loses interest quickly. If Mum was here, we would be kicking mud at each other's backs. I glance back at Rose. I probably shouldn't. She wouldn't appreciate it.

Near the bottom of the third field, I notice Bonnie is no longer carrying her Frisbee.

"Bonnie!" I call to catch her attention. "Where's your Frisbee? What've you done with it?"

The gormless look on Bonnie's face disappears at the sound of the word Frisbee. Her ears prick up and then she starts looking around frantically, nose to the ground.

"You dumb dog. Where is it? What have you done with it?"

"I can see it. Hang on. I'll grab it."

Rose walks across the field. Expecting her to balk at the state of the muddy, saliva-covered plastic ring, I call

Bonnie and point at where her ring is so she can fetch it, but to my surprise Rose picks it up, calls for Bonnie's attention and then hurls it. It flies in a beautiful long flat descent. Bonnie chases after it, jumping once it gets close enough to the ground and catching it in her mouth.

Nice throw, I think, but I don't say anything as Rose re-joins the footpath, wiping her hands on her leggings. I'm not sure why. It would be more awkward to break the silence now than to maintain it.

We scramble over a few more stiles and reach the Lion King rock field. Right on cue, Bonnie drops her Frisbee and goes sprinting off into the distance. I sigh and pick it up. When will dogs ever learn how to carry their own stuff?

"Errr," Rose says, "shouldn't we call her back?"

"Nah," I say, "she's just gone to the pond."

"The pond?"

"The pond," I reply.

Rose finds out what I mean when we reach Lion King Rock. It's something I named as a kid on the walks Mum and I used to do out here. It's basically a man-made mini – and when I say mini, I mean waist-high – waterfall. Apparently for some reason I thought the overhang of the waterfall looked like Pride Rock. I don't understand why now. It looks nothing like it. Bonnie has pushed her way through the fence around the top part of the river and is already swimming. There's nothing that can stop her from getting in the water when she gets it in her sights.

We throw sticks for Bonnie for a while, making her jump in and out. Just watching her is exhausting. Not a word passes between Rose and I directly, but we talk to Bonnie, shouting at her when she loses the stick we've thrown for her. She lets us knows she's had enough by slipping back through the fence into the field.

Back on the footpath, I call Bonnie back and put her on the lead before we reach the herd. The cows raise their heads as we approach. They've done that annoying thing where they've spread themselves out across the narrow field and over the footpath, meaning we'll have to walk through the herd. At least they're bullocks and there aren't any calves. But it's still a pain.

"Erm," comes Rose's nervous voice from behind me, "we're not walking through there, are we?"

"Yeah," I say, suppressing an eye roll. "How else are we meant to get into the next field?"

"Is that safe?" There's panic in Rose's voice now, but I wave it away.

"Perfectly."

But even my own heart gives a little jump when the herd starts walking towards us. I take a deep breath and press on.

Rose's voice rises several pitches. "Are you sure?"

"It's fine. Come on. They'll back away if we get too close."

Then Rose is close behind me and I can hear her heavy breathing. A pang of sympathy goes through me, because I can remember doing that to Mum when we used to walk puppy Bonnie through the fields. The sight of the herd of cows running towards us is making my chest tighten. But years of walking these fields has taught me what a bunch of scaredy cats bullocks actually are.

"They won't hurt us," I say. "They're just curious because they think we've come to feed them."

"Should we run?" Rose whispers.

I sigh and hold Bonnie's lead out to her. "Watch," I say.

Holding my arms out, I walk towards the herd. The cows at the front of the herd stop and then as I get closer, they bow their heads and start to back away.

"Ha!" I scream and clap my hands at the closest cow. The herd turns and scatters, running towards the other end of the field. "See?" I grin at Rose as I take Bonnie's lead back from her. "They're more scared of us than we are of them. Remember, we're the predator here."

"That was mad," Rose says, glancing back at the herd, who have come together again and are watching us.

I laugh. "I learnt from the best. Mum showed me how to do that. I used to be dead scared of them."

The cows follow us at a safe distance across the field, but once we reach the stile, they lose interest and go back to grazing.

Chapter 6

Rose

I will never look at a cow the same way again.

Instead of teaching kids at school, "The cow goes moo," they should teach them, "The cow goes charging towards you and is also FRIGGING HUGE!"

Seriously, they're monsters. And they're even more monstrous now I'm no longer looking at them from behind a windscreen.

I don't know why they bother inventing new monsters for video games and fantasy fiction - they should just make cows the boss battle.

Why did early humans think it would be a good idea to *farm* those creatures? Why didn't they take one look at them and think, "Nope. I rather like my head to stay in one piece, thank you very much." What made them think they could control them?

Although, I guess they were cow whisperers like Clover or her mum, or that farmer. People in the sticks really are as scary as the media makes them out to be.

The green space on every side is sort of lovely, though. In a strange sense. I mean, I would hate to live out here forever. It's eerie, there's way too much mud, and there's no one here. Just fields and boss battle cows. But it's also beautiful in a way and the air is cold and clean.

Clover and Bonnie obviously love it.

The surly Clover from the house has disappeared and has been replaced by someone with bright eyes and sure feet. She looks like she belongs out here. I mean, she's not talking to me, but she *looks* less surly.

We scramble over another stile, Bonnie squeezing herself through a gap in the side, and come out onto a muddy track. I follow in Clover's footsteps, walking along the edge of the track on the field where the grass keeps the soil together. Bonnie splashes through the mud and water in the middle of the track, her ring Frisbee pushed over her head like a clown collar.

At the top of the hill, the track finishes and we come out onto a narrow road. A red tractor is rolling up the hill. Clover stops and stares at it, and then she starts jumping and waving. The tractor flashes its lights at her. As it gets closer, I'm surprised it's the guy I saw on the back of the quadbike driving it. And to hear K-pop blasting from the cab. The black and brown dog that was balanced on the back of the quadbike is barking behind him.

When the tractor stops alongside us, Clover opens the door and steps onto the outside step. The dog in the back leans around the side of the driver's seat, trying to get to her, but the guy pushes it back with scolding words. With his man bun and checked shirt, he really does look like he belongs in a hipster café rather than in the driver's seat of a tractor. All he needs is a beard.

"Fine. Fine," he says and leans to the side to allow the dog to scramble through and jump out. My eyes turn into hearts as it gets closer to me. I hold out my hand, which he sniffs and then starts wagging his tail. Then he spots Bonnie and goes bounding over. Soon the two are sniffing each other's butts.

"Hey, Rose," he says, turning off the music.

Clover is balancing on the tractor step, looking out across the fields, and the hipster farmer - who I was sure is our age, but now I'm not sure since he's driving a tractor - is looking at me with an open face.

"How are you enjoying the countryside?"

"Err..." I look down at my mud-covered wellies. "Muddy?"

He grins back at me. There's nothing flirty about it, just friendly. He's the sort of guy you would spill your heart out to if you met him drunk one night in a bar. He's the exact opposite to closed-off Clover. "This is only the beginning. Just you wait until December. I'm Leon, by the way. And that—" he points to the black and brown dog who has his nose stuck into a patch of grass, "—is Alexander. I think we glimpsed each other a few weeks ago."

"Oh, yeah. You were riding a quadbike and I was about to get trampled to death by cows."

He laughs. "Oh, I know that feeling. Hasn't happened yet, though. Touch wood." And he raps Clover lightly on the head. To my surprise, she doesn't bite back, just gives him a narrow-eyed look that he smiles back at. It's so cute my heart flutters. Is there something more than friendship between these two? There's a warmth in Clover's eyes now that she's around him that I haven't seen before.

"How's the new school?" Leon asks.

"Remote," I say. "But OK. It's strange having to take such a long bus ride every day, and then essentially being stuck in the middle of a bunch of fields."

"I mean you're essentially stuck in a bunch of fields all the time out here. What subjects are you doing?"

"History, English, politics and French."

"Wow. That's a brainy bunch."

I give him a tight smile. "What about you?"

"Business, product design, food science and biology."

I frown. "That's a strange mix."

Leon laughs. "I'm hoping they'll help me take the farm forward when my parents retire. You know, a bit of a mix between understanding the science and then actually making some money out of what we produce."

"Just don't turn it into a food factory," Clover says.

"Don't worry. I'm not going to go that far, but I want to make things more interesting. Dad's been thinking about doing school visits, like the Cotters do, but Mum's got her sights on renovating one of the barns and turning it into an Airbnb."

"What do you produce on the farm?" I ask, hoping that

"produce" is the right word to use.

Leon's eyes brighten at the question. He obviously doesn't get asked it often and wishes he did more.

"We keep cattle and sheep, which we raise for meat. And we also grow grain - oats for cereal, and also grass for cattle feed."

"What happens to your cattle and grain once you've produced it?"

"Our beef gets sold to M&S after it's been through the abattoir. And then our grain get sold to Jordan's for cereal."

I blink and stare at the fields. I always knew that the food I bought in supermarkets had to come from *somewhere*, but it's strange to think that the fields I just passed through is where that food is produced.

Leon turns to Clover. "You still on for this weekend?"

"I sure am."

They knock the side of their forearms together in some sort of strange handshake, then Clover jumps down to the floor. Leon calls Alexander into the tractor with a whistle, then he's driving away up the hill, blasting girl band K-pop, while we cross the road and head into the next set of fields.

Clover and I don't talk to each other for the rest of the walk, which takes us through another village - this one is larger than Harboury and even, *gasp!*, has a bona fide British village pub - and then in a loop back across the fields.

Staring at Clover's back, I can't help but puzzle over her. I mean, I thought she was pretty moody, but seeing her eyes light up talking to Leon, or watching Bonnie play, or how at home she looks walking across the open fields, somewhere underneath all that defensive armour is a nice person.

Why won't she be that person around me?

Chapter 7

Clover

Why are eyes so hard to draw?

I erase the mess that is the Suga's left eye and start again. His hair looks pretty slick, if I do say so myself – I've managed to find the perfect shade of grey and nail that strange parting with all the stray pieces shooting off everywhere. Now I just have to get his big anime eyes not looking like they're stuck on with glue that is starting to fail.

It doesn't help when "Kyouran Hey Kids!!" by The Oral Cigarettes comes on my playlist and I start punching the air, dancing in my seat and mouthing along with the few English phrases.

My phone buzzes on the desk. I glance at it, and then unlock it when a message from Leon flashes up on the screen.

Lee-kun
Good news! Genny's sent me the trailer for their next game Want to see?

Ko-chan
When have I never not wanted to see a game your sister's worked on? Her stuff's always on point

Lee-kun
Just thought I'd check :)
I'll forward it on but it's not public yet so no forwarding this onto anyone
Seriously Genny's made me promise to delete the message after you've watched it
This is top secret shit

Ko-chan
Crosses heart
Will watch it now

I take my headphones out of my laptop and plug them into my phone. My heart beat quickens as the Celtic music begins to play at the start of the trailer. It's for an RPG - Genny and Paige have only produced platformers so far, so this is awesome - set in a village built among the trees, with a story that follows a young woman searching for a cure for a disease that is sweeping through her settlement. She goes around the forest slaying monsters and gathering herbs, mixing them together to try to find the miracle cure. And the graphics look amazing! Looks like the two new employees they brought on last year are really paying off. By the time the trailer ends, my hands are shaking with excitement.

I want to play it. I want to play it so bad.

Ko-chan
IT LOOKS SOOOOOO GOOOOOOD!!
I WANNA PLAY IT NOW!!
Can you ask Gen if I can play it now?!?!

Lee-kun
I'll see what I can do!
No promises
Right gonna delete the video now

Ko-chan
How long until it comes out?

Lee-kun
Not sure
Sounds like it's still a while yet
Likely next year sometime

Ko-chan
I don't think I can wait that long

Lee-kun
You've literally just watched a one minute incomplete trailer How can you be so desperate to play it?

Ko-chan
I felt an emptiness inside me I didn't know was there until I watched that trailer
Now I fear I will never be whole until I have played it

Lee-kun
rolls eyes

Ko-chan
:D

Lee-kun
They're hoping this game will be their big break – one that will get them signed with a publisher

Ko-chan
For sure! It looks awesome
If I was a game publisher I would sign them up

I'm composing a new message to Genny, letting her know how amazing the game is, when Leon says:

Lee-kun
Rose seems nice :)

I frown at the screen and sigh as I reply.

Ko-chan
She's OK I guess
But she doesn't have a clue
She was going to wear her trainers to go for

a walk
And tights! Who wears tights to go for a walk?

Lee-kun
She's fresh out of London
Give her a break
She'll soon learn that you don't dress up in your Sunday best to go for a walk

Ko-chan
Whose Sunday best is a pair of denim shorts, tights and trainers?

Lee-kun
Hey Genny went to church once dressed in black goth trousers complete with metal chains
We don't have a concept of Sunday best in this household
But you can't expect Rose to know what it's like living out here after a few weeks when she's come from an urban metropolis
Harboury is extreme even for the countryside
It must be quite a shock for her to come to a village without a local shop or anything really
Just cows and mud

Ko-chan
You love it though?

Lee-kun
100%
But this must be a huge shock for someone

who's grown up with endless distractions on their doorstep
I mean how awesome would it be if there was a comic shop down the road we could walk to?
Or a bunch of Japanese restaurants to choose from, that aren't just Wagamama?

Ko-chan
I guess it would be rather cool…

Lee-kun
Or having a little independent cinema we could go to to watch anime films?
Or having enough people living close by that we could start a manga book club?

Ko-chan
But would you give up living in the countryside for all that? Would you give up the farm?
I wouldn't give it up for anything

Lee-kun
Me neither
But I wish there was some sort of middle ground…

Me too, I find myself thinking.

Every time I see photos from the cosplay meet-ups that Paige and Genny go to on Facebook, or photos from their visits to Forbidden Planet, or from their manga book clubs, my heart hurts with longing to be in that moment with them.

To have a group of friends I could call on to meet me

at those places, and to be able to get to them without begging Mum for a lift to the train station, and then an hour-long train ride there.

Ko-chan
But we have each other to talk to about animanga?

Lee-kun
Of course :)
I'll always be here for weekend anime binge sessions and for you to talk my ear off about your newest ships

Ko-chan
fist bump

Lee-kun
fist bump

Chapter 8

Rose

I'm listening to a past French listening test about hot air balloons – and feeling sorry for those who had this as their actual exam – when Ari throws himself onto the stool next to mine. I try to keep listening to the track, but his eyes on my back is off-putting. Even though I'm giving him my best withering look, he grins when I take off my headphones.

"What's up?" he asks.

"Hot air balloons, apparently," I reply, which morphs his grin into a confused frown.

"Am I missing something?"

"A desire to take French A level." The frown deepens,

so I put the poor boy out of his misery. "What you just come out of?"

"Computer science, but I have economics next." He groans. "I don't suppose you want to pretend to be me and go in my place?"

"Nope."

He sticks his tongue out at me. I mirror the gesture and then pop my headphones back on. Ari's eyes slide over to my notebook, which is covered in scribbles.

"Are you studying?" he asks.

I sigh and lower my headphones again. "French listening."

"I swear you're always studying."

"Because there's always work to do," I say, pushing my glasses up my nose and immediately feeling very self-conscious.

Ari blows out his cheeks. "I guess you'll need to do a lot of it if you want to become a lawyer."

A cramp seizes my stomach and for some reason I notice what the other people in the sixth-form common room are doing. Not that I don't notice them normally, but I usually spend my free periods with my eyes glued to whatever essay I'm writing, or textbook we're meant to be reading. For the first time I notice how people aren't studying – how many are chatting to each other, or scrolling through their phones. Henry and Rory are in the corner playing cards on the top of Henry's briefcase.

The first ripples of an anxiety tsunami start to lap inside me, but I quickly smother them. I don't care what other people are up to. I know what I want.

I'm *sure* I know what I want...

Then the sixth-form common room door opens with a bang that makes everyone turn their heads. Natasha strides into the room like a model down the catwalk. Without glancing around the room, she strides over to Ari and I, and throws herself down onto the nearest comfy chair.

"I can't cope," she says. "I just can't anymore. How the fuck are we meant to keep up with this amount of homework? Like, do they want us to be glued to our screens all weekend? I have plans. Plans. Don't they understand that I have a *life* outside this prison? If I get set another friggin' essay today, I am going to scream. And, *and*—" she reaches into her bag and pulls out a copy of *Tess of the D'Urbervilles*, which she shakes, making the pages flop back and forth, "—I have to read this piece of trash by next week."

"Why are you even taking English Lit?" Ari asks.

"Because I needed a fourth subject and Mum told me to take it. Said it might—" she holds up her fingers to air quote her next words, "—expand my mind. All it's doing is making me want to smash my head against a wall."

"Wow," Ari says. "OK."

I pull my headphones out of my phone. I won't be getting anymore done with Ari and Natasha here. The door opens again and a stream of people come into the common room. I glance at the clock. It's just past two, so lessons will be changing over. Another hour and then I'll have my last lesson of the day.

A familiar figure catches my eye as they enter the room along with everyone else. Clover heads to her usual corner of the room and squashes herself into a comfy chair, headphones already on. No one joins her. I glance around the room, looking for the people in her group, but I don't see any of them.

She looks so small on her own. If I hadn't seen her enter the room, then I would have likely not noticed she was there.

"You're Clover's cousin, right?" Something about the tone in Natasha's voice sets off a fresh prickling of anxiety in my stomach, but I nod. Natasha leans forward. "Is she OK, like..." She taps her head.

Dear Universe. I am very uncomfortable right now and I'm not sure what to say. A little help here?

But, of course, the Universe remains silent. So I say, "Yeah. She's fine."

And immediately feel like I haven't said enough, because Natasha sighs and glances over at Clover with a pitying look I don't like one bit.

"She's so quiet," Natasha continues. "I don't think I've ever heard her speak. I mean, she sits on her own all the time."

"Perhaps she likes her own company," Ari says.

Natasha waves his comment away – like literally waves her hand in the air – and says, "What's she like at home?"

I frown. "I don't know. She spends most of her time in her room, but she makes a mean apple crumble."

While Natasha frowns, Ari laughs.

"But what is she *like*?" Natasha insists. "You know. Is she... like, weird?"

“No,” I insist and then struggle to find any further words to describe my cousin.

I remember the sparkle in her eyes as she looked out across the fields, her expression opening up like a flower turning towards the sun. How brave she looked staring down those cows, arms outstretched, and the joy on her face when she stepped up on the tractor to talk to Leon.

But is that all of what she is like?

I don’t think so somehow, especially when she insists on keeping me at arm’s length.

“But I don’t know anything else about her, really,” I say.

Natasha leans back, her expression twisted into something like disgust.

“Creepy,” she says. A flush spreads to my cheeks.

Dear Universe. Have I just made the situation worse?

“She’s just quiet, Nat,” Ari says, and the guilt in my stomach doubles in strength. Because Clover’s my cousin. I really should be the one defending her, but I like Ari even more for standing up for her.

“Isn’t there some saying about the quiet ones?”

“Leave her alone, Nat,” Ari says, with such firmness in his voice that it takes me by surprise. I’m even more surprised when Natasha presses her lips together and leans back in her chair. There’s a moment of awkward silence, and then Natasha starts rummaging through her bag. “Hey.” Ari leans forward. “You got any smokes?”

“They’re in my car.” Natasha’s withering look doesn’t make Ari smile. “And what makes you think I’m going to give you any?”

“Because you smoked most of mine last week. Come on.” He nudges her with his foot. “Let’s take a break.” Natasha rolls her eyes but stands up. Ari flashes me a grin before they leave. “See ya, Rose.”

“Bye,” I say. I watch them walk across the car park to Natasha’s car, grab the cigarettes and then disappear into the woods. I turn back to my French notes but I am no longer motivated. I glance around the room. Clover’s again huddled in her chair in the corner, headphones in, sketching something on a pad. When everyone else is sitting in groups or pairs, she looks so isolated.

I should go over to her, check she’s OK, or just sit with her for company. But the moment the thought comes into my head, a stab of anxiety pierces my stomach, because what if she blanks me like she does at home? What if she tells me to go away?

So I check my planner to see what other homework I can get on with for the next hour.

Chapter 9

Clover

"Veggie maki rolls," I say, pointing to the open containers, checking them off the list. "Karaage. Mini hambagu. Omu rolls. Aaand, chocolate tofu muffins."

As I put the lid on the maki roll container, Bonnie whines from her bed. I've already had to chase her back there a dozen times while I was cooking after she got under my feet sniffing around for scraps.

"You can have the leftovers, if there are any. No promises, though."

"This all looks amazing," Mum says as she comes into the kitchen. She peers hopefully at me, so I sigh and hand her a piece of karaage and a chocolate tofu muffin. "Thank you, sweetie." She takes a bite of karaage and makes appreciative noises while I pack the containers into the cool bag. "Did you ask Rose if she wanted to come to Leon's?"

I zip the cool bag up with perhaps too much force and say, "No. She doesn't watch anime."

"I feel awful for the poor girl, stuck here every weekend without being able to go anywhere. I was going to say to her she can have some friends down from London one weekend. What do you think?"

The idea makes me feel physically sick, so I don't say anything.

"Or you could do something with her and Leon – something non-anime related. Or perhaps the three of us could go for a pub lunch? I'm looking free the first weekend in October."

I'm only half listening to what Mum's saying, so I make a non-committed noise, but my ears prick up when she says, "Or we could go see Grandma" and then laughs at the look of panic on my face.

"Don't worry." She plants a kiss on the top of my head. "I wouldn't willingly submit you to that torture."

I'm putting my shoes on in the hallway when a car pulls into the driveway. It takes a glance out the window to drain all the blood from my face.

"Mum," I croak, backing away from the window. "Mum!"

The panic must be evident in my voice, because Mum dashes into the hallway. On our driveway, Grandma, who looks like she has been plucked off the streets of the 1950s, steps out of a 1970s black and white long bonnet open-topped car. She takes off her sunglasses and turns her eagle gaze towards the front door as Mum and I duck out of sight.

"Speak of the devil and she will come," Mum says, pushing me back into the kitchen. "Out the back door. I'll intercept her at the front. Go!"

As I crack open the back door, Bonnie lifts her head and cocks it to the side, her ears up. The word, "WALK?!" screams out of her face.

"I'd never leave a man behind," I say. "Come on then."

As I shut the backdoor, I hear Mum open the front one and greet Grandma with a voice that is louder and more enthusiastic than usual. I swear, I will not forget her sacrifice as long as I live.

While I climb over the fence into the back field, Bonnie crawls under the barbed wire. Once there is a hedge between us and the house, I take my phone out of my pocket and call Leon as I run.

"Draw your curtains and get your arse down to the backdoor to let me in," I gasp when he picks up. "This is an emergency situation and I need sanctuary."

Chapter 10

Rose

I'm buzzing as I stop outside the house. I check my watch and smile when it confirms that I just beat my PB of ten kilometres in fifty-three minutes. I'm on the verge of collapsing, but I make myself stretch at the end of the drive, grinning all the time. I'm so delirious that I don't notice the Panther car parked in the driveway until after I've finished cooling down my calves.

Great. Grandma's here.

I sigh. I'll check the post-box before going inside – anything to delay the inevitable. The checking pays off because I find a couple of parcels stuffed inside, one of which is for me. All the others are for Clover.

I stand for a moment with my hand on my keys in the front door and take a deep breath. I twist them and step inside. "Hello!" I call.

"Rose!" Helen's voice coming out of the living room is the most strained I have ever heard it. "Your grandma's here, but take your time having a shower."

"Yes, take your time," Grandma says, "because when you're my age you have all the time in the world."

I wince as I place Clover's pile of parcels on the hallway table, but I take my aunt's advice and go upstairs to take a long shower, shaving and then squeezing the mud out of my running clothes to make it last longer.

When it's time to face the music, I find Helen and Grandma in the living room drinking coffee. Clover isn't here. Clever girl must have escaped before Grandma got here. I can't deny I am extremely jealous. A look of relief washes over my aunt's face as I enter the room. The moment I step over the threshold, my shoulders rise up to my ears from the tense atmosphere.

"Rose," Helen says, her voice too high, "did you have a nice run?"

"Yes," I reply. "I beat my PB."

"Your what?" Grandma snaps.

The smile on my face pulls too tight around my eyes. "Personal best. I knocked a minute off it."

"Coffee?" Helen asks, her hand already on the percolator handle. I nod.

While Helen pours the coffee, my grandma's sharp eyes turn on me, looking me up and down, searching for something to comment on. Anything to bring me down from whatever pedestal she thinks I've put myself on. As her eyes roam, I hold myself very still, waiting for her to speak first before I move or say anything. This is something I learnt from watching Mum every time Grandma came to visit. Mum once explained to me that she's always been this way – when she and Helen were children she used to check them over before they left for school, before they went to church, before they went to a family meal, or even stepped foot outside the house.

"She's very worried about what people think," Mum said.

I find it strange that my mum – a woman who is nearly forty, and is one of the fiercest litigators in London – still allows her mum to treat her like this, but this old woman scares her more than any difficult law case ever could.

When Grandma takes a sip of her coffee and asks, "How are you settling into your new school?" I allow myself to relax. I take my coffee from Helen with a thanks and settle on the sofa beside my aunt, back straight, ready for my interview, or, rather, my interrogation.

"I'm enjoying it. It's a good school."

"What are you studying for your A levels?" Mum has already told my grandma what subjects I am taking, but I tell her anyway. She nods with approval. "A sensible list. Unlike art, photography and *media studies*."

From the look on Helen's face, I guess those are the subjects Clover is taking. Looks like I've just unravelled another thread in the mystery that is my cousin. There's a tartness to my aunt's voice that I haven't heard before.

"There's a lot of demand for people with creative skills these days."

I take a sip of hot coffee as my grandma's eyebrows rise, although her face somehow stays impassive.

"It's no life living hand to mouth," she says. "Being a starving artist might be a grand vision, but in reality, it'll just bring her misery."

Helen opens her mouth and for a moment it looks like she's going to shoot Grandma down, but then she closes it and raises her coffee cup. My stomach flips as Grandma turns her eagle eyes to me. A flash of pride shines in them, which makes me more nervous than pleased.

"Now, being a *lawyer* is a worthy career goal. You will never want for anything if you go down that path. Helen, you should guide Clover more - steer her away from the ridiculous notions in her head."

"Clover is perfectly capable of working out for herself what she wants from life."

"Don't be ridiculous. She's a wild child that needs a firm hand to take her down the right path."

What the fuck?

What the actual fuck?

I've always known Grandma has a nasty side to her - the side that made snide comments about our house, about how tired Mum looked, about how she always had to drive down to London because we never came to her, about how her and Helen still weren't talking - but never, *never*, has she been this vicious towards us.

Helen peers at her mum over the top of her coffee mug. "Right for who, Mum?"

I want to punch the air and shout, "Go Aunt Helen!" but I take a drink instead and squeeze my fist in triumph as the minutes of awkward silence drag on. Grandma and

Helen are staring at each other, Grandma looking as cool as ever and Helen looking like she's holding herself back from throwing Grandma out the window.

At last, Grandma puts her coffee cup down on the table and stands up.

"I must get going," she says and strides out of the room without so much as a thank you. Helen lets out a breath and then sees her out. Helen watches her mum get into her car and drive away, but when she closes the front door she slides down it with her back pressed against the wood.

"I need a drink," she says, dragging her hands down her face. "Or a yoga session. Shit." She glances at her watch. "I need to get going."

"I'll clean up the coffee stuff," I say.

Helen gives me a grateful smile. "Thank you, sweetie, and sorry you had to see that."

"I'm glad you hit back at her. When she comes to visit us, Mum always wants to hit back at every comment she makes."

My words make my aunt stand a little taller. "Claire was always a peace keeper. I try my best, but there are times I just can't let the things she says slide." She pauses on the stairs. "There's a chocolate tofu muffin in the kitchen if you want it. They're a Clover special."

I'm not sure how I feel about having tofu in my chocolate muffin – I'm sorry, that sounded awful – but I grab one and head upstairs to watch something chill before I start my homework.

Chapter 11

Clover

"So, this is just turning out to be a regular boxing match?"

"Yeah," I say, as Yuri and Joe stand opposite each other in the ring. "Doesn't that kind of make the whole megalobox thing obsolete?"

Leon frowns as he scratches Alexander's belly, making the dog's back leg twitch. "Think it's some sort of metaphor about the strength of the human body?"

"Maybe?"

The match gets underway, and Leon and I spend the majority of the episode shouting at the screen as if we were watching a real boxing match. And then become very confused when the last punch is thrown and the show cuts to a beach scene without the match results being shown.

"Well," Leon says, as the credits roll. "Who would have seen that coming?"

"I'm so confused," I admit. Then the final shot comes up on the screen, showing the results of the match and we breathe a sigh of relief.

My phone buzzes. I expect it to be Mum letting me know Grandma has finally left, but it's a Facebook message from Fran – one of the girls in the group I hang out with at school. She joined at the start of this year and I've barely said two words to her. Why the hell is she messaging me?

Curious, I click on the notification.

Fran
Hey Clover
I was wondering if you'd had a chance to look at the homework for media studies?
Did Mr Yew want us to do all the questions and then also write two case studies by Monday? Or are the case studies for later in the week?
Sorry for disturbing your weekend!

Clover
Hey
I think it's just the questions for Monday and then the case studies are for Wednesday

Fran
Thank you :)
I hope you're having a nice weekend?

I stare at the message for a few moments and then turn my phone face down on the bed.

"I'd better look at my biology homework tonight," Leon says, with a stretch. "Feel free to stay if you think your grandma's still at home."

"Nah," I say, snapping the first lid back on the container. "She never stays for very long. She always complains that the incense and the fracturing light from Mum's crystals give her a headache."

Bonnie and I walk down the road this time. I keep myself between her and the road, but Bonnie, being the sensible dog that she is, trots along contentedly beside me and the hedge. The driveway's free of any cars. I breathe a sigh of relief. I let us in with my house key and dump the containers in the kitchen to wash up.

I glance at the time. Four o'clock. It's too late to start homework, but at the same time I should really do something. Otherwise tomorrow's going to be a shit storm. Although, it *is* four o'clock. It's nearly dinner time. Will I really be able to get anything done in... an hour and a half? OK, that is quite a long time. I should try to get *something* done. No promises though.

With a fresh cup of tea, I head upstairs and am surprised to find Rose's bedroom door open and her music – something instrumental – playing on loudspeaker. I stop at the top of the drop down into the sunken landing, listening, because I know that song. I have no idea where from, but the sound of it tugs at something at the back of my brain.

The answer is on the tip of my tongue when Rose comes out of her bedroom carrying a plate covered in crumbs. The answer slithers away before I can grasp it.

"Your mum gave me one of your chocolate tofu muffins," Rose says, holding up the empty plate.

"OK," I say, although a stab of annoyance cramps my gut because Mum gave Rose the muffin that I gave to her. The annoyance is quickly replaced by a fear that grips my stomach – fear that Rose is about to say something awful about my baking, that she'll say how weird it is to put tofu in muffins, and then she'll ask me where I got the recipe from and I'll have to say I got it from the Japan Centre website and then she'll *know*.

But instead Rose says, "It was really good. I'm hopeless at baking. And whatever you were making this morning also smelled amazing."

"Thank you," I say, because what else am I meant to say? If I tell her I was making karaage and omu rolls, her expression will go all blank and confused, and I'll have to explain the whole thing to her and I... I really don't want her to know what a huge Japanophile I am, because I don't want that shit to start at school again. Not when this year has given me a fresh start.

"Alright, well—" Rose raises her plate again, "—just gonna pop this downstairs, then better get back to it?"

"Yeah," I say and stumble towards my bedroom. A flood of relief washes over me after I shut the door and slump in my desk chair. As I set my mug down on my *Seraph of the End* coaster – yes, it's of MikaYuu, and no, don't judge me – a thought enters my head: perhaps Rose isn't so bad after all. She was actually nice just then.

The tension I felt rise in my shoulders when I thought she was going to make comments about my tofu muffins has gone. She could have made some comments about them - plenty of people at school who would have done - but she just complimented them.

It felt good, being told something I'd made tasted nice rather than having it picked apart and questioned.

I hear Rose come back upstairs and go into her room, but her bedroom door doesn't close. I have a feeling she is keeping it open as a peace offering, but as nice as she has been about my cooking, I still don't trust her enough to have my bedroom door open.

So I keep it shut.

Chapter 12

Rose

Zoe
So when ARE you coming back?

Rose
For good or for a visit?

Zoe
Just for a visit although for good would be good too

Sienne
WE MISS YOUR FACE

Rose

Not sure
Soon maybe?

Maryam
You're always welcome to stay at mine :)

Rose
:)
My aunt did say y'all welcome to come stay here if you want to

Zoe
Hmmm...how expensive are trains?

Rose
I don't think they're toooo bad
Should be fine at the weekend

Zoe
Maybe then?

Jayden
Will have to be a maybe from me

Sienne
AND ME

Maryam
And me
Can't do a weekend but a school holiday would be OK

Rose
No worries

Completely understand
Hopefully won't be too long until I can come visit

Kai
What about next weekend?
My brother's got a gig in Camden
He can sneak us in

Sienne
PARTY! LET'S DO IT!

Zoe
Girl you really need to get your phone fixed
The constant caps is really starting to get annoying

Sienne
NOT UNTIL I GET PAID NEXT MONTH

Rose
It depends if I can get a lift to the station
My aunt works most weekends
I could see if I can get a train on a Friday night after school

Kai
Couldn't you get a bus?

Rose
There's no bus stop in the village
The closest one is an hour's walk across muddy cow infested fields

Zoe
Wow

Sienne
WOW

Jayden
That’s extreme :O

Kai
Taxi to the bus stop? Or to the train station?

Rose
Maybe
I might have to empty my bank account to do it
Think taxis out here are expensive

Kai
Sounds like it might be easier for you to walk all the way here

Rose
Yeah right
Just give me a day and I’ll be with you

Sienne
YOU COULD DO THE WHOLE DICK WITTINGTON THING AND CARRY YOUR STUFF TIED IN A HANDKERCHIEF ON THE END OF A STICK

Zoe
OMG cute

Maryam
Have you got a cat you could nick to take with you on your journey?

Sienne
IT ONLY COUNTS IF THE CAT IS WEARING BOOTS

Maryam
Is that the same story?
I thought they were two separate ones?

Rose
I have a dog I could possibly nick…

Kai
Do it
Dogs are better than cats anyway

Sienne
UM EXCUSE ME?

Kai
Got a problem?

Zoe
Oh no

Maryam
Please

Rose
Don't

Sienne
FIGHT ME!

Kai
draws sword

Sienne
draws gun

Kai
How dare you bring a gun to a knife fight!

Jayden
OK bye guys

Zoe
Take this off the group chat you two!

Maryam
Bye guys
Don't kill each other
Both your opinions are valid
Miss you Rose <3

Rose
Miss you all <3

Sienne
TAKE THIS!
conjures tornado

Kai
I see how it is
In that case…

Ha!
summons meteorite

Sienne
WOMAN DOWN! MEDIC! MEDIC!

Zoe
OMG GUYS TAKE THIS OFF THE GROUP CHAT!!

I laugh as I roll onto my back, holding my phone above my head. Zoe's last irate message has driven Sienne and Kai away, because the group chat stops buzzing. I turn off my phone and lay it on my chest. I need to do some work, but after staying for ages on my back staring at my desk, I know it isn't going to happen. So I start doom scrolling instead.

I see a photo Maryam posted last night. It's a selfie of her, Jayden, Zoe, Sienne and Kai, crammed onto one chair at GBK. Jayden has a chip sticking out of his mouth like a stereotypical farmer chewing wheat, Kai and Sienne are pulling mirroring stupid expressions, while Maryam and Zoe smile their best Instagram smiles. The pain in my chest grows more acute the longer I look at it. But instead of being sensible and putting my phone away, I click on everyone's profiles and scroll through their feeds – Kai and Jayden going to the cinema, Maryam, Sienne and Zoe chilling in Westfield with milkshakes.

Dear Universe. Why am I putting myself through this torture?

By the time I've had enough, I'm so lonely I'm on the verge of tears.

I'm looking up how much it would cost to get a taxi to the nearest train station, when there's a knock at my door. I swipe my finger under my eyes to check that my make-up hasn't run. All's clear so I say, "Come in."

It's Helen. She has what looks like dried candle wax clinging to her hair and also splattered across her apron. Grandma's visit last weekend has made us grow closer through our shared trauma of the incident. In the moments when our eyes meet, we share a knowing smile and there's a sense of connection that I've only felt with my parents. If this is a family connection, it's nice. Although there's nothing of the sort with Clover.

"Hello," she says, "fancy a pub lunch this afternoon? If so, leave in half an hour?"

"Sure," I say.

"Alrighty. See you downstairs." She starts to go but then says, "Oh, best to borrow my wellies again. The fields should be dry at the moment, so trainers will be OK, but, well, you never know."

Because of course we'd be walking across the fields to go to the pub. But the excitement of going somewhere other than school or down the road for a run makes me excited enough not to care.

At the appointed time, I head downstairs and find Helen and Clover pulling on their walking boots. Bonnie is running madly around the garden.

"Is Bonnie OK?" I ask.

"Just fine. Clover wound her up."

"Couldn't help it," Clover says but still doesn't meet my gaze.

We head out in a different direction to the way Clover

and I went for our walk, walking down the lane where I run at the weekends and then off down a footpath. We come across a field of sheep, clamber over countless stiles and gates, walk under an electricity pylon – I hear the crackle of electricity above me and fear a bolt of lightning will strike me – before we come to a single-track lane that leads to a village. This one is full of beautiful old cottages as well as more modern red-brick houses.

When we come across the pub, it's not what I expected. Seeing all the old cottages has made me expect the pub to also be old, maybe with a thatched roof and that white paintwork with black wooden beams on the outside. And it is like that, but it looks new, and it has a red-tile roof. The lettering on the outside of the building reads The White Hart. Inside we sit at a table underneath a high-beamed triangular ceiling. We have to leave Bonnie tied up outside.

"They built it so it would one day age to look like an old Tudor building," Helen explains. "Pretty cool, right?"

I nod, because I guess it's cool? I mean, it's the sort of place you can imagine Instagram influencers posing for photos when they talk about their country retreat. But without massive spiky seed things stuck to their clothes and in their fingers after walking through the fields. Influencers must drive everywhere so they don't mess up their hair and clothes.

Helen chats to me as we look at the menu, umming and ahhing over what to have. Clover holds her menu over her face, blocking herself out of any conversation. The waiter takes our order and brings us our drinks. Clover starts scrolling through her phone.

"We're having harvest festival at the church tonight," Helen says while I pour my Diet Coke. "There's no pressure for you to come if you don't want to, but the invitation's there if you do."

"I've never been to church before," I say.

Helen waves a hand as she takes a sip of her lager and lime. "We're not very religious in Harboury. Dawn - she's our vicar - knows not to make the services too religious otherwise she'd send half the congregation to sleep. It's just an excuse to get the village together for a bit of fun. And as the church is our only communal building, we have to use it, and to keep using it we have to raise money to keep it going." She sighs and takes a long drink. "But the auction's good fun and we have a meal together afterwards. No one really cares about the religious side."

"Sure," I say, "I'll come."

Helen smiles. "Great. If you hate it, don't worry about coming to any of the other services."

"Do you do many?"

"Only a few a year." She grimaces. "Thank god. It's like pulling teeth to get anyone in the village to do anything for them."

The waiter comes back with our food. It's good, but for the price on the menu I expected the portion sizes to be double what they are.

"It's a shame, really," Helen muses. "Harboury's turning into a commuter town. The village used to be so supportive - I wouldn't have been able to cope if I moved to Harboury now in the state I did a decade ago. There were so many more people in the village back then who were willing to help out - these days most people spend all their time in London and then stay in their houses during the weekend." She sighs and pops a roasted purple carrot into her mouth. "Oh well, shouldn't complain really. At least they turn up to the things we organise."

"Do you know everyone in the village?" I ask.

"Of course," Helen says. "It's hard not to know everyone in a village this size."

I think about the street where my parents' house is, about how there must be the same number of houses on that street as there are in the whole of Harboury, yet I only know the names of the neighbours who live on either side of us. I've only spoken to them a handful of times.

We don't bother with dessert because Clover made apple and blackberry cakes last night that I'm hoping we'll get to eat when we get back. Bonnie is very glad when we emerge from the pub. Clover makes a big fuss of her and then we set off back across the fields.

"I'm going shopping on Monday," Helen says, as she and Clover wait for me to clamber over a stile. "Is there anything you want from the supermarket?"

I pause for thought. "I'd love some blackberries," I say.

There's a strange silence, then Clover and Helen glance at each other and burst into laughter.

"Sorry," Helen says when she sees my confused expression, "it's just that we can get some on the way home."

How we can do that when we didn't pass any shops on the way here? Unless there is one in another village close by, but on the other side of another stile, Clover stops beside the hedgerow and calls out, "Here."

The hedge is covered in blackberries. Helen and Clover

get to work stuffing their pockets. Clover throws one to Bonnie who catches it mid-air. I hover behind them, anxiety churning my gut.

"Is it OK to do this?" I ask. "Doesn't someone own those?"

"It's fine," Helen says. "Take your fill."

So I fill my hoodie pockets with fruit. Bonnie tries to pull a couple off the hedge but gives up after a while and wanders off, nose to the ground. When we get home, we tip the blackberries into a bowl which goes into the fridge. Helen reminds us to wash them before eating them and then dashes off to the church to help clean ahead of the service.

Leaving Clover and I alone, again. But Clover disappears up to her room with a cup of tea, and the ache in my chest that disappeared during the afternoon returns again.

Chapter 13

Clover

Back home from the pub lunch – seriously, I don't know why we bother going out for pub lunches, because the food is never any better than what we cook at home and is always overpriced – I hole up in my room sketching my next composition piece for art while I watch anime. This means that when it's time to go to the church, I've barely drawn anything, but I have now reached episode twelve of *The Heroic Legend of Arslan*. I've binged so hard the opening song is going to be repeating itself in my head all the way through the service.

When I wander downstairs to make a cup of tea, Mum's packing her candles into a bag.

"Don't suppose you want to help with set up?" she asks with hopeful eyes.

"Sure," I say.

"Thank you. I'm heading down now, but if you could be there in twenty that would be a-maze-zing. Oh, and make sure you check with Rose when she wants to come down. OK?" She gives me a kiss on the cheek and dashes back out the door.

I consider if I can make and drink a cup of tea in twenty minutes but it's not worth the risk. Not with our toilet-less church. I don't fancy running up the road in the dark with a bursting bladder.

Instead I watch another *Arslan* episode, which means it's twenty-five minutes later when I'm pulling open my bedroom door and find Rose walking across the sunken landing with a fresh cup of tea. She pauses when she sees me.

"Heading down to the church now," I say. "Service doesn't start until five thirty, so you can come down later, if you'd prefer."

Rose looks down at her fresh cup of tea and sighs. "I'll come down now. I don't suppose you have a thermos I could borrow?"

I find Mum's travel mug. Rose pours her tea into it over the sink with difficulty while I pack up my auction offering for harvest festival – a couple of small apple and blackberry cakes with a Demerara sugar crumble topping.

"Those look good," Rose comments.

"Thanks."

There's a small silence. "Are they for the supper?" Rose asks.

"The auction."

Rose pauses as she screws the top onto the thermos. "Should I bring some money with me?"

"Are you going to buy something?"

Rose eyes the cakes. "Well, I skipped dessert at the pub for these so I will." I'm about to point out that I can just make more of these for Rose to eat, when she says, "Wait a moment," and runs upstairs.

"You'll want to wear warm shoes!" I shout up the stairs after her.

I give Bonnie a big fuss to make sure she knows we love her and also grab a torch before we head out the door. Rose offers to take one of the cake boxes and together we carry them through the village to the church.

The inside has already been decked out with bunches of wheat, flower arrangements, strings of conkers, bunches of herbs and a lot of other things that would probably look more at home inside a witch's house than a church. The heating's been on for a few hours, but the air is still cold. It's never really warm until the church is packed with bodies. I put my offering on one of the tables in the chancel behind the choir stalls. Rose follows my example and puts her box beside mine. I glance at her out the corner of my eye as she takes in the harvest decorations, the Victorian box pews, the organ, the wooden balcony and pulpit. Our church is plain, not like the stain-glass and wide-aisle churches they must have in London. My hackles rise in preparation of her saying something awful about it.

"I've never been inside a church," she says instead. "It's... colder than I imagined."

The side of my mouth pulls up into a half-smile. "Hence the warm shoes warning."

"Clo!" Mum's head pops around the side of the vestry door. "Are Leon and Robert here yet? They're meant to be helping me bell ring."

"Nope," I say, just as the church door opens and Leon and his dad step inside.

"Sorry," Robert says. "We had a bovine emergency."

Leon gives me a smile as he and his dad disappear into the vestry. Soon the noise of disjointed bell ringing sounds out from the bell tower. In the chancel, Lola's set up a table by the choir stalls, on which there are two slow cookers filled with steaming stew, as well as a whole mountain of bread.

"Those cakes for the supper or the auction?" Lola asks, setting out a stack of plates.

"Auction," I say.

"Then put them on the other table," Lola says.

Rose and I dump the cakes on the other table, which is full of produce – Mum's home-made candles, bottles of apple juice, a punnet of blackberries, a basket of pears and another home-made cake, which doesn't look as good as mine.

"Best grab a pew," I say. "They fill up quickly."

My favourite pew under the stairs up to the balcony is still free, so we dump our stuff in there.

Dawn arrives while the bells are still ringing, her vestments in a dry cleaner's bag over her arm. She pauses outside the vestry, watching Mum, Leon and Robert pulling on the bell ropes, a pained expression on her face.

"They never get any better, do they?" she says and barges inside. "Alright, I think they've heard you."

"Clover!" Carrying a stack of hymn books stuffed with orders of service, Deborah bustles in from the chancel. She dumps them down on the bench inside our box. "Can you and..." She stares at Rose, who stares back at her. "Sorry, I can't remember your name."

"Rose," says Rose.

"Rose, nice to meet you. Can you two hand out the hymn books? It's one between two. And you'll do the collection during the last hymn? Great, thank you."

Rose's panicked eyes turn to the stacks of hymn books. "But we didn't say anything," Rose whispers as Deborah walks away.

"Just go with it," I whisper back.

"So, what are we doing?"

I hand her a stack of hymn books. "Give those out as people come in. They're rationed one between two."

As people start arriving, I'm worried about leaving the pew empty in case someone nicks it, but Leon and Robert come back from the vestry to hold the fort.

"Don't suppose you want to hand out hymn books?" I ask Leon.

"Nope," he says and takes the one at the top of the stack.

The villagers pile into the church. I say hi to everyone as they come in. Everyone knows who I am, but I don't know everyone that comes in. A few of them are interlopers from outside the village.

At six thirty, Deborah closes the church door, signalling

it's time to start.

"It's amazing," Rose says as I shut the pew door behind me and squidge between Leon and Mum. "You know everyone."

"Well, everyone knows me. And there's not really a lot of people to know."

Dawn appears from the vestry dressed in her vestments and the church grows silent as she takes her place on the pulpit.

"We stand for our first hymn, 'We Plough the Fields and Scatter'."

Lola presses the keys on the organ and we start to drone out the first song.

Chapter 14

Rose

I'm glad I brought money with me, because during the auction I get very carried away. Soon after the auction starts I have a giant loaf of plaited bread sitting across my lap - which also includes an adorable dough mouse - a bottle of apple juice, one of Helen's candles and a jar of honey. I get so caught up in the high of bidding, and the suspense of waiting to see if I've won, that I find it hard to stop.

Dear Universe. Please don't let me become a gambling addict.

"I would have made you your own candle if you wanted one," Helen tells me, as I come back with my candle, grinning.

"Shhh," Leon's dad says. "It's all money for the church."

Clover wins a basket of damsons. Leon and someone on the balcony get into a bidding war for one of Clover's cakes. Leon wins, but pays £5 more than the starting price.

"Worth it," Leon says as he comes back with the cake.

"I want the box back, though," Clover tells him.

The moment the auction ends and the vicar announces supper is served, Clover and Leon dash out the pew door. I sit still, confused about the rush. There's plenty of food and no one else in the church is making any quick movements to get to the front.

"Better go before the queue forms," Helen says.

Still confused, I join the line behind Leon and grab a bowl of beef stew and a roll, which smells herby and looks like it has some sort of dried fruit baked into it.

"So hungry," Clover moans as she walks back to the pew, already taking a bite out of her roll.

By the time we've finished our plates, there's a long queue for the food that makes me understand why Clover and Leon were so quick to get up. The church is full of people milling around, talking and eating. There's a nice atmosphere. It's not noisy like a pub, it has that sort of relaxed atmosphere. You can tell everyone is enjoying themselves.

"Do you do this every year?" I ask.

"Yeah," Leon says. "Harvest festival is better than Christmas, in my opinion. It's more chill."

"But we get a candlelit service at Christmas," Clover says, dipping her bread roll into her stew. "And there are drinks after the service across the road."

"Mothering Sunday and Easter Sunday are dead ducks," Leon says. "Hardly anyone goes to them."

"Heard Mum saying they'll probably not bother with them anymore," Clover says.

"Easter Sunday's pointless unless there's an Easter egg hunt." Leon twists in his seat and looks at me. "Has Clover showed you around the graveyard?"

"No?" I reply. Why anyone would want to be shown around a graveyard?

"Get her to sometime," Leon says. Clover rolls her eyes. "There's some really interesting gravestones around here."

"Really?" My voice comes out high with disbelief. "I mean..."

"Really. There's a whole family buried out there – from the parents to their family of ten children – and a woman who drowned in the village pond."

"I haven't noticed a pond."

"It's all dried up now. And there's also a servant who poisoned one of the past owners of the big house."

"He's not buried in the graveyard," Clover says. "They didn't allow murders to be buried on consecrated ground back then."

I lean forward. "Why did the servant poison their employer?"

"It doesn't say in the village records," Clover says. "But it's thought it was a lover's spat."

I sing, "He had it coming," which makes Leon laugh. I take another spoonful of my stew. It's going cold fast, so I shove the last few mouthfuls in.

When the three of us have finished, Clover yawns and then asks, "Ready to head back?"

"Alright," Leon says.

"Sure," I say.

As we step outside, arms heavy with our auction wins, something strikes me as strange. I'm not sure what it is until Clover turns on the torch she brought with her and Leon brings up the torch on his phone.

"There are no street lights," I say out loud as we walk down the dark pavement.

Leon laughs. "Means we can see the stars."

I look up at the sky. There are way more stars visible out here. In London, the sky is always light with the glow of the millions of people that live there, and the thousands of businesses that operate there. I slow my pace as I take in the blanket of glowing lights above me.

"Bet Halloween is pretty cool here then," I say.

"No one does anything for Halloween 'cause there are no kids in the village," Leon says. "There used to be loads my sister's age – we went trick and treating around the village then, and one house had a massive Halloween party. But it's just Clover and me now under the age of thirty-five. We've done horror movie nights before. Perhaps we could do that again this year. What do you think, Clo?"

"Hmmm," Clover says. "Maybe."

By the non-committed sound she's making, I'm

guessing that won't happen this year or I won't be invited.

Dear Universe. It's becoming harder and harder for me to keep my mouth shut around her. I want to demand why she's so determined to keep me at arm's length. And why the hell she won't involve me in anything. Because, to be honest, it's starting to make me feel a bit shit. Being stuck out here all weekend studying by myself, watching films by myself, running by myself... I just want to do something *with* someone.

But I keep my back teeth squeezed together.

I don't know what to make of my cousin.

"What about bonfire night?" I ask, trying to change the subject. "Do you do fireworks?"

"Not in the village," Leon says, "because there are too many houses with thatched rooves, and also too many cattle and horses. Leighton has a display, or there's usually a good one at MK. Martinmas is more our thing here."

"What's that?" I ask.

I catch the edges of Leon's and Clover's faces in the torch light as they turn their faces towards each other to exchange grins.

"Just you wait and see," Clover says.

I don't know whether to be scared or excited.

Chapter 15

Clover

I wake up on the first day of half-term at 10 a.m. Glancing at the time on my phone I consider going back to sleep. But the pressure in my bladder is too much to ignore, so I haul myself to the bathroom.

Heading down to the kitchen, I glance into Rose's room. She has a small suitcase open on her bedroom floor, with clothes and toiletries neatly placed around it.

Oh, yes. That's right. Rose's going away for the weekend to stay with her friends in London.

A whole weekend with the house to myself to do all the things I haven't been able to do since she moved in. Like blasting my music, watching anime in the living room in a duvet fort, or inviting Leon round to game all day.

A whole weekend to be as loud and trashy as I want.

I'm still smiling from imagining the days ahead when I walk into the kitchen. Bonnie's muddy paws signal that Mum's taken her out before heading to her morning yoga class, but she stills looks up expectantly when I walk into the room.

"You've been out," I say. "I can see the mud on your paws... and on the kitchen floor."

But Bonnie thumps her tail on her bed and cocks her head to the side, eyes bright and hopeful.

"Fine," I say, which makes Bonnie jump up from her bed and start whining at the back door. I let her out and then shut the door behind her. I fix myself some porridge and take it outside. Wrapped in my walking coat, I sit on the back step and throw the ball for Bonnie, eating a spoonful of my porridge while she retrieves it.

"How do you have so much energy?" I ask her, throwing the ball for what must be the thirtieth time, but she runs after it with as much enthusiasm as the first.

"Can you imagine how hectic society would be if everyone had Bonnie's personality?" I tip my head back. Rose is standing behind me, red-faced and in her running gear, watching Bonnie sniff around the fuchsias. "Everything would get done in a burst of speed and then everyone would have to nap for the rest of the day."

"Getting out of tricky situations would be so much easier," I add, already smiling at my punchline. "You'd just have to throw a ball to distract the other person."

Rose laughs, and before I know what I'm doing I scoot over to the side, making space for her to sit. Which she does, even more to my surprise. When Bonnie comes back, she drops the ball at Rose's feet. Bits of dog spit fly from the ball as Rose hurls it to the end of the garden. She makes a face and then wipes her hands on her leggings.

"Everything would be covered in drool, though," she says. "And chewed. Can you imagine going into a shoe shop to find someone's been gnawing on the display?"

"That's only if you'd let the kids near the shoes. Bonnie hasn't chewed anything since she was one. We got her out of that habit pretty quickly. Although, it did keep Grandma away from the house for a few months."

"She's..." Rose's mouth presses into a thin line while she thinks. "She's not the easiest person, is she?"

I snort. "That's the biggest understatement of the year." Bonnie blesses me with the ball this time. It rolls off her tongue and lands at my feet with a soft *splat!* I can tell she's getting tired, but I throw it for her anyway. Her heart's in it even if her body's on the verge of giving up. A strong wind blows through, ripping a load of leaves off the tree. They spin through the air before landing on the lawn.

"I think I might hate her a little bit." The words come out quiet, sort of half spoken and half realised. They're words I've thought about for a long time – a thought that's been squirming in the back of my head for years, growing in size with every unkind word she's said towards me and Mum. It's something I've always felt but never voiced to Mum because it would upset her. But hearing Rose mention Grandma has made me realise that I have another person in my life I can talk to about the old eagle.

But Rose says nothing. I shift in my seat while anxiety takes its first bite out of my stomach. "Is that awful of me?" I ask. "To hate the last grandparent I have left?"

"You shouldn't have to love someone just because they're your family," Rose says. "Grandma doesn't—"

She stops herself before she can say something along the lines of, "Grandma doesn't give me the same shit as she gives to you." Rose isn't trying to hurt me, but Grandma blasted them into oblivion long ago.

She's constantly going on about how many nines Rose got on her last exams, or all the amazing and important law matters Claire and Myles are working on. She never asks Mum how her classes are going, or about her yoga exams, or asks to see my paintings (not that I would have wanted to show them to her).

In her mind, Mum and I aren't worth bothering about.

"I don't have the same relationship you and Grandma have," Rose says at last, "but even I can see that she's awfully judgy."

My surge of affection towards Rose makes me raise my chin and straighten my back.

Huh?

Wait. What?

My shoulders slump forward again as my heart begins to beat faster.

What am I doing?

Why the hell did I just open myself up to Rose like that?

Bonnie flops on the ground in front of us, panting heavily, the ball between her front paws.

"She's done," I say. I pick up my empty bowl and head back into the house, shaken. I can't allow myself to get close to Rose – can't allow myself to forget the rules I set for myself all those years ago. It'll only end in misery if I do.

"Rose! You ready?"

"Coming!"

From the other side of my bedroom door I hear Rose lug her bag down the hallway, then the opening and closing of the front door. Once I hear the car engine roar into life, I let out the sigh of relief.

She's gone.

For two blessed days I have the house to myself.

Punching the air, I let out a squee as I spin around in my chair. As I pass my laptop, I smash play and blast OLDCODEX into the house.

It's been so long since I could do this.

So long since I could just be me as loudly as I want.

I jump up and down on the landing, singing along to the English lyrics and then butchering the Japanese parts, shredding on an air guitar. I blast it so loud I can hear Ta_2's vocals downstairs in the kitchen when I go to get a drink. Bonnie gives me a pleading look from her bed.

"Alright, alright," I say to her. "I'll turn it down."

As I go back upstairs, I instinctively glance towards Rose's room, and my heart sinks to find her desk empty.

Huh?

I'm sad that she's not here?

The feeling catches me off guard and I trip on the rug in the middle of the landing, sloshing tea on my feet. The anger and pain overwhelms my confusion and the moment

– and what it might mean – is pushed from my mind.

But during the day I keep finding myself glancing at her room every time I walk past it. Or listening out for her footsteps on the stairs. When Mum and I sit down for dinner, I expect it to feel like old times, but instead Rose's chair feels empty and not just a spare piece of furniture like it used to.

"Has it been nice having the house to yourself again?" Mum asks me on the second night – the day before Rose is due to come home – come *back*, I mean. We're having a very us meal – liver, bacon and onion gravy with crusty bread. Rose mentioned she didn't like liver, so we haven't had it since she moved in. I never really missed eating liver until having Rose in the house meant we couldn't have it. Now it tastes all the better.

I want to say, "Yes."

I want to say that I've enjoyed being able to sing my awful renditions of BABYMETAL, LiSA, Survive Said the Prophet and GRANRODEO at the top of my lungs and having my bedroom door open without running the danger of Rose seeing my den of sin.

And I *have* enjoyed all those things, but for some stupid reason I feel like there's something missing.

And it's peeing me off because with Mum and Bonnie here nothing is missing.

The next day when Mum and Rose pull into the drive, my heart leaps a little when I hear the car door shut. I peek out the window onto the drive. I get a strange flashback from two months ago, seeing Rose and her mum stepping out of their car. But instead of feeling dread in my stomach, it flips with excitement.

What the hell is wrong with me?!

I try to go back to my religious studies homework, but I get distracted by listening to Mum and Rose moving downstairs.

"Clover!" Mum shouts up the stairs. "Tea?"

I hesitate for a moment and then open my bedroom door. "Yes please!" I shout back and then clatter downstairs.

Rose is fussing Bonnie, and they both look equally delighted to see each other. She stops when I enter the room. A guilty look enters her eyes and she takes her hands away from Bonnie's ears, which makes me guilty. Is she that afraid of me?

We stand there like muppets for a few moments.

"Welcome back," I blurt out at last.

Rose blinks. "Thanks," she says.

I swear Mum smiles as she fills the kettle at the sink.

It's not until the Tuesday of half-term when I decide I should probably do some art coursework.

I set everything up in the kitchen and am about to get to work when I notice my phone is on very low battery. Not that I need it to get any painting done, but I will do anything to delay starting.

I'm heading upstairs and grab my phone charger. Outside the postman's popping something into the post-box at the end of the drive. Something that looks suspiciously like a manga-shaped parcel. I hang around the front door until he drives onto the next house and rush outside. My heart skips a beat when I open the top to find a white parcel inside.

An angel's choir sounds in my head as I lift it out. I rip into the package as I walk to the front door.

It's here!

It's *finally* here!

My copy of *Haikyu!!*, volume 28 is fin—

Huh?

Because instead of five volleyball dorks staring out at me, I find myself staring at Cardcaptor Sakura dressed in a cute golden jester's outfit. OK, she's super cute, BUT THIS IS NOT WHAT I ORDERED!

I've been waiting for the new *Haikyu!!* volume for two weeks. How could they be so slow at getting my order sent out and then send me the wrong volume? Or perhaps the postman put the parcel through the wrong post-box?

I flip the envelope over to check, but my address is definitely printed on it. I sigh and shut the front door behind me. And I was so looking forward to reading that volume tonight.

But as my foot hits the first step on the staircase, my eyes fall on the name at the top of the address on the envelope.

It's not my name.

It's Rose's.

Chapter 16

Rose

It takes me watching a video of someone pulling off a face mask along with their blackheads to make me realise that my brain is fried and I need to take a break from my history coursework.

Admitting defeat, I put my phone face down on my desk and then stretch my arms back behind my head. I should go play with Bonnie for a bit - her slobbery happy face always cheers me up.

Then my bedroom door bangs open and I scream and fall off my chair.

"Fucking hell." I lie on my back, staring at my bedroom ceiling, my hand pressed to my chest. My headphones have slipped off my ears and are at a crooked angle across my face pushing against my glasses. Clover's standing in my bedroom door, a book clutched in her hands.

"Sorry," she says, with a wince. "Did I scare you?"

"Just a little," I say, pulling myself up.

Why is she in here anyway? It's super critical of her to barge into my room without knocking when she's been on my case since I got here not to go into her room. But I'm more curious to find out what caused this, so I take a breath, right my chair and sit back down on it, wincing at the new ache in my hip.

"What's going on?" I ask.

Clover holds up the book.

For a few moments I just stare at it, confused as to why Clover is showing me a book. It's a volume of *Cardcaptor Sakura: Clear Card*. The volume of *Cardcaptor Sakura: Clear Card* I've been waiting to arrive all week. What the hell is Clover doing with my book?

Oh.

My stomach drops out from under me as my bowels turn icy.

Oh, shit.

"I accidentally opened your parcel," Clover says, as my heart beat begins to pound in my ears. "I'm sorry – I didn't check the name on it and thought it was something I've been waiting for."

Oh, shit.

Oh, shit.

Clover is grinning as she holds the book out like she expects me to take it, but I'm frozen to my seat. Because she knows.

She knows.

"I don't want to watch that weird stuff."

It's fine. I can still pass this off. I can get away with this.

"Er, yeah," I say, trying to keep my voice level while my hands move to my face to adjust my glasses, "I ordered that for a friend... as a birthday present."

"Oh." Something in Clover's face changes. The spark disappears from her eyes and her face grows long with disappointment.

She wanted me to say the opposite thing.

She's disappointed that I didn't order that manga volume for myself.

"OK," Clover says. "I'll just..." She leans forward and places the book on my desk. Like an idiot, I watch her and say nothing. I really should say something. "Sorry, again, for opening it."

It's not until Clover is walking down the steps onto the landing that I finally blurt out, "Wait! I lied. Look."

Without waiting to see if Clover is watching, I crawl underneath my bed and pull out a box. I open it and lay bare a part of my soul I've never shown anyone - not since *that* time. Clover's eyes widen at the sight of my volumes of *Sailor Moon* and *Cardcaptor Sakura*, my Kero and Luna plushies, my deck of Clow Cards and my Clow Staffs, my Sailor Moon keyrings, and matching Luna and Artemis mugs, and everything else I've managed to track down over the internet over the past few years.

The longer her silence drags on the heavier the dread

grows in my stomach. Have I got it all wrong?

But then Clover says, “It’s like the equivalent of a teenage boy’s porn stash.”

I grin at her. “I don’t own any yaoi volumes, if that’s what you’re implying.”

Clover laughs and I find myself laughing with her, because I can’t believe that I just said the word yaoi out loud. And that someone else knew what it meant and found it funny.

“That’s the first time I’ve heard anyone say that word out loud,” Clover says.

“That’s the first time I’ve ever said it out loud.”

Our laughter fades and I become very aware again we are sitting on my bedroom floor, staring into the deepest part of my soul. The silence is so acute, it’s like I can hear Clover’s brain processing the revelation. I mean, I’m surprised she can’t hear my brain processing it. Sirens are going off in every part of it.

“Come with me,” Clover says at last and stands up.

Chapter 17

Clover

My heart slams against my chest as I flip the latch up on my bedroom door. When looking down at Rose's box of otaku trash this seemed like such a good idea, but now I'm on the verge of opening a portal into my soul it's the worst idea I've ever had.

What if I've got all this wrong?

What if Rose isn't actually into animanga? What if this is some trick Natasha put her up to, and the moment of connection I felt back in her room was all a lie? What if I turn around now and tell her I've changed my mind? It would be better, wouldn't it, to not risk hurting myself?

Or I could open this door and take the chance that the

moment of connection I felt was real after all. And that what I've been wanting for so long could have been under my nose for all these weeks.

I don't so much make up my mind as act on an impulse when I think, *fuck it*, and throw open the door. My palms start to sweat as I watch her taking it all in – the two bookcases crammed with manga volumes, anime DVDs and Switch games, the shelf of figurines and anime Funko Pop!, the Nintendo Switch in its charging cradle on my bedside table, the Totoro and Jiji pillows on my bed, the anime and gaming posters plastered on every wall, and the display of anime weapons to the right of my desk.

The longer Rose stays silent, the lower my stomach sinks.

She doesn't understand. She thinks I'm so weird.

Oh god, now she's going to tell everyone at school and it's going to stir up all that shit again.

"Wow," Rose says. "This is awesome."

The wave of relief makes me giddy and light-headed. I laugh. "Thanks. I'm glad you like my room of otaku trash." Silence passes between us. "I didn't peg you for an otaku."

Rose shrugs. "I guess I am, a little. My babysitter, Suzie, used to put the *Sailor Moon* and *Cardcaptor Sakura* anime on when she was looking after me. We watched every episode we could together. She would do all the poses with me and run around the house capturing Clow Cards. A few years ago I started picking up the manga." She smiles. "It was kind of cool reliving the stories all those years later, and finding out that Tori and Julian are together."

I put a hand to my chest. "That really tugs on my heart

strings." I sniff, pulling back the emotion threatening to burst from me. "She was like a fairy godmother who showed you the true path in life before disappearing. You a dubs girl?"

"What?"

"You called them Tori and Julian, rather than Touya and Yukito."

"Ah, yeah. I find it strange calling them their Japanese names when I first encountered them with their English names."

"No worries. I find it strange watching Studio Ghibli films with subs, even though I'm a subs girl since I first watched them all in dubbed." I throw myself down onto my bed and then wave at my desk chair. Rose perches on the edge, like it's about to bite her. She looks like she's in a job interview. Do I really make her that uncomfortable? The thought makes me feel pretty crappy.

"So," I ask, "you like magical girl anime?"

"Yeah," Rose replies, pushing her glasses up her face, "I guess."

"Do you watch or read anything else? Romance? Shonen?"

"Hmm, not really. Just stick to those two." Her eyes sweep across the posters on my walls and the bookshelves groaning with manga volumes. "I guess you like most genres?"

"Apart from mecha – I don't really get robots. And I haven't watched *Dragon Ball*." I lean back, kicking my feet out. "I know it's like, the 'king of shonen', but it looks too much like a male bravado show. Leon loves it, though. He's a little bit obsessed, to be honest."

"Leon also likes anime?"

"Yeah. Although he's sooooo slow at getting through a series. I have to sit him down to get him to watch anything. We watched *Megalobox* the other weekend." A stab of guilt impales my stomach and I can't look at Rose when I say, "I would have invited you if I knew you enjoyed animanga."

"Animanga?"

"Oh, it's an internet thing. It's a bit of a mouthful saying 'anime and manga' all the time, so you can smush them into one."

"Oh, OK, I didn't know if it was a technical term or something."

I shrug. "Well, it's an internet thing."

"Don't worry about leaving me out the other weekend – I understand why you didn't invite me."

"I would never have guessed you were into animanga."

"What do you mean?"

"Well, you don't look like someone who would be into nerdy stuff." Something crosses Rose's face – it only lasts for a second, but it penetrates my gut when it does. She looks hurt? Or confused. I've obviously said something wrong so time to change the subject. "Leon and I are going to have a Halloween anime night on Saturday, if you want to join? We're going to watch the *Junji Ito Collection*."

"Sure."

"Cool. Oh, we're also going to cosplay. I was just going to dig out my Kiki dress and hat. I've still got my broom somewhere..."

"I don't really have anything I could wear as cosplay."

I wave Rose's fears away. "No worries. Just come as you are. Leon's probably going to dress up as Goku." I sigh. "Again, because that boy is so predictable."

"Have you ever cosplayed?"

"Not publicly. Just for stuff at Leon's house. Have you?"

"I've dressed up for Halloween and stuff, but not really as a character. I'm guessing you have since you have an outfit ready?"

"I just have Kiki – Leon's sister, Genny, had a Studio Ghibli party one year, so I made it for that. Ever watched any Studio Ghibli?" Rose shakes her head and my mouth drops open. "OK," I say, "perhaps that's where we need to start your education."

Rose's eyebrows raise. "My education?"

"Yeah. Magical girls are just the tip of the iceberg." An excitement starts to rise inside me so intense my hands shake. "There's a whole backlog of anime for you to watch in so many different genres." Grinning I spread my arms wide. "And I can show them all to you." The perplexed look on Rose's face makes me catch myself. I lower my arms. "That's if you want me to."

"Yeah," Rose says with a small smile, "that would be nice."

I can't contain my grin. I'm surprised it doesn't blind Rose when it bursts out of my face. "Great! We'll start with the classics and work our way up. Want to start tomorrow night? *Spirited Away*'s always a good one to start with."

"That works for me."

"Great."

"Great."

There's a pause, which leaves the two of us without words. The atmosphere between us is still awkward AF, but at the same time a few hours ago the thought of sitting in my room with Rose would have been enough to give me nightmares. I still can't believe this strange twist of events.

Rose gets to her feet. "I'd better get back. Got homework to finish."

"Alright. Cool. Yeah, I'd better do some homework..."

As soon as I hear the floorboards in Rose's room creek, I pick up my phone and open my chat with Leon.

Ko-chan
Tell me
This is reality right?

Lee-kun
Err...yeah?

Ko-chan
And I'm not dreaming?

Lee-kun
Well if this was a dream I could easily tell you that this wasn't a dream
But no this really isn't a dream
Why? What's happened?

Ko-chan
So I opened a parcel that I thought was for me but turns out wasn't
It was for Rose

But I thought it was for me because it looked like the volume of HQ I've been waiting for FOREVER!!
But it wasn't HQ
It was Cardcaptor Sakura
BUT IT WAS FOR ROSE!
She reads manga!
And apparently she's watched Sailor Moon
SHE'S AN OTAKU!! :O

Lee-kun
Well...there you go...

Ko-chan
Why are you not more shocked?!?!
I can't get my head around this!

Lee-kun
Well I told you not to be so judgy
If you'd talked to her earlier, then you would have found out she liked animanga
So this means that you're happy to invite her on Saturday?

Ko-chan
Yes
Already done it

Lee-kun
Great

Ko-chan
Although she doesn't have a costume

Lee-kun
Doesn't matter
We're just going to be sat in my room
There's probably something of Genny's hanging around that she can borrow if she wants
What awesome baked goods are you bringing?

Ko-chan
Hmmm... not sure yet
Maybe cake?
Or brownies?

Lee-kun
Something chocolate orange?

Ko-chan
Maybe

Lee-kun
Mum's making her frogspawn punch

Ko-chan
YES!
HYPED!

Lee-kun
Looking forward to it

Chapter 18

Rose

Back in my room, I sit at my desk. I stare at my notes for a bit, and then decide it's a lost cause. I stack them to the side and drag my laptop towards me.

In my Amazon account I click into a private list called "Shojo Magic". In it, I keep listed all the *Sailor Moon* and *Cardcaptor Sakura* stuff I've found across the internet that I've thought about buying. I scroll down to the middle until I reach it and move my cursor to hover over "Add to Basket".

I mean, I've been considering buying it for ages, but I've talked myself out of it every time, because when am I ever going to wear it? But now Clover's and Leon's

Halloween thing gives me the excuse I've been waiting for.

Dear Universe. I want to wear it so bad, but...

My finger is halfway to pushing the button when I sigh and shut my laptop lid.

What the hell am I thinking? There's no way I can ever wear it.

The rest of half-term goes by too quickly, as always.

I expect things between Clover and I to go on as always, but they don't. Instead of blanking me when we pass each other in the house, or leaving as quickly as she can when we're in the same room together, she starts saying hi to me. Two days after our conversation, she offers to make me a cup of tea.

It's like a switch has been flicked inside her.

Dear Universe. It's a good thing that she's changed and I much prefer this version of Clover, but I can't help but feel a little disturbed by it.

Why did she suddenly become so friendly to me? Just because she found out I like *Sailor Moon* and *Cardcaptor Sakura*?

On Saturday morning, I come back from my run and find the house smelling delicious. My empty stomach rumbles, and even though I stink of sweat, I stick my head into the kitchen. Clover is mixing something together with her hands. Bonnie looks up from her basket and starts wagging her tail. I can never resist that face so I head over and start massaging her ears.

"What's cooking?" I ask Clover, while Bonnie makes appreciative grunting noises.

"Pumpkin rice balls." Clover places a ball of orange rice on a plate. "And inari sushi and chicken karaage mummies." Bonnie gives out a hopeful whine, which gets her a flat look from Clover. "None for you."

The recipes are displayed on a tablet propped against the counter tiles. She's on the recipe section of the Japan Centre website.

"I've been there," I say, nodding at the tablet.

Clover stares at me blankly for a moment, and then looks at the tablet. Her eyes widen a little when she gets it. "Oh, really?"

"Yeah. It's cool. They sell loads of different sake, manga magazines from Japan, cooking equipment and ingredients, counters full of convenience store food, and you can eat in their restaurant."

Clover sighs. "You're so lucky having all that stuff on your doorstep in London."

I laugh, because that's such a non-Londoner thing to say. "It's not really on my doorstep. It takes an hour on the train to get from my house to Leicester Square."

"Yeah, well." Clover picks up a fresh handful of rice and starts pressing it between her hands. "At least you *can* get there. Like, you just hop on a train and there you are. You don't have to worry about trying to get a lift to the train station. I really wish there was at least a bus stop in this village, then I could get to places. Instead of being stuck here most weekends while Mum's at work." She sighs and puts the third rice ball down with a little too much force, squashing it into the plate. "I can't wait to get a car."

"When's your birthday?"

"June." Clover mimes a tear rolling down her face. "When's yours?"

"New Year's Day."

"You gonna learn how to drive?"

I shrug. "I wasn't planning to, but since coming here I'm starting to change my mind. Although, not sure what I'm meant to do about learning when I don't have a car to practise in."

"Mum can get you insured on hers."

"Really?"

"Sure. That's the plan for when I learn to drive anyway. I'm sure she wouldn't mind." She smiles. "When you pass your test, we can go to the Asian supermarkets in MK. There's a really cool one near the Buddhist temple. They've got a small Japanese garden there as well."

As nice as that all sounds, Clover is getting a little ahead of herself. And of me.

"Well," I say, "it's still a long way off until I pass. *If* I pass."

Clover waves her hand. "Everyone passes. Think about all the idiots that are allowed to drive on the road – they've all pass their tests. There's no way you won't pass with your grades."

I laugh it off and go to have a shower, doing my best to ignore the nerves squeezing my stomach. Because that's me, isn't it? Brainy Rose. Always perfect at everything. Not allowed to fail anything.

Laden down with bags full of food and sleepover stuff, we head to Leon's. Clover is in full Kiki cosplay, wearing a billowy dark blue dress, red slip-on shoes and a big red bow in her hair. From the umbrella stand by the door she pulls out a broomstick, which looks home-made. She hooks one of the bags over the end of the stick and rests it on her shoulder, like a Dick Wittington sack.

As we put on our shoes, Bonnie sticks her head around the kitchen door and gives us a hopeful look. My eyes must be giving the same hopeful expression as I look at Clover, waiting for her to say whether or not Bonnie is allowed to come with us. Clover reaches for the keys and glances towards the kitchen, seeing Bonnie staring at us.

"Come on, then," she says. Bonnie wiggles her bum as she walks towards us and my heart gives a little leap as the three of us leave the house.

I've glimpsed Leon's house on the way to catch the bus to school. It's set back from the road, behind an old stone wall - the type that looks like it's held together by nothing but the expectation that it *should* be there - and a load of knobbly trees. It's a big house and looks *old* - like it might have seen a few plagues sort of old. There are some rickety stables or barns around one side, and then some larger newer barns set further back. As we walk up the drive, I hear cows mooing and a cat walks along the top of one of the low barn roofs.

So it's a little surprising when Leon opens the door dressed in full Goku cosplay, with his blonde hair spiked up into super Saiyan mode.

"Wow," I say.

He grins and shouts, *"Kamehameha!"*. He does the pose and everything.

"Damn nerd," Clover mutters and pushes past him into

the house.

The inside of the farmhouse is just like I expect it to be. The floors are stone, the walls a mixture of brick and plaster, and there are a couple of shelves full of trophies and medals from some sort of farm-related competitions. It smells like wool, coal and dried herbs. There are family photos decorating almost every wall and cats draped over almost every surface and curled on every sofa. The hallway leads into a small kitchen with a low brick archway dominating one wall, under which is a long Aga. There is a bona fide metal kettle sitting on the top, spouting steam. I kid you not. All I need now is the metal bath in front of the fire to complete the image.

Leon's parents sit at the kitchen table. Hearing us enter, they set down their papers.

"Hello," Leon's mum says.

"Hi, Lou, Robert," Clover says for my benefit.

"Hi, Clover," Leon's dad says. "And Rose. Sorry for the scare we gave you and your mum the other week. The cows don't mean any harm."

I laugh and my cheeks burn – Leon's parents must have been in stitches after seeing us react to the cows. "That's OK."

"We're heading upstairs," Leon says.

"Do you want any tea?" Leon's mum asks.

"I think we're good."

Leon's room is less... intense than Clover's. He has a *Dragon Ball* poster above his desk and a shelf full of Goku figurines, but those are the only flags that show he's into anime. He has a small bookshelf stuffed with fantasy novels, and also some Marvel and Star Wars stuff –

including a Lego Millennium Falcon. Clover dumps the food boxes on Leon's desk, alongside some tubs of M&S snacks and a big jug of something green and slimy looking.

"Oh my god." Clover grabs a glass and fills it with the sloppy stuff from the jug. "I look forward to this every year."

"What the hell is that?" I ask, because that really looks like nothing I would want to drink. But Clover looks very pleased as she downs half her glass.

"Frogspawn punch," Leon says, "but don't worry, it's just kiwis, lime jelly and lemonade."

"Want some?" Clover asks.

I consider it for a few moments and then say, "OK," because I'm pretty sure these two wouldn't go to such extreme lengths to get me to drink something that was actually disgusting. I'm glad I take the risk, because it's decent. Looking right at home, Clover sprawls out on Leon's bed, munching on a chicken karaage mummy. Out of place, I stand awkwardly to the side, sipping my drink while Leon sets up the TV. Alexander wanders in while Leon is unplugging and replugging various wires. I go to say hello, but he's more interested in sniffing Bonnie's butt.

"Clo says you didn't have a cosplay," Leon says.

"Um, yeah," I say. "I haven't really done cosplay before."

"Hang on a mo." Leon gets up and disappears from the room. When he reappears, he's carrying a clothes hanger, on which is hung a blue skirt, a giant red bow and a white top with a blue sailor cape. "It might be a bit big on you."

I raise my eyebrows at Leon, which makes him laugh.

"This is my sister's – despite the fact she moved out six years ago, her room's still full of stuff."

"You could totally rock those," Clover says.

Leon holds the hanger up against his body sticks a hand on one hip. While he and Clover are grinning at each other, Leon extends the clothes out to me. "I can't find the wig and gloves, so Genny might have taken those with her."

My heartbeat quickens as I take the hanger from him. "Thanks."

"Bathroom's down the hall and on the right."

My fingers tremble as I turn the lock in the bathroom door. I turn my back on the full-length mirror hanging on the back while I change. When I've finished, I take in a couple of deep breaths and turn around to face my reflection. The skirt and top are about two sizes too big for me, and I wish I did have the wig and that I was wearing contacts, but I still see Usagi Tsukino staring back at me out of the mirror. No, I feel like Usagi, Sailor Moon, protector of Earth.

I hold up a hand with fingers spread and whisper, "Moon prism power" and twirl around. When I come to a stop facing the mirror, a wide smile spreads across my face.

I hurry back to Leon's room. Clover and Leon look around as I step inside.

Sticking my left hand behind my back and holding my right over my forehead in a peace sign, I say, "Moon prism power!"

"Ooh!" Clover says, while Leon claps. "You look amazing."

Heat flushes in my cheeks and suddenly I feel very foolish, but the smile won't leave my face.

"Ready to start?" Leon asks, holding out the TV remote.

"Wait." I lunge for a plate and pile it up with food. I refill my glass with frog spawn and settle on Leon's bed beside Clover. "Ready!"

"It's so much more fun being trash when you have other people to be trash with," Clover says, as a moonlit forest appears on the screen.

"It wasn't scary," Leon says, gathering up the used glasses and plates. "I'm just a bit… freaked out? I can't move my tongue around in my mouth without thinking there's a slug in there. Clover, don't." Clover stops flapping her tongue at him and starts pulling out her sleeping bag.

"I'm just glad you don't have another house that's close to you," I say, flicking aside the curtain to look out.

"Yeah," Leon agrees, "that one was creepy. Could you help me take this stuff downstairs?"

All the lights in the house are off, so I guess Leon's parents have gone to bed. Leon turns one on at a time as we make our way down to the kitchen, where we dump all our dirty plates and glasses on the side and put some stuff in the fridge.

"Watch out for the cats in the morning," Leon whispers as we make our way back upstairs. "They might bring a live mouse in during the night, or they'll crunch through one on the landing and leave the guts. It's best not to walk around barefoot in the morning."

"Thanks for the warning," I say.

There's just enough space in Leon's room for Clover and I to sleep on the floor on blow-up mattresses, and for Bonnie and Alexander to lie down as well. It's very squashed but also comforting.

Leon pulls the light chord above his bed and plunges the room into darkness. We lie in silence for a while, the sounds of the wheezing dogs the only noise.

"I can't unfeel it," Leon says.

Clover makes slurping noises and gets a pillow thrown at her.

"I'm keeping this," she says.

"I'm not sure I want to watch horror anime again for a while," I say.

"That wasn't even proper horror," Clover says.

"It's not slasher horror," Leon says. "Supernatural horror's a valid subgenre. What sort of anime do you usually watch, Rose?"

My stomach squirms with embarrassment when I say "I've only watched *Sailor Moon* and *Cardcaptor Sakura*", because it's obvious that Clover and Leon have watched way more than just two anime series.

"Ah. You're a magical girl fan then?"

"I... guess?"

"I'll show you some new stuff," Clover says. "There's loads of awesome shojo anime out there at the moment. *Yona of the Dawn* is a-maze-zing. *Snow White with the Red Hair* is super cute."

"Sure," I say. "That sounds fun."

"Clover watches anything," Leon says. "If anyone can find you a new series to love, it's her. Shonen's my greatest love. As you might have been able to tell from the *Dragon Ball* shrine."

"All hail the *Dragon Ball* shrine," Clover says.

"Hail," they say at the same time.

"Knew this village had to have a cult in it somewhere," I mutter.

"You haven't seen Martinmas yet," Leon says.

I'm pretty sure Leon and Clover mentioned this at harvest festival. Whatever this thing is, it sounds like it's going to be something big. Hooded robes and blood sacrifices kind of big? I hope not.

"What was the first anime you guys watched?" I ask.

"Take a guess," Leon says.

"*Dragon Ball*?"

"Yup."

"*Fullmetal Alchemist* for me," Clover says. "I still remember the day Genny – that's Leon's sister – sat us down to watch it."

"She was determined to corrupt us," Leon says.

"She converted us to life's one true religion."

"Hail," they say together.

One of the dogs yawns and it sets off a chain reaction around the room.

"Night, then," Clover says.

"Night-night."

"Night."

While I listen to the dogs snore, and Clover and Leon's breathing start to slow into a steady rhythm, the warming glow that has been growing all evening starts to disappear. I'm excited about having many more evenings like this one, but, at the same time, a familiar uneasy feeling appears inside my stomach.

Why is Clover being so nice to me now when she was so... hateful when I first arrived? Why was she so determined to keep me at arm's length before, and now she's desperate to get as close to me as she can?

Best not to think about it, I tell myself and snuggle down into the blankets to fall asleep.

Chapter 19

Clover

The last word of my religious studies essay crawls out of my mind and onto the Word document. I hit ctrl and s, and then slide off my chair onto the floor.

It's a pile of shit and I'm not really sure I understand what I've just written, but it's done.

I'm so done.

My brain is literally about to melt out of my ears, and even though I am so fucking tired, I want to get *out*. I can't stand the sight of this room anymore today.

Standing up is too much effort, so I drag myself across the floor and slide my fingers around the side of my bedroom door to pull it open. I flop down at the top of the stairs.

"Rose!" I cry. "Rose!"

Even though her bedroom door is open, Rose doesn't appear. I figure she must have her headphones in, so I drag myself back to my desk and grab my phone. As I wait for her to accept my call, I hear her phone vibrating on her desk. The buzzing stops, and Rose wheels into view with her phone pressed to her ear and her headphones around her neck.

"You rang," she says. It's strange hearing her voice from across the room and also in my ear at the same time, but I keep the line connected for the novelty of it.

"I need. To. Get. Out. I can't stand the sight of my room anymore. Wanna go for a walk?"

"Let me finish this paragraph and I'll be there."

"Cool."

"Cool. See yah downstairs then."

"*Ja ne.*"

We hang up and Rose wheels back to her desk.

Downstairs I pull on my waterproof trousers, wellies, coat and scarf. Bonnie starts whining so I let her outside. Rose is still upstairs, so I break off a row of chocolate from the emergency tin – which we have to refill every week because there are far too many emergencies in life not to eat chocolate every day. And it's not helped by the mountain of school work I permanently find myself buried under.

I try my hardest not to think about all the photography coursework I should have done this weekend, and also that media studies homework I've got to do by Tuesday, but my mind turns to it anyway. I find myself crunching down on the chocolate squares so hard my jaw aches. To distract myself, I pull my phone out, open YouTube and pull up my *50% Off* playlist.

I've watched these fan dubbed episodes so many times I can recite the lines by heart, but they never fail to make me laugh. By the time Rose comes down I'm in stitches. She pauses in the kitchen doorway, looking very confused as she listens in.

"What the hell are you watching?" she asks.

"*50% Off*." I close the app and slip my phone back into my coat pocket. "I assume you haven't seen *Free!*?"

"No. Is it good?"

I scoff. "It's only one of the best anime of all time. Although, perhaps we should watch *Yuri on Ice* first, since it's winter. *Free!* always makes me want to go swimming. We'll turn you into a fujoshi by the new year."

"Is that a good thing?" Rose asks, looking concerned.

"It is when you live in this house."

Outside Bonnie starts barking so I go to calm her down while Rose changes into the new walking boots her parents bought her when she told them we had started walking together at the weekend.

It's a misty November day, so misty we can't see the bottom of the first field and the trees stick out of the thick gloom like fingers out of a grave. The fields are now empty of cows, but they've done their damage, churning up the soil so our shoes sink down into the mud with every other step. At one point I put my foot down and the mud rises up to the middle of my calves. I have to take hold of the top of my wellies when I pull it out so I don't lose my shoe. The arable fields are bare of crops and slick with mud, so when we take one step forward it's like we slide two backwards. I give up on the footpath, which has been trampled down into a mud slide, and walk on the stubbly crops to the side.

"You got much coursework to get in before the end of term?" Rose asks.

"A shit ton of photography and art coursework, and an essay each for media and religious studies." I sigh. "Not sure how I'm going to get it all done to be honest. What about you?"

"Four essays each, and then I need to get revising."

My foot slips on a piece of slick mud and I stumble to the side. "*Pfftt*. Revision."

Bonnie's picked up a stick from somewhere and is trotting along with it, looking very pleased with herself. I call her over, make her drop it and then send it spinning across the field. Bonnie chases after it. I glance at Rose to see whether she's watching Bonnie, but she's staring at her feet. There's something guarded about her expression.

"Do you have any idea what you want to do after A levels?" Rose asks.

I kick a clump of mud and shrug. "Don't know," I say, as the familiar sense of panic starts to build in my chest. I have no love for that prison, but the thought of having to decide what to do after school, to move away from home, away from Leon and Bonnie, to find a sense of purpose that pays me money, leaves me feeling sick.

I swallow down the acidic burn in my throat and add, "But I'll work it out. It always happens in anime. You know – the protag is feeling listless and uneasy about life, and then 'Boom!' A stranger turns up who changes everything and makes them realise their goal. I'm sure I'll have an epiphany like that soon... When did you decide you wanted to be a lawyer?"

Rose shrugs. "It just felt like the best choice, since my parents are lawyers and all."

Silence descends on us as we clamber over the second stile and across a bridge over a shallow river. Bonnie races ahead of us and splashes in the water, looking as happy as an otaku in the manga section of a bookshop.

I begin to take after her when Rose says, "Why have you suddenly started talking to me?"

A cramp seizes my lower stomach. Rose sits on the top of the stile, looking at me. Am I having a nightmare? I pinch my arm, but the scene stays in place. Dammit.

Although I really should have known we were going to have this conversation at some point, I was hoping this day wouldn't come. I knew at the time I was being an arsehole, and now I am super embarrassed for how I acted. But I don't want to talk about it.

"You were so cold towards me when I first moved in," she continues, "and then you only started talking to me when you found out I had those manga volumes under my bed. Why? Why did it make such a difference?"

I shrink under Rose's gaze. Guilt squeezes my stomach.

"Sorry," I say and then wince at how pathetic I sound. "It was awful of me to treat you like that, and I'm a right arsehole now for doing it. And I felt like an arsehole at the time, but... I was scared of you."

Rose's forehead wrinkles and she jumps down from the stile. "Scared?"

I nod. "Home is the one place where I can be myself. I can wear geeky t-shirts, blast my anime music while I cook, or curl up in the living room and binge a series in an afternoon, or read a stack of manga, without anyone asking me a barrage of questions about what I am doing or making dumb comments. But when you arrived..." We start walking again, side by side. Bonnie's gone so far ahead she's been swallowed by the fog. I kick another clump of mud. "I panicked, but you looked like one of... *those* girls."

Rose's voice pitches higher when she says, "*Those* girls?"

"Y-you know," I say too quickly, "like the ones who always hang around in the toilets at school, re-doing their make-up and talking shit about other people. Like Natasha."

"Natasha's OK," Rose says.

The words hit me so hard that I blanch. Did I hear that correctly? Natasha's OK? *OK*? Are you shitting me? I kick a stone so hard it smashes through a clump of mud.

"You only think that because she's not constantly bullying you," I mutter. "She might seem 'OK' this year because most of her posse moved to other schools."

There's a pause.

"Did she do something to you?" Rose asks.

I scoff. "Yeah. In Year Seven she rummaged through my school bag and found my anime journal. I guess I shouldn't have brought the thing to school with me, but I used to work on it on the bus. I came out of the toilets in the changing rooms, and she was READING from it. Out loud."

The memory of her standing on the changing room bench, that smirk on her face as she read out my gushing feelings towards *Samurai Champloo* and my complicated crush on Mugen, and the sound of her dumb posse laughing along with her, makes my lower stomach cramp once more. I grit my teeth and kick the next stone that comes across my path.

"I'd written some... personal stuff in there. Just boy stuff, but it was shit. I'd never told anyone at school I was into anime - never really told anyone much really - and hearing Natasha say all the stuff I'd written down made me so ashamed."

Especially when Natasha had thrown the journal on the floor and said, "Guess it makes sense. You're never going to get a boyfriend in real life, so you might as well stick to fictional ones."

"Then for *weeks* afterwards they kept asking me how my boyfriends were. Then they must have done some research because they started asking me if I watched ecchi anime, or yaoi anime. I never answered them back, but they would keep asking me and then talking loudly about how disgusting anime is and that anyone who watches it was rank."

"Did they stop?" Rose asks.

"Eventually. To be honest, it was only Natasha and her bitch parade who gave me any grief, but I couldn't help but notice the looks people would give me when they were laying into me." It didn't help me make any friends. I was already struggling to fit in and join the social circles that everyone else had developed in the lower schools. Everyone else knew someone else other than me. "They got bored eventually and stopped because I never answered back. Made me feel like shit, though... I almost stopped watching anime because of it. Genny's the only reason I kept at it." I laugh as a different memory resurfaces. "She even threatened to come to school and beat them up for me."

"I didn't know any of that about Natasha," Rose says, her voice quiet.

I take a deep breath, calming myself down as memories resurface to the forefront of my head. I slam the gates on them, trapping them like Kurama in his cage, and cover the gates in ofuda.

"I know," I say, "and that's not your fault. And it was wrong of me to think you were like them because you like some of the same things as them, but when I first saw you, you looked like someone who was going to invade my only private space and make my life a living hell. I mean, just because I don't talk a lot and I'm not into 'popular' stuff like getting a fake ID to go out drinking, or smoking in the woods, or listening to Taylor Swift, or Ed Sheeran, of whatever generic love song is in the charts at the moment, or don't keep up with whatever TV show everyone's raving about, doesn't make me boring, or give everyone the excuse to mock me to make themselves feel better.

"And now that most of those girls who bullied me have gone to other schools, I want a fresh start this year. Because everyone's finally stopped giving me strange looks. I don't want everyone at school to be reminded of what they did to me that time. It would give them something else for them to single me out. I mean, I don't care if people find out I'm otaku trash – I'm not ashamed of what I like – but it makes life a lot easier if everyone doesn't know. You know?"

"Yeah," Rose mutters.

As if sensing my mood, Bonnie comes over and drops the stick at my feet. I let out a loud shout as I throw the stick as hard as I can across the field, putting all my frustration and anger into the throw. It doesn't go very far, but it improves my mood.

We head into the next field, another quagmire of cow-churned mud, which also hasn't been made any better by the farmer driving his tractor through it. I hop over the wave of mud created by the tyres and jump into the water collected at the bottom. The last part of the field to the stile is an obstacle course of jumping between the last solid pieces of ground. I scramble over the stile first. Rose hops between the remaining grassy patches and then cries out as she throws herself at the stile.

"Well done," I say as she climbs over.

"Thank you for going first."

I stick my tongue out at her and she gives me a sly grin.

"So," I say, "did you have any otaku friends in London?"

"No," Rose replies. "None of them know." The look she gives me is very pointed. "And I would prefer that no one outside you and Leon knew."

We hold gazes for a few seconds.

"Of course," I say, because if there's one thing I understand – it's the need to keep your true passions a secret.

Chapter 20

Rose

The house stinks of petrol. It's so strong I swear an arsonist must have soaked the house during the night. I reach for my phone and keep my finger hovered over the emergency call button while I slide out of bed and crack open my door.

Dear Universe. Please don't let the house be on fire. Mock exams are in eight weeks and I can't be dealing with any shit right now.

The morbid thoughts - too morbid for a Saturday morning - stop when I stick my head out of my bedroom door and see the house devoid of an intruder carrying a petrol can with a mask over their face. The sound of Helen singing somewhere downstairs makes me relax.

Outside, I find the source of the smell. My aunt sits in the garden pouring a white liquid that smells like petrol into a bucket.

"Morning!" she sings.

"Morning. Something smells... strong?"

"It's kerosene for the torches."

"Torches?" Helen nods at a bucket. It's filled with what look like unlit medieval torches.

"For tonight - Clover has told you about Martinmas, hasn't she?"

"She's mentioned that it's happening, not what it is."

"It's our replacement for Bonfire Night, but it's a lot more fun."

"Does it involve a ritual sacrifice?"

Helen laughs. "Maybe next year. It's trouble enough getting the torches, bonfire and food sorted."

Not sure whether Helen is being serious, I let out a nervous laugh and back into the house.

When I return from my run, I find Leon, his dad and Clover on the village green. They're building something that looks like a small high-walled pen. Leon's dad is hammering nails into planks of wood, which Leon and Clover hold in place. Clover waves as I approach, causing her end of the plank to drop.

"Look sharp, Clover," Leon's dad says.

"Sorry!"

I jog across the road to join them. "What you building?"

"The bonfire for tonight," Clover says.

“For the sacrifice?” I ask.

“The what?”

I blink. “What?”

“This isn’t *Hot Fuzz*,” Leon says. “We’re not that backward out here.”

“At least not in public,” Leon’s dad adds and drives the nail home. “Next plank.”

“See you later,” I say and jog back to the house.

I have a shower and stare at my homework list. I feel guilty at the thought of sitting at my desk all day when everyone else is outside prepping for tonight. I should be helping in some way.

“I’ve got time,” I tell myself and go to find Helen.

I end up helping Lola lay out chairs and tables on the village green. By that point the last planks on the bonfire are being hammered into place.

“Done!” Clover yells. The trio step back and look at their work.

“We’ve got to build it up now,” Leon’s dad says. “Come help me kart the wood down the road.”

“Whaaaat?” Clover moans. “Don’t we get a break?”

“Not yet, lazy.” Leon takes Clover’s arm and starts dragging her down the road.

“Roooose!” Clover reaches out with pleading eyes. “*Tasukete*!”

“I don’t speak Japanese!” I call after her.

“You dub-watching traitor!”

The next time I see Clover it’s lunchtime. I’m dipping pitta bread into my hummus when she comes in to the kitchen and collapses on a chair.

"Otaku are not built for physical labour," she moans, resting her forehead on the table.

Helen pats her on the back. "You're doing great, sweetie."

The house phone rings. Helen jumps up and answers it. She has a short conversation, hangs up and says, "The beef man's here!", and rushes out the house, abandoning her lunch.

"The beef man?" I ask.

"For dinner," Clover explains, sitting up. "He's roasting on the green. I need to make a salad after lunch to take with us."

Now with a full stomach, I force myself to look at my French homework while Clover makes a salad, then we head down to the village green together. Helen and Lola are laying out tablecloths and cutlery. There's a van parked alongside the green and a man pulling something that looks like a massive circular BBQ out the back. Once it's on the green, he opens it to show what looks like half a cow. I'm guessing that's the beef man. I help Helen lay out stuff for dinner and by the time darkness falls, the long tables are full of food offerings - bread rolls, green salads, potato salads, rice salads, couscous salads, falafel and veggie burgers, and a couple of sweet baked goods and desserts. Clover's eyeing up some really jammy looking blackberry crumble slices. I've got my eye on a toffee apple trifle.

The villagers start to trickle onto the green, wrapped in their winter clothing. Like at harvest festival, they all start talking to each other. I stick by Clover and Leon, who are watching Leon's dad get ready to light the bonfire. Then Helen pushes one of her unlit paraffin torches into each of our hands.

"Hop in the queue," she says and points to the end of the green where the post-box and village noticeboard are. There's a line of people holding torches, stepping up to someone at the front who sets them alight. There's already a couple of people walking down the road towards the church with flaming torches.

Leon, Clover and I are one of the last to have ours lit, so by the time we've stumbled down to the church – these things really do not give off as much light as books and films make them out to – there's already a circle of people standing around in the graveyard. Our journey time is not helped by the fact we keep stopping to take photos. We slot into place. As I take my place in the circle a strange shiver runs through me. With the 900-year-old church standing tall and solid behind us while the flames from our torches lick the air, the history permeates me right down to my bones. And then I ruin the moment by snapping another couple of photos.

"Is this the point where we sacrifice someone?" I whisper, which makes Leon and Clover laugh.

"Well," Helen says, who stands on my other side, "you know what they say..." She flashes me an evil grin. "First in, first out."

The vicar emerges from the church and makes some sort of speech, which I only half listen to. Then we're given metal buckets of sand to plunge our dying torches into. We make our way back down to the village green by electric torchlight. The smell of roasting beef when we get there makes my stomach grumble. More food has been added to the tables, this time hot stuff covered in tin foil to keep it warm. There's also drinks. Lots and lots of drinks.

"Grab us a good spot by the fire," Clover says. "Leon and I will source the drinks." She gives me a wink and disappears with Leon into the small crowd of people. Bless her if she thinks this will be my first foray into alcoholic beverages.

Most of the chairs by the bonfire have been taken, but I find three and spread myself over them, making it clear they're taken. Clover and Leon return with something hot and appley.

"It's an apple rum toddy," Clover explains. "Jan's speciality."

I take a sip and the heat runs down to my toes.

"So you survived your first Martinmas," Clover says. "You're lucky we've had a good harvest this year and didn't need to sacrifice anyone."

"You're doing better than the family that joined the village last year," Leon says.

"Which family?" I ask.

His eyebrows rise as he lifts his mug to drink. "Exactly."

"Beef's ready!" Helen shouts from beside the giant BBQ.

"Let's go!" Clover places her mug down on her chair and rushes up to the food table. Just like harvest festival, she's the first to move.

"Where's the fire?" I ask.

"That girl is ruled by her stomach." Leon sighs.

Clover comes back with a plate piled high with food

and starts tucking in while Leon and I finish our drinks. Then we join the small queue for food that has formed. While we wait, I ask Leon about school. He goes to a boys grammar school that sounds closer than Clover's and mine. He's in the top-tier cricket team and can't wait for summer to come back so he can stop playing football and rugby. Turns out he and Clover went to the same primary school, which is a local one in the village where Grandma lives. He's going to go to agricultural college after doing his A levels, which he didn't really want to do, but his parents thought it would be a good idea for him to get some. He wanted to jack in school as soon as he could to start working on the farm.

Clover gets up for seconds while Leon and I eat our first plates, then all three of us go up for dessert and end up coming back with a second rum toddy. I was worried we might get judgey looks for underage drinking, but no one bats an eyelid.

"Can you tell me who everyone is?" I ask Clover.

"What," Clover replies, "all one hundred people?"

"OK, perhaps not everyone, then. Point out the key players to me."

As she raises her mug for another drink, Clover points to the man behind the rum toddy cauldron. "That's Jan – he lives in the big rectory house with Roger, who is... over there talking to Mum. Both of them work in London doing something. The other lady with them is the vicar, Dawn. Next to them is Deborah – that's the lady with the short curls. She helps Mum out with church stuff a lot. She's talking to... Kevin, I think he's some sort of investment banker in London. He lives with his wife Lola a couple doors down from us, at that house with the big conifer tree out the front. Lola makes and sells luxury chocolates to posh boutiques in London and she plays the organ for us in church. Lola is... not here, but you saw her at harvest festival."

"She's talking to Mum and Dad over there," Leon says, nodding towards the other side of the fire. Leon's parents are talking to a woman with a sharply cut bob.

"Anyone else you want me to point out?" Clover asks.

I shake my head.

It must be nice living somewhere you know everyone who lives on your street. There was one man on our street in London who organised the odd litter pick or community event – we closed our road once for some big national occasion when I was little. We went to one or two of those events, but afterwards I would never be able to name anyone. But this... this is really nice. I guess I can understand the benefits of living in a village. And OK, maybe it's not all that bad, but maybe they should consider doing something to bring this place out of the dark ages, like some street lamps and maybe a shop.

By the time my second rum toddy has disappeared, I feel more balloon-like. Everything looks a little unfocused around the edges, and I'm swaying in my seat. Leon and Clover get up at some point and start throwing things into the fire to burn – like dead leaves and bits of branches. They shout Japanese phrases and they throw them in, which I guess are anime references that I don't get yet.

I scroll through the photos I took on my phone. Most of them are blurry, or the lighting is so poor you can't make out what's happening. But there are a few that would be passable for the Gram. I snap a few more of the bonfire, and then call Leon and Clover over for a group selfie. Clover pulls a stupid face, while Leon stares neutrally at the camera. I can tell these two rarely take photos.

"You look constipated, Leon," Clover comments when I show them the photo. The two of them start bickering and chase each other around the bonfire while I edit the photos and upload them. There's little signal out here so the upload takes forever. The photos have only been up a few seconds when my phone vibrates with a comment. It's from Zoe.

zozo02 HUN ARE YOU OK? DO I NEED TO COME RESCUE YOU?

Another one comes in from Sienne.

siennecouture Have you joined a cult?!

I smile as I reply.

LondonRose02 @siennecouture @zozo02 It's too late. They already got me. Don't come here. They'll only get you toooooo...

zozo02 @siennecouture @LondonRose02 OH GOD SHE'S GONE. I TOLD YOU THE COUNTRYSIDE IS FULL OF WEIRDOS

siennecouture @zozo02 @LondonRose02 Does that mean I can take your spotty Phase Eight dress?

LondonRose02 @siennecouture@zozo02 Over my dead body

siennecouture @zozo02 @LondonRose02 Good thing you've been murdered by a village cult then!

LondonRose02 @siennecouture @zozo02 My ghost will haunt you if you dare take my Phase Eight dress

siennecouture @zozo02 @LondonRose02 But if you're dead, surely you don't need it?

LondonRose02 @siennecouture @zozo02 I want to be buried in that dress

zozo02 @siennecouture @LondonRose02 GUYS! GUYS! CHILL.

LondonRose02 @siennecouture @zozo02 You telling us to chill in all caps doesn't really work Zoe

siennecouture @zozo02 @LondonRose02 When are you going to get your phone fixed?

zozo02 @siennecouture @LondonRose02 AS SOON AS I GET PAID!

zozo02 @siennecouture @LondonRose02 BTW. MISS YOU ROSE!!!

siennecouture @zozo02 @LondonRose02 Catch up soon, yeah?

zozo02 @siennecouture @LondonRose02 NEED TO ENSURE YOU HAVEN'T BEEN BRAINWASHED BY THE CULT

LondonRose02 @siennecouture @zozo02 Yeah I would love that. Miss you too <3

There's an ache in my chest as I put my phone away. I do miss everyone back in London, but the pain is less acute than when I first moved here. If Zoe, Sienne and I had had that sort of exchange back in September, I would likely be a crying mess right now. Instead, I laugh at Leon and Clover chasing each other around the fire. Clover slows down first. Leon wrestles her to the ground and sits on her back.

"Want another drink?" Leon asks me, as Clover

struggles beneath him shouting, "*Yamete*!"

I consider it for a few seconds, and then say, "Alright."

The third drink is really the clincher. Everything gets a little bit fuzzy and a lot funnier. Part of me is aware Leon, Clover and I are being way too loud in our seats by the fire, and we're definitely now drawing looks from the rest of the village, but I don't really care. Clover gets up and starts dancing around the fire again, calling on the spirit of St Martin-sama. I join her in her dancing and chanting, at which Leon laughs his arse off so much he falls off his chair.

At some point, I look around and find that the village green is almost empty. Most people have gone home and the beef man has also packed up.

"What time is it?" I ask, even though my phone is in my pocket.

Leon squints at his watch. "Half eleven."

"Blegh," Clover says and then burps. "That's not late."

A cold wind sweeps across the green and I shiver. It's been months since I felt the cold. Suddenly I want my bed.

"Shall we go home?" I ask and realise that I've just referred to Clover's house as "home" for the first time. The thought strikes me so hard that I sit ridged on my seat. Then I see Clover and Leon are walking back without me and jump to my feet. Instead of continuing down the road, Leon follows us up the drive towards the house. It takes a bit of fumbling with the keys but eventually Clover gets the door open.

"Shhh!" Clover giggles as we pile inside.

"WHY?" Leon shouts. "There's no one here!"

"Shhh!" I say, and Clover laughs like it's the funniest thing in the world, which makes me start laughing.

"Ugh. I don't get this!" He turns dramatically and catches the hallway table. The table wobbles and then the ugly brown-frilly-couple-kissing-vase falls and smashes on the tiled hallway floor. The three of us stare at it in silence.

"Oh," Leon says. Looking at Clover he points down at the vase. "Is that OK?"

"Hmm." Clover nudges a shard with her foot. "I guess not?"

"Um?" I raise a hand. "Why aren't you more worried?"

"About what?" Clover asks.

"The vase? Won't Helen be mad?"

Clover waves a dismissive hand while Leon picks up two pieces and tries to fit them together. "Nah. She'll be pleased. We hated that vase, but Grandma gave it to us, so we couldn't get rid of it."

"It did look out of place," I say.

"Shouldn't we at least try to fix it?" Leon asks. He clacks the two pieces together. "I mean, wasn't it really old? And I feel pretty awful about breaking it, even though your mum will be cool with it, Clo."

"Hmm." Clover crouches down beside Leon and knocks two pieces together. "Looks pretty hopeless to me."

"What about..." Leon whispers, his eyes wide with excitement. "What about if we used alchemy?"

Dear Universe. What is going on right now?

"Alchemy?" I ask, unable to keep the disbelief out of my voice.

"Leon," Clover whispers back, "you're a fucking genius. Move everything into a pile. We can't miss a single piece."

Still really bloody confused, I copy Leon and Clover and help them gather all the vase pieces into the middle of the hallway. Clover then kneels over the pile. Looking deadly serious, she claps her hands together and then slams them down onto the floor, one either side of the broken shard pile.

Nothing happens.

Not that I was expecting it to, but Leon's and Clover's infectious excitement made me believe that something might.

"*Kuso*," Clover says.

"We need to draw a circle," Leon says. "We haven't seen The Truth, remember?"

"Remember what?" I ask.

Clover nods and stands. "You're right, Leon. Look up the circle to use. Rose."

My body jumps to attention. "Yes?"

"Come with me. We need chalk. A lot of chalk."

I literally have no idea what is happening, but I'm interested enough to follow Clover up to her room. She shoves a box into my hands and tells me to search through it for chalk. We find a couple of packets, most of which are half used, and take them downstairs. Leon hands Clover his phone and then Clover kneels on the floor and starts drawing something on the tiles with the chalk.

"What's happening?" I ask Leon.

"We're going to use alchemy to repair the vase," Leon says, like it's the most obvious answer.

"OK," I say slowly.

"It didn't work before because we hadn't drawn the circle."

"OK."

"Just watch and see."

Clover finishes drawing an intricate circle on the floor. She throws the chalk across the room and says, "Right!" For a few moments she stands over the circle, staring intensely at it and then starts clicking her fingers.

"Burn!" she yells. "Burn!"

"Um," I say, raising my hand, "I thought we wanted to fix the vase, not destroy it?"

"Let me try!" Leon presses his hands on either side of the circle and cries out like he's powering up to make a magical attack. Clover joins him and I hear Bonnie howl in the kitchen.

"Perhaps we need to try another circle?" Leon suggests.

Then an idea strikes me. And it's so brilliant I can't believe that I didn't think of it before.

"Wait!" I yell. "I have a Clow Card that can fix this!"

"Rose," Clover says, "you're a fucking genius."

I'm only halfway up the stairs when I hear the unmistakable sound of the front door clicking open. Leon, Clover and I turn in unison and watch Helen enter the house.

Everyone freezes in place as a cold blast of air from outside sweeps around the hallway.

Helen stares at us - me halfway up the stairs, Clover and Leon on the floor next to the chalk circle - and I can almost see the question mark over her head. Then she notices the pile of pottery shards on the floor.

"If you can still pull off that nerdy stuff," she says, shutting the door, "then you haven't drunk enough."

Still on the floor, Leon looks up at Helen with plaintive eyes. "I broke your vase. I'm really sorry. We were trying to fix it."

"*Pfftt.*" Helen waves his apology away. "It's going to be a blessing not to have to look at that ugly thing every time I walk through the door." She comes into the house and shuts the door. "Your dad's on his way home, Leon. I told him you might be crashing here tonight."

"Sleep o-ver! Sleep o-ver!" Clover chants, and my heart leaps with excitement. "Let's drag all the mattresses onto the landing!"

"OK," Helen says. "But at least clean up the mess you've made first."

We clean up the broken vase, hoover and wash the chalk off the tiles. Upstairs, Clover and I drag our mattresses onto the landing. Leon grabs one from the spare room and puts it on Clover's right, while I'm on her left. I'm in my room grabbing my duvet and pillows when I hear Clover throwing herself onto her mattress.

"We should build a blanket fort," she says. "Like we used to when we slept here all the time. Oh! We should watch some anime!"

"I want to watch *Little Witch Academia*," I say. "I keep seeing it on Netflix. It looks really cute."

"Let's do it," Clover says but doesn't make a move. And, to be honest, my eyelids are starting to droop as I throw my bedding onto the landing.

"It's too late." Leon yawns and collapses onto his mattress. "And I'm too drink, *drunk* to build one. Let's just sleep."

"You need a duvet and pillow first," I say, dragging mine down the stairs to the landing.

"Grab mine for me, will you, Rose?" Clover yawns.

"No way."

"Please?"

"No. Get it yourself."

"But I'll be cold without one."

"I know. So deal."

"Come on." Leon forces himself off his mattress and then drags Clover off hers. By the time I'm finished in the bathroom, Clover and Leon have sorted their duvets and pillows. While Clover is in the bathroom, Helen goes into her bedroom, wishing us goodnight. Leon is last to finish in the bathroom, so he turns the light off on his way back. He stumbles back to the sardine can.

"Guys," Clover says, "I don't know whether it's the alcohol, or the fact the lights are out, but I'm feeling really emotional."

"Oh, god," Leon says, and then "Ow!" when Clover hits him.

"And I want to let you both know... that I'm really happy to have you both as friends. I would be really lonely without you."

Something in Clover's voice cracks and my chest tightens. I reach out and find Clover's searching for me. Our fingers interlace and I give her hand a squeeze.

"Same, Clo," Leon says.

Chapter 21

Clover

My head is thumping and my mouth is like sandpaper. The light streaming in from the skylight burns my eyes.

Is this a hangover?

Leon and Rose are still asleep, Leon curled on his side with his pillow hugged to his chest, and Rose on her back, snoring softly. Mum's bedroom door is open. She must have gotten up without disturbing us, like the hippy ninja she is.

The house is cold and it's warm under my duvet, but I need a piss and my dry mouth is crying out for water. I count down from five and haul myself out of bed. Mum's sitting at the kitchen table and wishes me good morning. I grunt something in reply and rush into the bathroom, where I take a piss a horse would be proud of. Bonnie's waiting for me when I come out the bathroom. I give her a quick fuss, then rush to the sink and pour a massive glass of water. There's stacks of unwashed plates and cutlery on the counter.

"Good night?" Mum asks.

I put my half drained glass down on the counter. "Yeah."

"How's the head?" She laughs at the face I pull.

"It'll feel better when I'm hydrated again." Bonnie sits beside me and looks up with expectant eyes. I scratch the top of her head. "Have you taken her for a walk yet?"

"Just out in the field. She could do with a proper one this morning if you're up for it."

"Sure. Rose and I can take her out. Later, though."

Mum sips her green tea. "I'm glad you and Rose are getting on."

My stomach clenches. "She's cool. I might... I might have judged her too quickly." I run the tap and refill my glass. "I wish we had known each other growing up – would have been cool having someone else to talk to about anime and manga."

Mum sighs. "That was my fault for falling out with Claire. I'm sorry our stupid spat kept the two of you apart."

That would be the perfect segue for me to ask Mum why she and my aunt didn't talk to each other for thirteen years. AND I WANT TO KNOW SO BAD, but my head hurts too much and Mum looks so tired from yesterday that I decide not to.

I'll ask her another time. She can't hide our family secrets from me forever.

Rose is sitting up when I go upstairs. She blinks at me, a hand to her forehead.

"Mornin'," she mutters.

"Mornin'," I reply.

"Mornin'," Leon mutters on the floor. Then he burps. "Remind me to never drink rum again."

"I won't be doing anything today," Rose says.

"Me neither." There's a pause where all three of us silently wallow in our hangover pain. "Want to have an anime day?"

"Alright then," Leon says.

I glance at Rose. She'll want to spend the day doing homework, but instead she nods weakly.

"*Little Witch Academia*?" I suggest.

"*Little Witch Academia*," she agrees.

Chapter 22

Rose

It's pelting down freezing rain, the sort you know would turn into hail if it was a few degrees colder. Ari and I run through it, our jackets over our heads. He screams and laughs as we barrel past the line of students lining up outside the lunchroom waiting to be let in. The teacher on duty waves us through. Ari smirks and sticks his tongue out at the waiting students, who give him hard stares. I give them a nervous smile and head into the narrow corridor where we squash against the end of the queue. The narrow hallway smells stale, wet and humid. I take off my steamed up glasses to clean them on my shirt.

"I do not miss having to queue for lunch," Ari says,

shaking out his jacket. "Waiting outside in the rain, while the sixth formers went ahead of everyone else." He puts his jacket on, tugging on the lapels, and then smooths back his hair. "Now it's finally my turn to gloat at the lower years as I walk straight in."

"Wet sheep," I say, as the line surges forward, heading into the canteen further up the hall. "That's what this hallway stinks of."

"It's the blazers," Ari says. "Those felty things the rest of the school have to wear. Look." He nods at the fresh batch of soaked students who have been let inside – or rather at their grey fuzzy blazers. "Again," Ari adds as we enter the canteen, "another thing I thought the sixth formers had good. Those things itched, as well as looking fucking awful."

It's tomato pasta for lunch. I look between the salad bar and watery pasta sauce. I choose the salad bar, piling my plate up with couscous salad. Ari sweet talks the lady behind the counter into giving him extra pasta and then adds some salad on top and also grabs the pudding – some sort of sponge with custard. We weave our way through the tables into the library, which is used as extra seating space for sixth formers and teachers during lunch. It's quiet in here compared to the rest of the lunch room. As we move into the library, someone spills their drink, washing the table, their laps and most people's plates with water. The table's outraged cry follows us into the next room. We bag a table next to the window.

"So," Ari says, "what was with those photos you posted at the weekend? What the hell were you doing?"

"It was just a village thing," I say, spearing a tomato.

"A cult village thing?"

"Don't all villages have weird traditions?"

A massive mouthful of pasta stops Ari from answering. He makes a thinking face while he chews. "Not really. We used to have a maypole dance at primary school – that was weird. But nothing with flaming torches and robes."

"There were no robes. Although I might suggest them for next year."

"Bet that was why you couldn't summon the devil – he didn't want to turn up with you all dressed in your peasant clothes."

"Who said we failed?" I wiggle my eyebrows at him from across the table, and I'm sure that his skin colour turns a shade paler. "Are there any other strange things that villages do around here?"

"My village just has a fête, with a coconut shy, tombola and wellie wanging."

I almost choke on my mouthful and have to take a drink of water to wash it down. "Wellie wanging?"

Ari grins. "Wellie *throwing*, then. Person who throws the wellie the furthest wins. But the next village over from me has a midsummer festival, with a maypole and a bonfire. It's all very pagan. Going back to your photos from the weekend," Ari says, "who was the guy in the photos with you and Clover?" He lowers his voice. "Is he Clover's secret boyfriend?"

"He's just a friend. They've been friends for years, I think."

"Clover's too boring to get a boyfriend." The chair beside Ari scrapes against the floor as Natasha pulls it out. Ari catches my eye as she dumps her plate on the table and sits down. We exchange weary looks. Natasha pokes her pasta with her fork. "How is it possible for the food at this school to have gotten worse over the last six years?"

Ever since Clover told me that story of how Natasha bullied her in Year Seven, when I see Natasha now I feel smaller. I hate to say afraid, but my heart is going at a hundred miles an hour. I'm super conscious round her, like I have I WATCH ANIME stamped across my forehead, and it's only going to take one moment in the wrong lighting for her to see it and plunge me into the same hell she put Clover through.

Hearing Clover's story has made me even more determined to never let anyone else at school know that I like anime and manga.

"Don't be cruel, Nat," Ari says.

"Oh, come on, Ari, you're always going on about how awful the food is."

"I wasn't talking about the food," Ari says.

"Oh." Natasha shrugs. "But it's true. You can't get a boyfriend unless you've got a personality."

My palms grow hot. I'm such a coward. While Ari's defending my cousin, I'm sat here chewing my food. I should be the one standing up for her, but I'm too afraid to speak in case it makes Natasha look too closely. But the flash of anger from Natasha's insult rekindles the heat I felt when Clover told me what Natasha and her friends did to her.

The anger gives me the courage to say, "Clover's not as boring as you think she is."

Nat's eyebrows rise so far up they look like they might fly off her face. But I turn back to my food and keep eating. The rest of my lunch tastes a little bitter.

But as hard as I try to forget it, Natasha's awful comment keeps coming back to me during the rest of the day. I channel my anger into my essay on Wilfred Owen, typing way too hard on the keyboard, enjoying smashing the keys under my fingers. I'm so absorbed in my writing that I don't notice the presence behind me until someone taps me on the shoulder. It's so unexpected I scream and almost fall off my chair.

"I'm sorry!" my attacker says. Her cheeks are bright red and her eyes wide. "Are you OK?"

The rest of the common room - even Rachel, who has looked up from her phone - is staring at us. My attacker - a sixth former who's wearing a matching dress and jacket, with her hair pulled up into two bunches on either side of her head - looks like she might explode from embarrassment. It takes me a while, but I recognise her as someone who hangs out in the group that Clover's normally with.

"Fine. You scared me, that's all."

"I'm sorry, but I didn't know how else to get your attention." She gives me a nervous smile. "Should have known better since you were so absorbed... Erm." She shuffles her feet. The smile disappears and she looks like a nervous Year Seven, rather than a sixteen-year-old. "Can I speak to you... outside?"

"Sure." Confused about what the hell this is about, I follow the girl outside into the freezing November air and around the side of the building. At least it's stopped raining.

"I, er, I heard that you're Clover's cousin," she says,

"and that you're living with her at the moment."

"Yeah," I say.

"I, er, I wanted to check with you, if it's OK, if she's, like, OK? I only started here in September, so I don't know her very well, but everyone says Clover's always been quiet and withdrawn, but I wanted to check that she's doing OK at home?"

Her eyes widen. "Sorry!" she blurts. "I sound like a teacher, don't I? It's weird, I know, but I'm... I'm just really worried about her. I was like her in my last school – I barely said a word to anyone all day, so I know how hard it can be at school."

"It's OK," I say quickly. The poor girl looks on the verge of having a heart attack. As taken aback as I am by this sudden and random show of intensity, this girl is kind of sweet. I'm touched by her show of caring towards Clover. It's the first show of concern I've seen for her at this school. "Clover's fine at home. She's... she's more herself there."

The girl nods enthusiastically. "Oh. Oh, good. I'm glad."

"She doesn't have anyone she can be herself with here," I say. The words sort of feel like a betrayal – like I'm bitching about my cousin to someone – but I'm sure this girl means well. And I want Clover to be happy at school. I want her to smile here like she does at home with Bonnie and Leon. "I think that's why she's withdrawn, because she's lonely."

"OK. I'll keep trying to talk to her."

"What's your name?"

"Fran."

"Thank you, Fran."

Chapter 23

Clover

“This just shows how fucked up our education system is.”

“It really does,” Rose says, reaching for another biscuit. “I didn’t know you could only pass the ball back in rugby.”

“I’m guessing you didn’t do rugby at school either?”

“The boys did. We did netball.”

“And rounders?”

“And hockey.” I pull a face. Rose snaps the biscuit in half. “I sort of liked hockey.”

“I couldn’t breathe with that gum guard in my mouth, and running around like that killed my back.”

Rose grins. “Alright, old lady.”

I throw a pillow across the room at her. Rose catches it with one hand and gives me a smug look.

"But, really," Clover says, "why have I just learnt the rules of rugby from an anime? I bet every boy that goes through the English education system knows them by the time they leave school."

"But wasn't it more fun to learn the rules by watching *All Out!!*? By investing in Gion's story to find a sport that proves his height isn't a disadvantage? By waiting for Iwashimizu to regain his love for rugby? By seeing the team develop into a powerhouse?"

"Yeah, but that's not the point." I blink at Rose. "Did you just have a bit of a fangirl moment?"

Rose blinks at me and then turns her face away. She clears her throat. "I really enjoyed the show, OK?"

There's a rap on the door and Mum pokes her head inside.

"Still watching anime?" she asks.

"Just finished," I say and stretch out my legs on the sofa. My hip sockets pop.

"We need something for dinner. I was going to walk over to the market. Want to come?"

"Sure. Rose, you game?"

"Sure," Rose says.

"Great," Mum says. "Let's grab lunch there as well."

Even though Bonnie's already had a walk this morning, she hops around in the garden with the same enthusiasm as if it's her first of the day. We set out across the fields, Mum with her rucksack on. The sky's thick with cloud, but at least it isn't raining. The fields are muddy enough as it is. I can't wait until the temperature drops enough to freeze the ground solid. By the time we arrive at the Sunday market, the insides of our legs are coated in brown. I want to tell everyone who walks past that, no, we haven't shat ourselves. It's just mud.

The Sunday market is set up in the car park in the town's centre - a half doughnut ring of stalls with people flowing in between, filling up their bags with cakes, bottles of juice, jars of preserves, cuts of meat, and bags of fruit and vegetables. There's a banner for Dale Farm Foods meaning Leon and his mum must be here. They're in their usual spot, standing behind a stall full of packaged sausages, bacon, and cuts of lamb, pork and beef. I snap a photo of him handing a bag to a customer and send it to him.

Ko-chan
I see you

My phone buzzes with his reply a few minutes later.

Lee-kun
Creep

I catch his eye as we move around the market. I tap two fingers to my eyes and then point them at him. He gives me a withering look and then smiles and waves at Rose. She waves back.

The ostrich man is here flipping burgers. The smell makes my stomach rumble so I grab some money off Mum to buy two. Rose and I stand out the way of the shoppers while we eat them, steam billowing out of our mouths as we chew each bite. I throw Bonnie a tiny bit of my burger, even though I shouldn't, but if she's as cold as I am, the hot food will warm her up.

"I must admit," Rose says, as she scrunches the paper wrapping up in her hands, "I was sceptical of the idea of an ostrich burger. But that was really nice. Have you ever bought one of those ostrich eggs?"

"I've been tempted to, but Mum always talked me out of it."

"What would you even make with one of those things?"

"Something that requires twenty-four eggs."

"It would make one epic fried egg sandwich."

My palms itch as my eyes slide over to the huge white egg sitting on the stall. "I want it so bad," I whisper.

We throw away our wrappers and set about people watching. Mum's chatting to someone behind one of the stalls – someone selling pies and tarts. I really envy her – how she can just talk to anyone like she's known them for years. I really wish I was more like her.

My thoughts must be showing in my expression, because Rose asks, "Clover, you OK?"

Mum is laughing at something the woman behind the stall has said. "Hmm," I say. "Yeah. Well, no, but it's fine." But Rose keeps staring at me, waiting for me to keep talking. I sigh. "I just wish I found it easier to... talk to people."

There's a pause and I start to worry that I've made Rose uncomfortable, but then she says, "The group you sit with at school – you talk to them, don't you?"

A knot tightens in my stomach. Everything is very tense. I stroke the top of Bonnie's head, rubbing her ears between my thumb and forefinger.

"Not really," I admit. "They're a nice bunch, but I don't really fit in with them. None of them watch anime, so we don't have anything to talk about. I've never felt like I belong with them."

"Perhaps you should give them another chance," Rose suggests. "Try talking to them."

About what? None of them watch anime, or read manga, or play games. What am I meant to talk to them about? Didn't Rose just hear what I said? You can't be friends with people you can't hold a conversation with.

"Nah," I say, "it's OK. I have you and Leon. I don't need anyone else. Less than two years, and then I'll be free of that shitty place. I'll get a car and travel to wherever I want to meet up with other otaku. Look."

I get out my phone and pull up the Facebook page for the manga club that Genny and Paige belong to. The photo at the top of the page is from last night, showing the club gathered around a table at a Korean BBQ restaurant. They're all smiling at the camera, copies of *To Your Eternity*, volume one held in their hands. Paige is making bunny ears behind Genny's head. Staring at the image makes my heart lighten.

"This is what I want," I say. "I want to be part of something like this."

"Are there no clubs around here that you can be part of?"

I sigh. "They're all London based. Even if there was one around here I wouldn't be able to get to it. Not until I get a car."

"You on social media?" Rose asks.

"Just Facebook, although I don't really use it."

Rose taps something on her phone and a few seconds later my phone buzzes with a friend request. I smile as I tap accept.

"You gonna add me as your cousin?" I ask. "Make it Facebook official?"

Rose zips her phone back into her mac. "I've read too many articles on Mark Zuckerberg to trust him with too much information about myself. I don't tend to use my account much either."

"Leon doesn't have Facebook - he's read too many conspiracy articles."

Mum's finished talking to the pie seller and is browsing the apple juice stall. I have a feeling we're going to be here a while yet. I'm about to suggest we go over to chat to Leon, when Rose says, "Have you ever thought about looking for an online community?"

"What?"

"You know, find people online that like anime and manga, and talk to them. I bet there are loads of people on Insta and Twitter you can connect with."

The idea takes me aback a little. I mean, I've seen photos online of other people's manga collections, anime memes and TikTok videos. I often check out the manga publisher's social media feeds for news, and I have read a few Twitter threads, but... I guess I've never thought about actually *talking* to these people. They were always over there and I was always here.

"Maybe," I say. "I'm not really a big social media person, but I'll think about it. Thanks, Rose." But even as I say "maybe" something kicks my stomach. The more I turn the idea over, the more excited I am.

"Follow me on Insta and Twitter when you set them up." Rose rubs her hands together and breathes into them. "I could do with an injection of anime stuff on my timeline."

"What are your handles?"

"@LondonRose02."

I check her timelines. Her Insta looks like an influencer's account. It's all photos of her posing in styled outfits in the mirror, photos of beautiful London streets, or meals out with her friends, or pre-run selfies. Since September her feed has slowed down. She posted one thing over October half-term – a photo in London of her squashed into the frame along with five other people, all smiling at the camera, and then a couple from Martinmas, which look so out of place in her timeline.

There's not a hint of her otaku side on there. Not that I was expecting there to be, after she told me that none of her friends know she likes animanga, but... I did sort of hope there might be. I click on her follows and have a scroll.

"I don't follow any anime or manga accounts," Rose says. "I check out cosplayer accounts from time to time, but—" she sticks her hands in her armpits, "—I don't follow them, or interact with their posts because... well, you know, in case anyone sees that I've done that."

I get it. I really do. I'm always so paranoid about someone at school seeing something they shouldn't, so I have rules: 1) Never bring manga to school; 2) Never look at animanga pictures or watch anime clips on your phone at school; 3) Never listen to anime openings, endings or soundtracks while at school; and 4) Keep your phone history clear of anything anime in case someone flicks through it. My only weak points are my messages to and from Leon, Genny and Paige. Because there's no way I'm wiping those.

But at the same time, knowing that Rose wants to keep her otaku-ness a secret still hurts. She's one of the few people in my life who shares the same obsession as me, and is set on keeping it hidden. Like it's some sort of dirty secret.

Not like I'm one to talk.

Since I know why it's sometimes necessary to keep what you like a secret.

I clear my throat. I reach for Bonnie's ears and start fussing them. "So, cosplay?"

Rose gives me a strained smile, which is more of a grimace. "Haha, yeah." She adjusts her glasses. "I guess it's sort of cool. Although that time at Leon's was the first time I'd tried it."

"You should give it another go."

Rose looks at her feet and the silence that stretches between us is the most awkward one that we've had since our connection over half-term. I might have pushed Rose a little too far.

But could it be that our little Rose is a budding cosplayer?

Hmm. Interesting.

Bonnie grunts as I find a good spot behind her ear to

scratch.

Mum appears beside us, her rucksack looking a lot fuller than it did than when we got here.

“Good ostrich burger?” she asks.

“Yeah,” Rose says. “It wasn’t what I was expecting, but it was still good.”

“Good. Ready to walk back?”

“Yeah.”

As we walk, I message Leon, letting him know we’re leaving, with a suggestion we meet up soon to binge-watch a series. Leon replies with a thumbs-up emoji.

Chapter 24

Rose

For some strange reason, school finishes at noon on the last day before the Christmas holidays. Clover says that they do it as well before Easter and also summer. Not that I'm complaining since we're finishing early, and especially since we get three weeks off rather than two. Although the school day doesn't finish until four o'clock, rather than half-three, which *sucks*.

But still: #privateschoolperks.

As an extra treat, Helen picks us up from school. Clover and I wait along with all the other pupils who usually get picked up by their parents. Helen's car comes crawling around the drive. We watch it together getting closer and closer, until she pulls up. Bonnie presses her panting face up against the back window.

"Freedom!" Helen cries, as we pull away down the drive.

"Thank fuck," Clover says, slumping in the front seat. Bonnie's wagging tail whacks me in the face. I push her bum down to make her sit. "Anime every day. Lie-ins every day. Long walks every day. Doing nothing all day every day."

"Revision for mock exams," I add.

Clover gives me a look over her shoulder. "Maybe."

"Try to do *some*, Clo," Helen says.

I'm all set to start my revision plan on the first day of the holidays. I smash my morning run, shower and shave, but as I sit down at my desk to start work Clover crashes into my room. Her hair is now a bright sakura pink. She dyed it less than two hours after we finished for Christmas yesterday.

"NO!" she says, yanking me away from my desk by the back of my chair. "No! It is *first* day of the holidays. We do not do school work on the first day."

"But I have a plan," I whimper, reaching for my colour-coded timetable. I have it all laid out. Every subject and every topic I have to cover before mock exams. If I stick to this, I can do it. I can cover everything. I can't afford to slip on the first day.

"Which you can start on Monday. But for the next two days we are going to be sitting on our arses in the living room, watching anime and eating brownies – the slutty kind with Oreos and a cookie base."

"I can't afford to miss two days!"

"Yes, you can! Now come on."

Clover made good on her promise and forced me to sit on my arse for two days to watch anime. We got through *Yuri on Ice*, and all twenty-five episodes of *A Lull in the Sea*, as well as a large pan of slutty brownies.

Dear Universe. I felt so guilty by the end of Sunday, but it was honestly two of the best days of my life. I hadn't realised how tired I was until the end of Saturday when I lay down in bed. When I woke up on Monday, it was the first time I had woken up not exhausted.

Damn Clover for ruining my perfectly colour-coded timetable, but I had to thank her for making me take some rest.

I get a promise from Clover on Sunday evening to let me get back to my routine the next day, which she keeps. So on Monday morning, I get my arse out of bed and get my running shoes on. It's a cold and frosty morning, the sort that bites at your fingers and toes, and makes your cheeks go dry. I take off along the pavement, slow and steady as the surface is shiny with ice. I hop onto the grass. The ground is hard with frost, and I find it a lot quicker and easier to run on. I look down the road at the miles of icy pavement and then turn my face towards the fields.

Dear Universe. I might regret this.

So I turn off the pavement and head for the fields.

The entrance to the first field is marked by a hedge tunnel that runs between two houses. When I reach the end of the tunnel, I stop at the sight of the misty rolling fields over the stile, with the white-frosted tree tops and silver grass. It's bitterly cold and every breath is like breathing in a lungful of needles.

At the top of the field a deer stands in the mist. I stop running and stare at it, grazing on the stubble left in the field. It's beautiful and magical, and it makes my heart rise in my chest. But when my muscles start to cool down, I have to take off again, which is when the deer hears me. It lifts its head, spots me and then bounds off across the field, kicking up its back legs.

Helen calls to me from the kitchen when I come in the front door.

"Nice run?" she asks.

"Yeah." I show off my mud-splattered legs, because even though the ground was frosty there were still plenty of places where the mud was still wet. "I went across the fields this morning. I saw a deer."

Helen takes a sip of her green tea. "From experience, I know how frustrating it can be growing up out here as a teenager, but there's plenty to enjoy if you look. It's just different from living in a city." Helen raises her mug to her lips again and then pauses. "Fuck." She puts her mug down and stares at the surface. "I'm starting to sound like my mother."

I go to London for a few days once the state schools have broken up. Maryam's dad is happy to have me stay at hers, rather than stay by myself at my parents' house. Helen drives me to the train station and, even though I can get to her house with my eyes closed, Maryam meets me at Highams Park station. We hug for way too long and get some strange looks from passers-by. But I don't care. I've missed her so much and don't want to let go.

Eventually we walk to her house. Her dad's at work and her younger brother's at a friend's house, but her mum is in her usual seat in the living room watching TV. I say hello to her but don't get a response today.

"She's not having a good day," Maryam says as we take my stuff upstairs.

We hang out in her room for the rest of the day, watching *Queer Eye* and catching up on life. Maryam heads downstairs from time to time to check on her mum, to bring her some water, or help her to the toilet. In the afternoon, Maryam's dad comes back with her brother in tow, which is our cue to head out to meet the others.

Because Kai is a super fussy eater and won't eat anything new, we meet at the nearest Nando's. Tears spring to my eyes at the sight of everyone sitting together at the table. It's been two months since I saw them all. And just like our reunion during half-term, Sienne is the first one who sees me. She screams in a way that makes the restaurant fall silent, but then everyone relaxes when she flies across the room and engulfs me in a hug.

"Roooooose!" she wails.

"Hello," I say and find my throat thick with emotion. It only grows thicker when Zoe wraps her arms around me. Kai picks me up with his thick arms and swings me around in the small space between our table and the next, making me laugh. I bump fists with Jayden – he's not a hugger, but I get big smile from him.

We're way too loud. Like waaayyy too loud. I'm surprised the waiting staff don't tell us to quieten down. I laugh at everything that is said and the smile on my face stretches wider and wider during the evening. By the end of the night, my cheeks hurt and I'm giddy with joy.

The waiting staff finally come over when we're the last ones in the restaurant and politely ask if we want anything else. I glance at my phone. It's ten minutes past closing time. I don't want to leave. I mean, I'll be seeing Zoe and Sienne tomorrow, but how many more times will all six of us be able to meet up like this? I brought up the suggestion again of them coming to visit me in Harboury, perhaps during the Easter holidays, but it was met with some less than enthusiastic responses. The photos of Martinmas might have put everyone off, but I'm sure I can persuade them in the summer. And if Clover is OK with it. I'm not sure she would be comfortable with five other people descending on her house.

Outside the restaurant I say a long goodbye to Kai and give Jayden another fist bump. I hug Zoe and Sienne tight while I gush about how much I'm looking forward to seeing them tomorrow.

"I've missed this," I say, when Maryam and I are in bed that night, me on the blow-up mattress on her floor, lights off with the sounds of London traffic outside her window. "I've missed you guys so much."

"We've missed you too," Maryam assures me. "But don't get all sappy just yet – we've still got the whole of tomorrow and some of Sunday to spend together."

But it all goes by way too quickly. The next day speeds by in a whirl of Christmas shopping crowds at Westfield. I buy way too many clothes – all clothes that I won't be able to wear back in Harboury for fear of getting muddy – and eat way too much when we grab dessert for lunch.

Then it's Sunday afternoon and Maryam is walking me back to the train station. We exchange another long hug outside.

"Love you," I tell her.

"Love you too," she replies and squeezes me extra tight.

On Christmas Eve, Clover allows me to study in the morning but then drags me into the living room in the afternoon to watch *A Place Further than the Universe*. I heard Helen get up before me, and all day she's been zipping in and out of the house, and running up and down to the church. When I come downstairs, the kitchen smells like mince pies and cinnamon. When I go in there to get a drink, I find a whole tray of baked cinnamon rolls and cooling racks heavy with mince pies.

"Can I have a cinnamon roll?" I shout through the house.

"Not yet!" Clover shouts back. "I haven't iced them."

"I don't care!"

"I care! Have a mince pie instead."

But I don't like mince pies, and I really don't understand why anyone would, so I take my tea and pout when I get back to the living room.

"Later," Clover tells me and presses play on the next episode.

We're six episodes in - and I'm so invested in these girls and their desire to get to Antarctica that I know I'm going to cry at the end no matter what - when Clover gets a message that makes her squeal.

"Genny and Paige are here," Clover says as she types a reply. "We're heading over there in an hour."

"With cinnamon buns?"

"They're technically for the church after party, but I'm sure one won't be missed."

I pump my fist and feel very smug, especially when I'm walking down the road licking my sticky fingers.

"Am I right in thinking that Genny and Paige own a gaming company?" I ask as we start walking down the farm driveway.

"Yeah, they've released a few mini games on Steam. Their next game is going to be released on consoles." Clover's eyes light up. "I can't wait to play it!"

I've seen photos of Genny and Paige, and heard stories, so I already have a strong impression of them - loud, cheery and the sort of ladies that would whisk you out at a moment's notice for a fun night out - but I do not expect to be scooped up in a tight hug the moment Leon's door opens. Which is exactly what happens.

"You must be Rose," says a loud voice. The pair of solid arms give me another squeeze and then let me go. Then I'm looking up into the smiling face of a tall curvy white woman, with long bright blue hair and a nose stud. She's wearing a low neck long-sleeved black top that shows off the hints of the tattoos on her chest, a red tartan skirt with a lace-up waist, and has the most perfect wings around her eyes I've ever seen.

Dear Universe. I'm staring.

A hand hits Genny on the shoulder, as a voice says, "You've frightened the poor love." I follow the hand and find Paige, a brown girl with a dark pixie haircut. She's wearing a pair of ripped jeans and a poncho which is covered in manga panels.

Dear Universe. I'm staring again, aren't I?

Paige's eyes follow mine to her poncho. She breaks into a smile and holds out her arms so I can get a better look.

"It's awesome, isn't it?" She twirls so I can look at the back. "My little bro made it for me. Do you recognise many of the panels?"

"I recognise some of the characters," I say. "Clover's been working on developing my manga knowledge."

"She is," Clover says, "but right now she's developing her own disbelief that she hasn't received a hug."

Genny laughs. "Sorry, Ko-chan. How about a GENNY AND PAIGE SANDWICH!" Clover shrieks with delight as she's enveloped in a hug between the two women.

"Trash sandwich!" Clover shouts and the three of them set about giggling. Inside the house Alexander begins to bark.

"Fuck it's cold out here. Let's get in." Genny ushers us all inside. We wave to Leon's parents as we pass through the kitchen and wish them a merry Christmas, and head upstairs, followed by Alexander, who tries to lick the remains of the cinnamon roll icing from my fingers. Instead of going into Leon's room, we go into another bedroom, which is twice the size of Leon's room but is filled by a double bed and more gaming stuff than a gaming shop. A massive flat screen TV dominates one wall, while all the others are covered in gaming posters, or shelves filled with figurines, game artwork books and guidebooks. On the stand under the TV are at least six consoles and a box full of jumbled controllers. I'm taking a guess that this is Genny's room.

"Wow," I say. "You like gaming, then?"

Genny laughs and her eyes take on that same glitter Clover gets in her eyes when she talks about anime. "Yeah, just a little."

Leon is sat in one of the two gaming chairs facing the TV, a controller in his hand, eyes focused on the TV screen. He pauses the game and swivels when he hears us come in.

"Merry Christmas," he says.

"Merry Christmas," Clover says and throws herself into the other gaming chair. She frowns at the screen. "Why are you playing *Little Nightmares* on Christmas Eve?"

"Because it's scary, and Christmas Eve is prime ghost story time."

"Now that everyone's here," Genny says, "let's play a multiplayer. What shall we start with? I brought all my consoles back from London. Even the VR stuff."

"*Mario Kart*!" Clover cries.

"Switch or Wii?" Genny asks.

"WII!"

"That's a dangerous game to play on Christmas Eve," Leon says, as he saves and quits his game. "Might ruin the goodwill vibe."

Paige makes a farting noise. "Screw goodwill. Clover and I have a score to settle."

"Damn right," Clover says and the two of them clasp hands. "*Makenai*!" Clover vows.

"Be prepared," Genny whispers to me. "This is going to get ugly."

I've played on consoles a few times – and I really mean a few. Jayden and Kai both have Xboxes. We've had a few impromptu gaming tournaments when we're at theirs, but mostly him and Jayden meet up with other guys from our year to play. We always play shooting games or ones where you just button mash to pull off a series of fighting moves. I sort of enjoyed it the couple of times I'd played, but mostly I just felt confused by what the hell was going on.

As there are five of us and only four controllers for the Wii, we take turns sitting out. I volunteer to go first so I can watch what I need to do when it's my turn. The idea was a good one on my part, but halfway through the first race I'm gaping open mouthed at the chaos.

Dear Universe. I'm not sure I'm going to survive this.

Paige and Clover's progress around each track is followed by a string of expletives. They sit in the gaming chairs, bent over their controllers, eyes fixed on the screen. Most of the time they jostle for first place. To my surprise, Leon and Genny don't engage in any sort of sibling rivalry I typically see around my friends. They sit calmly next to each other, laughing occasionally at something that happens on screen or that Paige or Clover has said. Once they have played four races, the final scoreboard comes up. Paige's character – a blonde lady in a pink dress – is at the top of the board. Clover is in second place. Paige stands on her chair pumping her fists, while Clover sinks to the floor on her hands and knees.

"I am shamed," she whispers.

Leon pats her shoulder. "You'll get her next time."

Clover passes her controller to me. "Here," she says,

looking dazed, "avenge me."

"OK," I say and sit down in her chair.

We go through the character and vehicle selection process. I have no idea what to pick, so I choose whatever looks good. Once the race starts, the chaos I saw is no comparison to what actually goes on.

I lose every single race, coming in last place for most of them. Clover hovers over my shoulder reminding me what button to press to release my box item, how to drift around corners, and how to accelerate. Most of the time I hit a box, I get the bullet thing which zooms me back into the middle of the pack. Each time I do, I get a chorus of, "Bullet Bill!" and everyone's radars begin to beep. I still drop to the back very quickly afterwards.

Leon and Clover swap next. Then Genny and Leon. Then Paige and Genny.

By the end of the final round, I'm finishing in the middle of the pack rather than at the end and have picked up a few tricks by watching the others out of the corner of my eye.

"Finish on Rainbow Road?" Genny asks, pointing her controller at the screen.

"Always!" Clover says. "Although I still think Wario's Gold Mine is harder."

"How you finding it?" Paige asks me.

I smile and, like the fool I am, say, "I'm getting the hang of it."

I don't even finish the next race.

I fall off the course countless times and get airlifted back on while the others zip around without a care.

Although I feel a slight surge of smugness when Clover tumbles off the course after taking a corner too hard.

"Don't worry," Paige says as my character comes to a depressing stop far from the finish line. "It takes a lot of practice to get any good at Rainbow Road."

"Can we play *Worms* next?" Clover asks.

I enjoy *Worms* a lot more than *Mario Kart*. I still lose but cackle along with everyone else at the ridiculous deaths.

We switch back to the Wii and play some party games, then Leon's dad shouts up the stairs that he and Leon's mum are heading up to the church.

"We'd best go too if we want good seats," Genny says. We switch everything off, put on all our layers and walk up to the church, phone torches lighting our way. We joke and laugh as we replay the best moments of the afternoon, and by the time we've reached the church my cheeks are aching from smiling so much.

The service doesn't begin for another twenty minutes, but there are already people sitting in pews. Helen and a couple of others are lighting the dozens of tea candles placed around the church, and also the candlesticks in the windows. There are flowers placed in vases around the building and a couple of pieces of greenery threaded through with fairy lights hanging down various parts of the wall.

Leon's parents have grabbed a box pew, but as we pile in, Leon's dad says, "Who wants to help with bell ringing?" Paige and Genny jump at the opportunity and the three of them disappear into the back room.

Deborah, who asked Clover and I to help hand out

hymn sheets last time, reappears, but she jumps on some other people and gets them to do it. Clover grabs us a couple of hymn books and some orders of service.

"Are we singing 'Ding Dong'?" Leon asks.

Clover flips to the back of the order of service. She breaks out into a grin. "Yes, we are."

By the time the service is due to start, the church is packed. I thought the church was busy during harvest festival, when all the box pews were full, but tonight there are people crowded on the balcony at the back of the church and the choir stalls in the chancel are also packed. Bell duty done, Genny, Paige and Leon's dad join us back in the pew along with Helen. It's all a bit of a squash, but it's also sort of cosy. Someone turns off the lights, leaving the church bathed in nothing but candlelight in time for the vicar to emerge from the back room.

I am strangely giddy during the service, like I'm slightly drunk. I sing the carols way too loudly, especially "Ding Dong! Merrily on High". But then everyone does. Genny, Paige and Clover break out into giggles a few times during the carols.

At the end of the service, the vicar says, "Roger and Jan have very kindly invited us to join them across the road for mulled wine and mince pies. I hope to see you there, but, if I don't, I wish you all a very merry Christmas and a happy new year."

The organ starts up again and everyone remains seated as the vicar walks between the pews to the room at the back of the church. Once she's passed, the pew doors open as everyone spills out and dozens of chatting voices echo around the building.

“You coming across the road?” Helen asks.

“Of course,” Genny says. “Clover’s cinnamon buns are there, ready and waiting to meet my stomach. There’s no way I’m letting them down.”

“It would be rude to ignore them,” Paige says, linking her arm through Genny’s.

“Indeed,” Leon agrees.

“I can already vouch for them,” I say.

Leon, Genny and Paige’s heads turn in my direction. Each one of them wears a look of outrage.

“Um, excuse me,” Genny says, turning to Clover, who has her eyebrows raised. “What is this favouritism? Why didn’t you bring some for us to sample?”

“There’s no time to waste! Quick.” Paige turns the pew lock. “Let’s get there before they all go.”

Paige and Genny push their way through the crowd of villagers and disappear out the door.

“Are they really likely to go so quickly?” I ask. “I was rather hoping to get at least another two before the end of the night.”

“Don’t underestimate how much a village full of farmers can eat,” Leon says. “Especially once they get on the cherry vodka.”

“Cherry vodka?” I ask, but I just get one of Leon and Clover’s knowing looks.

As we leave the church, the vicar shakes our hands and wishes us a merry Christmas. We walk across the road to a big old house, which is all lit up and decorated with Christmas lights. With the herd of glowing electric deer on one side of the lawn, the inflatable Father Christmas and

Rudolph on the other, the strings of Christmas lights trimming the edges of the house and every tree outside, and the waving gingerbread man and snowman outside the front gates, the house looks like it would be more at home in an American suburb. The sign on the wall outside says it's called The Old Vicarage. The front door is open and we walk straight into a grand hallway with black and white tiles, and half a set of stairs at the back. A small chandelier hangs down from the ceiling in the middle of the hallway, casting fractured light on the oil paintings on the walls. On the right is a modern kitchen, with gleaming counters and a big island. We head into a living room on the left, and I follow Clover's and Leon's example by throwing my coat over the back of a sofa, which looks too expensive to be discarding coats onto. There are already a few people milling around, drinks and mince pies in hand. Genny and Paige are talking to a well-dressed middle-aged man in front of the lit fireplace. Each of them have a cinnamon bun.

Soon I also have one in hand, as well as a champagne flute filled with something purple and bubbling that was handed to me by another middle-aged man dressed in a nice shirt and felt reindeer antlers. I recognise him as Jan, the man who was serving rum toddies at Martinmas. Then I remember the man Genny and Paige are talking to is Roger, who I am guessing is Jan's husband?

"Merry Christmas, nerds," Clover says and we click our glasses together. I take a sip and can taste cherries and lemon.

A couple of hours and cherry vodkas later the five of us are stumbling down the road, belting out Christmas

Carols. At some point Genny and Clover start singing "The Twelve Days of Christmas" but swap out the traditional items for anime references, which sends me, Paige and Leon into hysterics. By the time they get up to "Seven wishing Dragon Balls" we've arrived at Clover's house. There's lots of hugs and I end up in a Genny and Paige sandwich. Clover and Leon knock the side of their forearms together in their weird handshake. We scream "Merry Christmas!" at each other as Clover and I stand outside our front door. Bonnie's waiting for us in the hallway. Clover and I make a massive fuss of her for a bit, let her out to do her business, then Clover says, "We need to hang our stockings."

We kick our shoes off and skid into the living room. To my surprise, my stocking is hanging on the arm of the sofa beside two I assume are Clover's and Helen's.

As I pick it up, I get a rush of homesickness, the kind I haven't had in weeks. It finally hits me that this is the first Christmas I won't be with Mum and Dad. The joy and excitement I felt a moment ago dissipates, leaving my throat thick and my eyes wet.

"You OK?" Clover asks. She's holding a knitted stripy stocking with Father Christmas skiing on one side.

"Yeah," I say, blinking. "Just had a realisation."

I hang my stocking beside Clover's over the fireplace and then we head up to bed.

"I know Mum fills them when she gets home," Clover says as we climb the stairs, "but I don't want it to stop. It's the one thing that makes me feel like a kid still."

While I wait for Clover to finish in the bathroom, I check my phone and find a message from Mum. It's a photo of her and Dad sitting out in the garden of their Dubai house. It's night time, but their faces are lit by the garden lights.

Mum
Merry Christmas. Speak to you tomorrow.
Love you loads xxx

The message was sent three hours ago, but I reply anyway, knowing they'll pick it up in the morning.

Rose
Merry Christmas
Miss you and love you and Dad loads
xxx

As I wait for sleep to take me, my mind replays the events of the night. I end up snorting with laughter. I sort of feel a little guilty. This is the longest time I've spent away from my parents, and the first Christmas we haven't been together – I should miss them. And I do, I really do, but not with the same intensity I should. Instead, I'm falling asleep with a grin on my face. Something I can't help after the Christmas Eve I've just had.

I guess if I'm not able to be with my parents, Harboury isn't too bad a place to be on Christmas Eve.

Chapter 25

Clover

I can't believe I'm here again.

You would have thought that after Martinmas I would have learnt my lesson. But it turns out that cherry vodka is lethal stuff. There's a whole belfry ringing in my head while my body is on a ship rolling on the high seas.

I drag myself through the silent house to the kitchen for a massive glass of water and hole up in bed. What time did Mum get in last night? It's 6.30 a.m., but I already have a text from Leon timestamped at 6.00 a.m.

```
Lee-kun
Yearly traditions never die
Genny just jumped on me and demanded I get up
```

```
I refused and then she stole my covers :(
I really hope one day she accepts that
Christmas Day doesn't have to run like
clockwork
```

```
                                          Ko-chan
     I'm in danger of this hangover becoming a
                                 yearly tradition
                           And Merry Christmas :)
```

The double blue ticks appear instantly and then Leon sends me a snap of him stretched out on the sofa. There's a cat on his lap, one on the back of the sofa and Alexander on the floor next to him. There's already scrunched up wrapping paper on the floor and sofa.

The caption reads: Merry Christmas :)

I hear the creak of Mum's feet on her bedroom floorboards, then the sound of her bedroom door opening and closing. I groan and roll myself out of bed in time to catch her on the landing. Wow. And I thought I looked rough.

"Did they get you with the cherry vodka too?" I ask.

She gives me a weak smile. "Just a bit. Has Rose emerged yet?"

Like she's been summoned, Rose's bedroom door creaks open.

"Morning," she croaks.

"Morning," Mum and I chorus back in the same tone.

The three of us stare at each other for a few moments, then Mum starts laughing.

"Lunch with your grandmother is going to be a real trial today," she says, pushing back her bushy hair. She sighs. "But perhaps a decent breakfast will make a difference. Come on."

I really don't want to eat, but when I smell frying potato cakes and mushrooms my stomach starts to grumble.

"This is the ultimate Carter hangover cue," Mum explains to Rose, as she puts our plates of potato stacks in front of us, piled with fried mushrooms, tomatoes and topped with a poached egg. Mine's already complete with black pudding, but Mum gives Rose a choice between that and bacon. Rose chooses bacon. She doesn't know what she's missing. I squirt HP sauce all over mine. By the time I put the last forkful into my mouth, the hangover is in full retreat. But the forthcoming day looms in front of me and makes the sickness swell again in my stomach.

"I really can't face Grandma today," I admit.

Mum sighs. "I know what you mean, but we can't leave the old woman on her own on Christmas Day – especially the first Christmas she's had her grandchildren together in over a decade. We just need to stick it out for a couple of hours."

I blow my hair off my face. "Still don't want to."

"Do it for the food," Rose says, scraping her plate clean with the side of her fork.

The prospect of Christmas lunch does make the day less of a dark cloud, but the dread still sits heavy in my stomach. Rose and I clear up from breakfast while Mum showers. Then we gather in the living room to open presents. Bonnie can sense the excitement in the room and sits panting at my feet while we tear into the wrapping paper.

Rose bought me a Pokémon terrain with Vulpix curled up asleep in a woodland. I love it so much I throw myself across the room to hug her. Rose breaks into a wide smile when she opens the Cardcaptor Sakura figurine I bought her.

"Thank you," she says, making my heart soar.

My present from Mum is a load of art supplies. I bought her a new pair of gardening gloves. Rose gets a load of walking and running gear from her parents. Mum whispers that she might have given her sister some ideas. I'm surprised to find a present from Aunt Claire and Uncle Myles for me under the tree. It's only an envelope, but inside is a card with a handwritten message and a note to say they have transferred some money to my bank account so I can buy a subscription to the OS Maps app.

It's unexpected and also a really nice gift. Tears gather behind my eyes.

"Walkies?" Mum asks.

It's a bright and crisp day. The grass cackles under foot and our breath spirals in white puffs into the air. The rabbits are out this morning, darting in and out of their burrows. Bonnie watches them intensely for a few moments and then gets distracted by a stick.

Rose and I shower when we get back. Getting out from under the hot water is a real struggle. I know it's Christmas Day, and that I'm meant to be *happy*, but, honestly, the thought of having lunch with Grandma – of having to sit for several hours while she prattles on about her friend's grandchildren and all the amazing things they're achieving – makes me want to smash my head against the shower tiles.

"Do it for the food," I remind myself and turn the water off.

"Are we taking Bonnie with us?" Rose asks as we pull on our coats and shoes.

"No," I say. "Grandma hates having dogs in her house."

"And it also gives us an excuse to come home early if we leave her here," Mum whispers. She picks up a bagful of presents. "Ready?"

"No," I say, but I pick up the bag of bottled drinks.

Grandma lives in an old bungalow a couple of villages over – the same house Mum and Aunt Claire grew up in. It's a huge village, with a primary school, a church and a chapel, two pubs, a town hall and a park. There used to be a library and a shop, but they closed a few years ago. The place is a city compared to Harboury.

I say that Grandma lives in a bungalow, but to be honest the place is more like a European villa, with a courtyard, lots of nice stone arches and a wisteria climbing up one of the walls. Inside everything is white and clean, with every surface devoid of "clutter".

I hate it.

It's like stepping into a show home, stripped of any personality. Every time I come here it always amazes me that Mum grew up to be who she became after living in a house like this.

Grandma comes out of the front door as we pull into the drive and watches us like an eagle watching its prey. Mum takes the fall and goes first.

"Merry Christmas," she says.

"Merry Christmas," Grandma replies.

They kiss each other on the cheek, while Rose and I stand in line behind and exchange a look. It comforts me that she's dreading this as much as I am. Rose steps up after Mum. I can't help but notice that Grandma's smile reaches a little further to her eyes and her voice sounds brighter when she greets Rose.

All of that disappears when I step up. Her eyes immediately flick to my pink hair. Crease lines form around her mouth as she holds back her comments. At least she does that. Merry fucking Christmas.

I tense when she presses her papery lips to my cheek. We mutter, "Merry Christmas" to each other and then I rush inside, kick off my shoes and hurry into the living room to get as far away from her as quickly as I can.

"You all stink of alcohol," Grandma comments.

"I can assure you, Mum," Mum says, "that we are all stone cold sober." She sniffs the air. "Lunch smells good."

"It's almost ready."

"Let me help you finish it." Mum shoots Rose and I a wink over her shoulder as she hustles Grandma into the kitchen.

"Now's our chance," I whisper to Rose and dash into the living room. I collapse onto the sofa. Grandma has put up a few Christmas decorations – some electric candles on the mantelpiece, a small tree, decorated with colour-coordinated tinsel and baubles, which is a far cry from our tree of mismatched ornaments – and her dozens of Christmas cards are strung up on ribbon around the room.

"I wonder if we'll end up with as many Christmas cards as this when we're in our eighties," Rose says, sitting down beside me.

"Doubt it," I say. "Can you imagine our generation sending stuff in the post in sixty years' time?"

Rose looks around at the cards. "It's sad, though, that it's a tradition that might die off."

"I wouldn't go that far." We stare around the room. "Tell me I'm not the only one who thinks this house looks devoid of life?"

"Apart from the Christmas cards?" A smile cracks Rose's lips. "Definitely not."

"Have you been here before?"

"No. Mum came here a few times, but I never came with her. Grandma always used to come to us. Was this the house where our mums grew up?" I nod. Rose's gaze sweeps around the room. "You wouldn't have thought it, would you? There's no sign they were ever here."

No, there isn't. Not a photograph, or a childhood drawing. It's all polished surfaces and minimalist art.

Rose sits up. "Can I see Mum's bedroom?"

"It's been turned into a Pilates studio."

Rose slumps back down again. "Never mind. Guess I should have expected that."

We sit in silence for a while. Then a thought pops into my head. The one I've been thinking about since August.

"Why do you think our mums stopped talking to each other?"

"Not sure," Rose says, pushing her glasses up her face. "I can't imagine your mum giving anyone the silent treatment. So it must have been something big for them not to talk to each other for... thirteen years."

"Maybe one of them murdered someone," I say, my voice deadpan.

Rose cracks up laughing. "I wouldn't put that past my mum when she's sorting out her billing hours."

I pick at a loose thread on my hoodie sleeve. "I keep meaning to ask Mum, but... it's never the right time."

"I've tried talking about it with my mum, but... it feels really personal. Too personal for me to ask about at the moment."

"If your mum tells you one day, will you tell me?"

"Of course. As long as you tell me if you find out."

"Deal." I hold out my hand. Rose stares at it for a second and then clasps it with hers.

"A pleasure doing business with you," she says as we nod at each other.

We watch stupid videos on my phone while we wait for lunch - using my mobile data, I would like to point out, because Grandma doesn't have Wi-Fi. I KNOW, RIGHT?!

We're cracking up over a compilation video of misheard anime openings, when Mum sticks her head into the room.

"Lunch is ready," she says.

We head into the dining room and find the table groaning with food. One thing I will say about Grandma - she can cook, and when it comes to Christmas she never stinges on the food. There's a tray of stuffing balls, pigs in blankets, crispy roast potatoes, parsnips, carrots, peas, Brussel sprouts, a boat of steaming gravy, cranberry sauce and bread sauce. The table at the back of the room has all the drinks on it. Rose and I help ourselves to some water and sit down. I know, water, on Christmas Day? Boooring. But that's what my pounding head demands.

Grandma and Mum come in from the kitchen. Grandma has a large glass of white wine in hand and Mum's carrying the roast chicken, which she puts in pride of place in the middle of the table. We sit down, Grandma at the head of the table, Rose and I on one side and Mum on the other.

There's a moment of awkward silence. I've been to enough Christmases at Grandma's to know how they work, but the rule is to always let her make the first move.

At last, Grandma picks up her cracker.

"Shall we pull them?" she says, crossing her arms.

Rose is thankfully sat next to her, so she grabs the other end of Grandma's cracker. I grab the other end of Rose's and stand up so Mum can grab the other end of mine. Mum crosses her arms and allows Grandma to grab the other end of hers.

When we are all linked, Mum counts, "Three, two, one, pull!"

There's a series of cracks and shouts of surprise, and pieces of plastic fly everywhere while paper jokes and crowns flutter to the ground. We read out our jokes and put our crowns on our heads – Grandma's wears hers with a regal pride, whereas Mum, Rose and I all wear ours at tilted angles.

We've only taken a few bites when Grandma starts telling us about her friend's daughter who has just bought a new house in Chelsea, and another who has booked a holiday to The Bahamas, and another who has been invited to lord so-and-sos party. Blah blah blah.

Rose and Mum are good at pandering to Grandma's whim; they nod along and comment in all the right places. I concentrate on my lunch and try not to let my ohmygodjustkillme expression show on my face.

Thankfully Mum knows how to deal with the situation and keeps topping up Grandma's wine glass throughout lunch. At first it's when she's not looking, and then she does it when she is and gets a confused thank you for it.

By the time we've eaten as much as our stomachs can hold, Grandma is a lot quieter and is swaying a little in her seat.

"Who wants pudding?" she asks and stands up so suddenly she starts to tip to the side. Mum catches her and puts her back in her seat.

"Why don't you sit there, Mum, and we'll sort pudding?"

"Oh, alright." Grandma pats Mum on the arm. I seriously can't believe she gets away with this trick every year.

I start to clear the table and Rose jumps up to help. We carry everything through to the kitchen. Rose and I load the dishwasher, while Mum prepares the Christmas pudding and gets the trifle out the fridge.

"Wow," I say, when Mum sets the trifle on the side.

"I know," Mum says.

"What?" Rose asks.

"It's finally taken Grandma seventeen years to accept that I do not like Christmas pudding," I explain. "Normally I have to go hungry."

“I don’t understand how you can claim to be hungry after eating all that,” Rose says.

“It’s Christmas Day,” I point out. “Unless my skin is starting to rip over my stomach, I have not eaten enough.”

Grandma is quieter during dessert, allowing the rest of us to talk about topics we want to talk about, such as what happened at last night’s Christmas Eve after party. Things got really wild after we left, with Jan and Roger busting out the karaoke machine, and Deborah getting a little too into her rendition of “Lady Marmalade”.

By the time I’ve eaten a large portion of trifle, my stomach is bursting at the seams. I’m glad I wore my trousers with the elasticated waistband. Rose pops the top button of her jeans and lets out a relieved sigh.

“Shall we go for a walk before it gets dark?” Grandma asks.

Moving is the last thing I want to do now – apart from perhaps eating anything else – but Grandma is already heading into the hall. We walk around the village, greeting everyone who walks past us with “Merry Christmas!”. Mum points a few things out to Rose as we walk, telling her stories from her and Aunt Claire’s childhood. At some point during the walk, Grandma takes hold of Mum’s arm. Mum puts her hand over Grandma’s without a word. As I watch them walk together, I notice for the first time how frail and old Grandma looks.

I’ve never thought she looked frail before, but holding onto Mum for support she looks like the old woman she is.

Back at the house, we follow our usual Christmas Day routine and open our presents from Grandma – Rose gets a really nice set of cashmere knitwear while I get some generic revision guidebooks... thanks, Grandma – while Mum gives her a present from us. When it gets to three o'clock Rose's parents video call her. When she answers the call, her face crumples and her voice becomes tight. She really misses them. I've never thought about how hard it must be on her to be so far away from them.

"Yeah, we're at Grandma's. Clover's here too." Rose turns the camera on me and I smile and wave awkwardly at Aunt Claire and Uncle Myles.

"Merry Christmas, Clover!" Aunt Claire sings.

"Merry Christmas," I reply. Rose's dad gives me an awkward wave. Rose turns the camera back to her.

They talk for a bit more and then Rose passes the phone to Mum, who holds it for her and Grandma to talk to. I start scrolling through my phone, half listening to their conversation, when I hear Grandma say, "You two better be here next year. We've wasted too many years of not being a family at Christmas because of that stupid argument."

An awkward silence follows Grandma's outburst, during which Rose and I exchange raised eyebrow looks. This is the first time I've heard Grandma so openly address the elephant in the room. Goddammit, Grandma, we already know that Mum and Aunt Claire didn't speak to each other for thirteen years because they had an argument. Why couldn't you have spilled some more details?

"We'll ensure we're there for Christmas next year, Mum," Aunt Claire says, defusing the tension.

"Wouldn't miss it for the world," Uncle Myles jumps in.

When we've said goodbye to Rose's parents, Mum says, "Shall we have a game of *Pitt*?"

My ears prick up. If I was Bonnie right now, my tail would be going like a Katherine wheel. *Pitt* is a family game we don't get to play often. You need at least four players to make it worthwhile, and on Christmas Day when it's just Mum, Grandma and me, we can't make it work. When Mum has people round for dinner, she busts out her deck and we end up shouting the house down. We've rehearsed Leon's family in it well, including Paige, so I often take our deck around there when she and Genny are visiting. Poor Rose. Learning to play *Pitt* for the first time is a distressing experience.

Grandma groans as she gets up from the sofa. "I'll go get my deck."

"What's *Pitt*?" Rose asks.

"A trading game," Mum explains. "There are different suits and you have to get a full deck, which you do by swapping cards with the other players. First to get a full set of nine cards wins."

"But you can't show what cards you're trading with other people," I add, which makes the furrows on Rose's brow deepen.

When Grandma brings back the cards, Mum, Rose and I kneel around the coffee table so Grandma can sit on the sofa. Mum shows Rose the cards and the different suits, which are all different agricultural crops, and explains how trading works – keeping your cards face down, you slide them into the middle of the table, shouting how many cards you have to offer. All the cards you offer have to be of the same suit, but you can trade as many cards as you want at one time.

"There is a version where you play a bear and a bull," Mum explains, extracting those cards from the deck, "but it makes it too complicated, so we don't play with those. And since there are only four of us, we'll only play with four suits." She picks out the corn, barley, oranges and wheat cards, and discards the other crops.

Rose nods like she gets it, but there's apprehension in her eyes. I pat her arm.

"You'll get it after a few rounds," I say.

Mum shuffles the cards and then deals them out so we have nine each. I have four wheat, two oranges, one barley and two corn. Looks like I'm collecting wheat. I extract the barley and lay it face down on the table, ready to trade.

"Ready?" Mum asks. Both her and Grandma have their first trading cards ready on the table. Rose's eyes are wide with panic, but she takes a card out of her deck and joins us. "Market open!"

A chorus of "Oneoneoneoneoneoneoneone!" fills the room. Mum, Grandma and I swap cards, checking each one in turn. Rose is frozen by the sudden burst of noise. I help her out by swapping cards with her. I've got one more wheat. Just four more to find. Mum starts shouting "Twotwotwotwotwotwotwo!" so I swap her two for my corn, but she has two barley. I trade those with Grandma, and get two more corn. In a rare moment, Grandma and I share an exasperated look across the table. Perhaps I should be collecting corn, then?

A few trades later, I get two more wheat, and then the third. Mum and I are trading our single cards back and forth, with no sign of that final wheat, when Grandma shouts, “Corner!” and spreads her houseful of corn on the table. Mum groans.

“Who had the last wheat?!” I demand.

Rose gives me a sheepish look and turns her cards around, which are a mix of oranges and barley, with my single wheat on the end.

“Sorry,” she says.

I give her an encouraging smile, feeling guilty for shouting at her when she’s a beginner. “Don’t worry,” I say. “You’ll get quicker.”

And she does, but Mum, Grandma and I slaughter her in every round. At one point someone trades me a mixed hand – a three group made up of two oranges and a wheat – and I stop the game in outrage.

“Don’t be a sore loser, Clover,” Grandma tells me, which makes me know it was her. We play another couple of hands, and I make sure I check every hand I get from Grandma. Rose scrapes a win, calling “Corner!” a second before Mum does. By the time we’re ready to wrap up, Grandma and I are tied for the highest number of wins. Mum knows that blood will be shed if we have a deciding round, so she tactfully suggests we should have some tea. I don’t care. I have won.

“Claire tells me you have your mock exams after Christmas,” Grandma says, as we sit sipping tea – in China cups, because of course Grandma doesn’t do mugs. My cup rattles as I set it back down on its saucer. Mum deliberately never tells Grandma when exams are coming up to avoid conversations like this one. She only tells her once they are over. Less bother that way. “Are you studying hard?”

"Of course," Rose says, because she is. I've seen her colour-coded timetable. It's a thing of beauty and a thing to be feared. There's no way I could create something like that, let alone stick to it. I revise when I'm ready. I paint or take photos when I want to, not when some timetable tells me to.

Grandma turns her eyes onto me when I stay quiet. The worst of the wine must have left her system because the eagle is back in her gaze.

"I'll be fine," I say, sinking down into the sofa.

I should have lied, because the moment the words are out of my mouth Grandma's back straightens and her chin dips down as she narrows her vision on me.

"'Fine'," she says, in a tone that makes me want to roll my eyes, "is not good enough. 'Fine' is not going to get you anywhere in life. If you want to succeed, you have to work hard, and that hard work has to start at school. Studying hard and getting good grades will open all sorts of doors for you later in life. This wishy-washy attitude cannot go on. Look at your cousin. Rose knows what she wants to be – and a lawyer at that. If you don't start making an effort soon, you'll end up like your mother."

The silence is so piercing I can hear it ringing in my ears. Rose is staring at her hands, her eyes wide. I can hear my heartbeat in my ears. I'm not sure whether I want to cry or punch the old woman in the face. I can't look at her to see if there is any sort of regret in her expression, because if there isn't I'm going to explode.

Mum stands up. "It's time for us to go. We have to get back for the dog."

Grandma doesn't say a word as we put on our coats

and shoes, and she still does not speak when Mum kisses her cheek and wishes her "Merry Christmas" again. She just stands in the doorway and watches our car pull out of the driveway. In that moment she looks older than I've ever seen her look before. The thought doesn't make me pity her at all.

Mum turns the radio on to fill the silence. I tremble inside all the way home.

I hate her.

I hate her with every drop of blood and shard of bone in my being.

That stuck up, self-righteous *kusobaba*.

"Mum," I say, "if I end up like you, I'll be the proudest and happiest person on the planet."

Mum catches my eye in the rear-view mirror. "Thank you, Clo. That makes me the proudest and happiest mum on the planet."

Chapter 26

Rose

Maryam
Sounds like your Christmas was eventful then!

Rose
I wouldn't call it eventful
More like Coronation Street drama
I still can't believe Grandma said that... in front of Helen

Maryam
Have you heard from her since?

Rose
Clover and I haven't spoken to her. Not sure

about Helen...
Told Mum about it
Apparently Grandma used to say that sort of shit to Helen all the time when they were growing up
I can't believe the two of them are still talking

Maryam
Helen sounds like a saint

Rose
She really is
She's so lovely and caring
She doesn't deserve to have that sort of crap thrown at her all the time

Maryam
I hope your grandma is having a good long think about what she said

Rose
I hope so too...
How's revision coming along?

Maryam
Not as structured as yours I'm sure
But I feel like it's sticking in my brain which is a good thing I guess!
I really envy people with photographic memories
Jayden makes such a frustrating revision partner
Have you managed to stick to your military timetable?

Rose
Had to do some juggling around after Clover bulldozed my plans for the first two days
But otherwise yeah
It's going well

Maryam
I'm glad she made you relax

Rose
I relax!

Maryam
Your idea of relaxing is going for a run

Rose
Runs are relaxing!

Maryam
Yeah sure…
When you coming back for your next visit?
Two days wasn't enough :(

Rose
:(
Not sure
I'm going to see the rents during February half-term
Maybe we can sneak a weekend in after mocks?
If not... Easter?

Maryam
Giirrrrlll I am NOT waiting another three

months until I see your face
If I get the OK from Dad I could come see you at Easter?
If your aunt's alright with it?

Rose
Yeah that should be fine
She said I could have people to stay
But I warn you there is not a lot to do out here

Maryam
So I've gathered
But you seem happier out there now than you were before

My fingers hover over my phone's keyboard, unsure how to respond.

Am I happier out here now?

I guess compared to how I was back in September, I am a lot happier. I still miss London like a piece of myself. But living out here, I guess it's not all that bad.

Rose
Yeah I guess I am

Maryam
I knew it!
You're turning into a country bumpkin
Next time I see you you'll be speaking in a West Country accent and brandishing a shot gun

Rose

Hahahaha
Just no

Maryam
Then you'll get married to that nice hipster that's been appearing in your Insta feed recently and become a farmer's wife

Rose
Have you ever thought about pursuing a career as a comedian?
Because YOU ARE JUST SO FUNNY!!
But seriously I miss London
I can't wait to come home

"I can't take it anymore!"

I scream and jump off my desk chair. Even with my headphones on Clover's voice got through loud and clear to me. While my heartbeat thumps in my ears, I slide my headphones off one ear. Clover's draped over my bedroom steps, like a drowning person dragging themselves aboard a lifeboat. Although her face is turned up to me, looking shocked.

"Sorry," she says, "I forgot how jumpy you are."

"What do you want?" I snap, pulling off my headphones.

Clover presses her face into the carpet and groans. "I can't hold any more information in my head. My skull is going to explode."

"*Ganbatte*," I say, turning back to my phone.

"Eugh."

"Fight on!"

"You can't force me to do more work by throwing generic shonen quotes at me."

"Go, go, Clover! Push it, push it, Clover!"

Clover gives out a load moan, pulls herself up onto my bedroom floor, where she rolls over onto her back.

"I don't understand," she says, staring at the ceiling, "how you can cope revising for four subjects? Two is too many." She pauses. "But then if you're going to be a lawyer you'll probably have to remember way more stuff than we do now."

There is it again. That strange plunge and twist in my gut. I take a deep breath and ignore it. Clover pushes herself off the floor and then pauses.

"What are you listening to?" she asks.

I must be playing my music louder than I thought. "It's the *Cardcaptor Sakura* soundtrack."

"Ah!" Clover plops her closed fist into her open palm – a gesture I have definitely seen in anime before. "That's what it was. I heard you playing this a few months ago."

"It's my studying music."

Clover laughs. "Your studying music is a lot calmer than mine. I need something to get me PUMPED! The *Haikyu!!* soundtrack is my saving grace." She sighs. "I'm going to take a break and do some photography coursework... if you can call that a break. You all ready for tomorrow night?"

"Yes," I say hesitantly. "Although I'm not sure if I'm excited or afraid for what you and Leon have planned. I hate surprises and I don't trust you two."

Clover holds a hand to her chest in mock horror. "And

what have Leon or I ever done to make you think we're untrustworthy? On second thoughts, don't answer that. Just be ready at seven tomorrow evening." She winks at me and leaves the room. "You're gonna love it!"

Dear Universe. Please keep that girl under control.

I wake up on the morning of my seventeenth birthday – known to everyone else as New Year's Eve – to a message from Mum telling me to ring her when I'm awake. I go to the loo first and then sit up in bed to call her. She answers after the third ring and immediately starts singing "Happy Birthday".

"Muuuum," I groan when she's finished, but I'm smiling. Even though we're four thousand miles away, she still kept up her tradition of singing to me first thing in the morning. Even if she's not coming into my room with my presents while doing it.

She grins at me from the screen. "It's tradition! Hang on a moment – let me grab your dad then you can open your presents."

I wipe my eyes while she goes off screen. But when Dad appears the tears well up once more, and I have to pinch my leg to stop them from spilling over. He blows me a kiss and wishes me happy birthday, then I grab their present and card from under the bed – Helen gave them to me last night with a smile and a wink.

"Open the present first," Mum says. "Your main present's in the card."

The present is a small box of make-up from my favourite brand, and a set of learner car plates. When I open the card – which has the traditional British seventeen birthday card image of a car on the front – a piece of paper flutters out. I catch it and hold it while I read the inside.

To get you on the road to freedom.

The piece of paper is a note saying I have been signed up to a course of driving lessons at The Blue Car Driving School in Aylesbury. A thrill of excitement rushes through me as I stare down at the piece of paper.

"Thank you," I say.

"Helen says you're more than welcome to use her car for practice," Dad says. "We'll sort the insurance out with her."

We have an hour long catch up. Once they've hung up, I let the tears out. There aren't many, but it's so cathartic. The tension I didn't know I had drains away, leaving me deflated but with a clearer head.

When I come back from my run, Helen is at her usual place at the kitchen table, having her breakfast and reading a magazine. Bonnie comes bumbling over to me, wriggling her bum.

Helen smiles when she sees me. "Happy birthday!"

"Thank you," I say, giving Bonnie a good scratch.

"I would give you your present now, but Clover is insistent we wait until this evening. If you don't mind."

"Do I have a choice?"

Helen laughs. "Despite what the maestro orders, it is your birthday, so you can decide what you would like to do."

"It's OK," I say. "I'll wait."

I return from showering and find my phone swamped

with notifications. Most are from older family members writing on my Facebook wall. I smile at the WhatsApp message from Ari that reads: *You're so extra you've got the whole world throwing one big party just for your birthday*

I reply with the GIF of Leonardo DiCaprio holding up a champagne glass against a background of fireworks. The group chat is flooded with happy birthdays and GIFs from Jayden, Zoe, Sienne and Kai. Maryam's messaged me separately.

Maryam
CALL ME!!

She answers on the second ring and starts singing before I can get a word in.

"I'm bitterly disappointed that I'm not there to sing to you in real life," Maryam says, once she's finished. "This is the first time in... what, our whole history of friendship that we're not together on your birthday."

"I'm sad you're not here," I say. A lot of traditions have been train-wrecked this year, but not seeing my parents and Maryam on my birthday is a bitter pill to swallow.

"Did you get anything nice?" she asks. I tell her about the car driving lessons, which she whistles at. "You going to get a car?"

"Not one of my own, but Helen says I can use hers to practise in. Don't think I'll be able to use it much once I pass anyway since she works at the weekend."

"The potential of freedom is exciting, though."

"Yeah. It is."

"You doing anything tonight?"

"Clover has some big plans. Not sure what they are. I've just been told to come downstairs at seven."

"Oh, a surprise." Maryam drops her voice to a conspiratorial whisper. "Any ideas what she's planning?"

I laugh, because I have my suspicions and they all involve anime, but I can't tell Maryam that. "Not a clue," I say.

"Whatever it turns out to be, send me lots of photos."

"Will do," I lie, which tastes like another bitter pill going down.

I spend a whole hour on the phone with Maryam, chatting about everything and nothing, and then say goodbye with a heavy heart. I do a little bit of studying after our call, but if there's one day I can take off, aside from Christmas, it's my birthday, so I shove everything away and pull myself onto my bed with my laptop and turn on Netflix.

Clover sticks her head around my bedroom door just before lunch, wishes me happy birthday and asks if there's anything I fancy doing. We end up playing on her Switch all afternoon in the living room sitting beside the blazing fire.

At five o'clock, Clover makes a big fuss of noticing the time and says with little subtleness, "Only two hours until seven o'clock." I take the hint and head upstairs with her following close behind me.

"Right." With her hands on my shoulders Clover steers me into my bedroom. "Stay here. Do not, I repeat, do not come downstairs until seven o'clock."

"OK," I say. Clover leaves my room, shutting the door after her.

I keep myself occupied by re-watching some of my favourite *Schitt's Creek* episodes. In the moments in-between episodes, I hear laughing and the sound of people moving around downstairs.

Dear Universe. Please don't let whatever they're planning turn into a viral video.

At seven on the dot, I open my bedroom door and find a parcel on the steps. There's a post-it note stuck to the top in Clover's loopy handwriting that reads: *Put this on before you come downstairs. Don't forget your key.*

A mixture of nervousness and excitement makes my heart thump as I open the parcel. The first tear of the paper reveals white cloth. The second, a glimpse of black cloth with a red stripe. Then I pull the whole thing apart and find myself staring down at a white skirt, a black top with white cuffs and a white sailor collar with a red stripe.

For a few moments I'm so shocked I just stare down at the costume, unsure if what I'm seeing is what I think it is. Then a grin pulls at my cheeks and I take my jumper off.

I'm about to go downstairs when I spot Clover's note again and re-read the line about the key. Of course. I dive under my bed and pull out the box. This time when I step out my bedroom, my Clow Key is hung around my neck.

At the top of the stairs I find scattered pieces of pink crepe paper cut into the shape of sakura blossoms leading into the living room. With my heart thumping against my ribcage I follow the trail.

The moment I step inside the living room, there's a soft *bang!* which makes me jump and shriek, and streamers rain down on me.

"Happy birthday!" Clover, Helen and Leon shout. They're standing on either side of the door, empty party poppers in their hands.

"Thanks," I say, and then I clock what they're wearing.

Leon's in a white top and trousers, with a green and gold hat and robe, with wide long sleeves. Clover's dressed in the same clothes as me, except she's got a long black wig on with a pink hairband.

"You're Li and Madison," I say.

Leon and Clover grin. "Yes we are, Sakura," Clover says.

"Cosplaying was a step too far for me," Helen says. She holds out her long skirt and twirls, showing off the cherry blossom print. "But I took the theme on board."

"We made someone else dress up, though," Clover says. "Bonnie! Come here!" The sound of Bonnie's claws on the hard floors grows louder, and then she appears in the living room doorway. I let out a little squeal and press a hand to my chest.

"Ohmygod," I gush.

Bonnie's wearing a pair of white wings and has a piece of grey painted cardboard around her neck, in the middle of which is a half oval of red shiny plastic that looks like a gem.

"Kero!" I cry and wrap my arms around her neck. "Never take those wings off, because you look too cute."

I finish my emotional display and notice all the other changes in the living room. There's Clow Card bunting strung around the room, fake sakura blossom thrown everywhere, teacups and saucers placed on the coffee table along with dainty cakes and rings of doily cloth. In the middle of the floor is a round piece of white cloth, on which has been painted a Clow Card circle.

"It's likely not the sort of party you're used to getting," Clover says, her cheeks darkening, which is so true. But the sight of all the effort that the three of them have gone to for me – to acknowledge my love for *Cardcaptor Sakura* – makes me start to tear up.

I take in a deep breath and say, "It's the best."

Helen makes us a pot of tea and we sit down to eat cake. There's also mini quiches and salad, but it's my birthday so I eat dessert first. Then Clover brings out a stack of board games.

We're in the middle of playing *Cluedo* when the front doorbell rings.

"About time," Leon mutters and goes to answer it. From the sound of their loud shrieks, it's Paige and Genny. But I'm the one who shrieks the loudest when they walk into the living room, because they're dressed in matching black trousers, white shirts, black ties and pale blue school blazers. Genny is wearing a short brown wig, and Paige is wearing a silvery grey one.

"Julian and Tori!" I cry, jumping up in excitement.

"Little sis!" Genny cries, not missing a beat, and she envelops me in one of her bone-crushing hugs. "Happy birthday!"

Paige holds up a bag. "We bought alcohol."

Genny gasps and holds my head against her chest. "Villain! How dare you ply my innocent underage sister with poison!"

"Did you make your jackets?" I ask. Being pressed this close to Genny, I have a very good view of the stitching. I'm suddenly very aware that I am staring at her boobs.

"We did," Genny says, releasing me. She stands still so I can get a better look.

"They're amazing," I gush. "How long did they take you to make?"

"About two weeks," Genny says. "Paige did most of the work."

"I'm a practised hand," Paige says. "All those cons we've gone to over the years."

"They're so cool," I breathe. "I wish I could create something like that."

The moment the words are out an itching starts in my fingers. The realisation makes the world stop around me, until Paige's laugh re-starts it.

"Happy to teach you if you like," she says. Then she hands me a white bag covered in sakura blossom. I peek inside and find a present wrapped in paper printed with swimming koi.

"Thank you," I say.

I have the annual treat of opening my presents in front of everyone – I'm very grateful for the gifts, but at the same time really wish I didn't have to open them with everyone watching. It's so awkward. All of the gifts are amazing, though, so the delight on my face is genuine when I open each one. Clover painted me a huge watercolour *Cardcaptor Sakura* art piece, but instead of Sakura in the clothing it's a girl with brown skin. It takes me a few moments of staring at the framed painting to realise that girl is me.

"You can cry," Clover says. "Either because you think it's awful or amazing. It's fine."

"It is amazing," I say and give her a hug while blinking back the tears.

Leon's bought me a Sailor Moon figurine, a beautiful tall model of Usagi, which I'm going to spend far too long staring at. I thank him without a hug – because we're not quite there yet – and set myself a mental reminder to ask Clover when his birthday is.

Genny and Paige's present turns out to be a stack of manga, all of them the first volume in their series.

"We're calling this the Shojo Starter Pack," Paige says, as I turn each one over to read the backs. There's five series: *Kamisama Kiss*; *Yona of the Dawn*; *Horimiya*; *Kiss Him, Not Me* and *Say "I Love You"*. "Apart from *Sailor Moon* and *Cardcaptor Sakura*, those are all the classics."

"Both new and old," Genny points out.

I thank them and go to hug them in turn, and end up being enveloped in another Genny and Paige sandwich, which leaves us all giggling.

We eat cake, drink spirits and play board games for a few hours. Then as it approaches midnight, we play loud music and turn the TV onto the BBC countdown.

When the last few seconds of the year fall away, we count them out together and cheer when the clocks strike midnight. Genny and Paige kiss, and Leon, Clover and I jump around laughing and singing to Queen's "Don't Stop Me Now". Helen slumps on the sofa with a green tea, smiling and scratching Bonnie's neck.

I go to bed that night giddy with happiness, my Clow Key still around my neck.

Chapter 27

Clover

The first three weeks of the winter term pass in a coffee-fuelled blur and a barrage of exam papers.

I refuse to let myself get too stressed about exams. As long as I do my best, I'll be happy with whatever results come out the other side. And doing my best means knowing when to stop before I trip myself into a stress pit.

I can tell on day one of the new term that Rose is going to find the next couple of weeks very difficult. Very difficult indeed. She's silent at dinner and on the bus she constantly looks at her notes. Ari, who usually chats with her all the way to and from school, gives up trying to talk to her after a few days when Rose blanks him.

During those three weeks of mocks, cracks form in my cousin's armour. When we get back from school after our first day of mock exams, I push her into the living room to chill with an episode of anime before we have dinner and she disappears into her room for the rest of the evening to study more.

I can't believe how much she's pushing herself.

Surely it's too much?

Surely one person doesn't need to study this much?

But then I guess if Rose is going to do law at university then her exam results matter more than mine do. School have been harping on at us since the start of the new school year to start going to university open days, and to think about what subjects we want to study there.

I have no idea what I want to study at uni.

I don't even know if I want to go to uni.

I just want to watch anime, read manga, go for dog walks, play games with Leon and draw fan art.

I wish somewhere did a uni course on being an otaku.

One evening, Mum and I are on washing up duty and I find the courage to ask, "When did you decide what you wanted to do for a living?"

With her hands deep in washing-up water, Mum shrugs. "I never really decided what I wanted to do. I just... started doing it, I guess." She pauses. "A friend asked me to do a tarot card reading at a festival and I did it to earn some extra cash. At the time I was working as a receptionist for a physio clinic and hated it. Then after I spent the day doing what I really enjoyed, I thought 'Fuck it', jacked in the receptionist job and did some training courses on yoga and meditation. Why? What's up?"

I finish drying the last saucepan.

"We're being asked to think about what we want to do at uni," I say, "and I don't know what I want to do."

I want her to ask me questions – to talk through all the options with me – but instead Mum just says, "You'll work it out."

And that's the end of the conversation.

I find Rose in the living room the first weekend free of mock exam revision, reading a fashion magazine. She looks so relaxed for once that I don't want to disturb her, but I need to talk to someone about the thoughts buzzing around in my head.

I throw myself onto the other sofa, making her look up from her magazine.

"Have you been looking into uni open days?" I ask.

"I've already picked where I'm going to uni," she replies.

Because of course she has.

I moan in despair and lie across the sofa like some fainting damsel. Rose puts down her magazine.

"Perhaps it would help if you looked at some prospectuses," Rose suggests. "I think you can get them for free online. Have a look at a couple and see if anything takes your fancy."

"I have. But... I don't know." I fling an arm across my eyes. "I don't feel anything when I look at them."

"Is there nothing you want to study at uni?"

For a moment I feel it. Something on the tip of my tongue, like a ladybird poised to take flight on the end of a finger. But then I bite my lip and the idea slips back away into its dark corner.

"Survey Corps training," I say.

Rose blinks at me, and then she breaks into a smile when she gets it.

"Can't you pick a profession with less risk?" she asks.

"Where's the fun in that? If you're going to pick an anime profession, might as well do something fun."

"I don't think there's anything fun about fighting titans."

"But learning to use the 3D manoeuvre gear would be so cool."

Rose wrinkles her nose. "I'd rather stay on the ground, thanks."

"What about if you were a Sailor Soldier? Or a Cardcaptor?"

"Alright," Rose admits. "If I had any of those powers, I guess I wouldn't mind having the ability to fly. As long as I didn't have to fight titans. If I'm putting my life in danger, I want cool powers to fight back with. Not just gas jets and swords."

"Being a pirate would be pretty cool, like in *One Piece*. Do they do uni courses in how to be a pirate? Then I could sail the Grand Line having lots of awesome adventures. Or I could do a ninja training course and work for one of the hidden villages, like in *Naruto*. Oh, or Pokémon training? Then I could go out and have adventures, battle in tournaments and see lots of awesome Pokémon." I sigh. "Why are IRL jobs so *boring*?"

"There are loads of exciting jobs," Rose says, "and there's nothing stopping you from going out into the world and having all the adventures you want. You just need to do some admin before you go." She thumbs the edges of her magazine pages. "But the idea of having an adventure and the reality are completely different. It's much easier to stay at home and read about or play as characters having these adventures. The reality of adventure is hard."

"Your logic hurts my head, and my heart," I say. Because she's right. There's no way in real life that I would want to have a job that involves any danger. Leaving my room can be a real effort sometimes.

"Leon's so lucky," Rose says. "Having the family farm to take over, I mean. He's had his life planned out since the start. It's like destiny."

"Not really," I say. "If Genny had wanted to farm, Leon wouldn't have been able to take it over. One farm can't support two families. Leon was so relieved when Genny told them she wanted to move to London and start her own gaming company."

Mum shouts from the kitchen, "It's snowing!"

Rose and I rush to the same window. We throw aside the curtain and find the world awash with white flakes.

"I can't believe they actually got the forecast right," Rose says. She pushes herself up onto the sill to peer down at the ground. "I can't see if it's sticking."

I cross both sets of fingers and also my toes for good measure. "Snow day," I whisper. "Snow day. Snow day. Please. Let there be a snow day tomorrow."

The next morning when my alarm jolts me awake, I lie in bed for a few moments and whisper, "Snow day," over and over, until I have enough courage to get up and open my curtains.

A world of white stares back at me.

I shriek and bolt out of my room.

"Snow day!"

Rose, who's on the landing on her way back from the bathroom, screams and drops her PJs on the floor.

"For the love of..." she mutters, as she picks her stuff up.

"The cascade hasn't called yet," Mum says, appearing at the top of the stairs. She's got the house phone in her hand, ready to answer the call to freedom. "So get ready as usual."

"There's no way they'll make us go to school in this," I say. "The buses won't run."

"They'll have gritted the roads last night," Mum points out. "So—"

The phone starts to ring. My heart thunders in my chest as Mum answers it and talks to whoever is on the other end. Rose glances at me out the corner of her eye. I hold up my hand, showing I've crossed all the fingers that I can.

At last Mum says, "OK. Thank you. I'll pass it on." She hangs up the call and grins at us. "Snow day," she sings. "Guess I'd better cancel my classes."

I yell and jump for joy. "Tobogganing!" I shout. "Rose, get dressed in your warmest, most waterproof clothes. We're heading out the moment it gets light."

Rose looks rather confused at the whole situation, but I dash into my room and call Leon. He answers on the third ring.

"I've been expecting your call," he says.

"Meet at the end of your drive at eight?"

"Roger. Over and out."

The sky has barely started to lighten when Rose, Bonnie, Mum and I leave the house, dragging two tobogganing sledges behind us. Leon waits for us at the end of his drive, Alexander on a lead and his own sledge dragging behind him. He has a proper wooden one that he is sure used to belong to his grandfather. It looks old enough to. Mum and I have a plastic one each. We drag the sledges up the slushy road. It's no longer snowing, but the wind is bitter on my exposed face.

We get to the top of Dirty Lane Hill – a single-track road that is really only suitable for farm vehicles but is sometimes used as a shortcut between our village and another. No farming vehicles have come through yet, so the snow is pristine and flat.

It takes a few runs to compact the snow down, but once it is we start flying. We take turns using the sledges to race each other, the dogs chasing us up and down the hill. On one of her runs, Mum tries to get Bonnie to come into the sledge with her, but she freaks when they start to move and jumps out.

"Bet you wouldn't have been able to do this in London," I say to Rose, as we watch Leon and Mum race each other down the hill.

"We would," Rose says. "It just would have been a lot busier. I'm amazed we've got such a sweet spot all to ourselves."

When are hands are numb and our clothes are soaked through, we drag ourselves back along the road to home.

Mum lights a fire, which we sit in front of in dry clothes with hot drinks clutched in our hands. Bonnie and Alexander curl up together on the rug and start snoring.

While Mum is making hot chocolate, my phone pings. It's a Facebook message, from Fran again.

```
Fran
Hey :)
Having a nice snow day?
```

Random. But OK.

Why would Fran be messaging me? Again?

Maybe she messaged me by mistake.

I close Messenger and say, "Wanna watch some anime?" I wiggle my eyebrows.

"What else are snow days for?" Leon asks.

Leon and I bicker over what series to watch, while Rose scratches the tops of Alexander's and Bonnie's heads. In the end we settle on *Kabaneri of the Iron Fortress*.

"We really should be watching this at Halloween," Leon says.

"It's a modern classic," I protest.

"And February is just as dark and depressing as October," Rose says. "Perhaps more so."

We binge half the series. Leon goes home with Alexander while Rose and I stay beside the fire. I have some chocolate left over from Christmas which we share between us – I only didn't binge eat it through mock exams because I lost it down the back of the bed. Don't worry, it wasn't open when I lost it.

"Have you ever tried making your own cosplay?" Rose

asks me.

"Nope," I say. "I've only bought my stuff before. Genny and Paige are amazing at making their own, though. Have you seen their Insta page?"

When Rose shakes her head I bring up their joint account – because they're that cool that they have a joint account – and show Rose all the cosplays they've done, from the earlier ones they bought most of the pieces for, to the most recent ones that Paige made from scratch.

"Wow," Rose says, as I show her the cosplay they did for the last con they went to – Ashiya and Abeno from *The Morose Mononokean*. "They're amazing."

"Genny even made Moja. I tried to get her to give him to me afterwards, but she said no."

"I wish I could make cosplays like that." She gets out her phone. "I don't follow any accounts, but there are loads of Instagram cosplay accounts I keep an eye on and save posts from. This is my *Sailor Moon* collection."

As Rose shows me her collections of cosplay ideas, something lights up in her eyes.

I remember the way Rose clamped up at the farmers market when I tried to push her on the cosplay subject, but maybe I should give her another subtle nudge.

"Why don't you learn how to make your own stuff?" I suggest, in what I hope is an innocent voice.

For a moment, I'm sure that the light grows in Rose's eyes, but it quickly dies. She turns off her phone and places it face down on the coffee table.

"Maybe," she says, pushing her glasses up her face, "after exams are over."

"Right," I mutter. "Exams."

"What about you?" Rose asks. "Have you ever been tempted to make your own cosplay?"

"Tempted, yes. But sewing isn't really my thing."

"Have you ever drawn fan art? Apart from the piece you gave me for my birthday, that is."

I want to laugh, but I don't because how would Rose know how many sketchbooks I have filled with fan art. They're all stored under my bed, out of sight. For my eyes only.

But Rose and I are having a Moment here. The sort of Moment that calls for things to be shared so relationships can grow.

I need to share something with her that I have never shared with anyone else.

I hesitate on the sofa for a few moments longer and then say, "One sec," and head upstairs.

Chapter 28

Rose

I'm hoping I haven't stepped on a tender spot asking about fan art so I'm relieved when Clover comes back to the living room with a couple of sketchbooks.

"So," she says, sitting on the sofa beside me, "I haven't shown these to anyone. Not even Leon."

"Don't feel pressured to show me if you don't want to," I say.

"It's fine." Clover starts flipping through the pages of one of the sketchbooks. "I want to show you."

She turns a few pages, pauses on one page for a few seconds, purses her lips and then flips through a few more. Then she stops and pushes the sketchbook towards me. I'm staring at a watercolour painting of the brothers from *Fullmetal Alchemist*. The younger one – Al, I think his name is – is being enfolded in pieces of armour. He's reaching through the plates, a look of desperation on his face, while the older brother reaches for him, their fingers centimetres from touching.

"Wow," I breathe. "That's amazing!"

Clover's cheeks flush. She mumbles, "Thanks," and flips to the next piece.

Thanks to Clover's education over the past few months, I recognise most of the characters. All of Clover's pieces are stunning – even the quick sketches. Most of her paintings are in watercolour, although she's done a few in pen.

"Clover," I say, when she's worked her way through the last sketchbook, "they're beautiful."

"Thanks," Clover says, and then she laughs. "I wish I could draw this sort of stuff for my art A level, or manga style art with pen and ink – I would get so much more work done if I could. But my art teacher said I couldn't – said they were illustrations, not 'art'." She sticks her tongue out as she makes air quotes. "Apparently the examiners wouldn't like them."

I scoff. "I'm not an artist of any sort, but I don't know how anyone can't see that is art. If I was an examiner, I would give you full marks for all those pieces."

"Thanks." Clover flips through her sketchbook. "I can't wait until A levels are over so I can draw as much as I want."

I watch Clover turn the pages, getting glimpses of colours and poignant expressions. For some reason my mind turns back a few weeks to standing with Clover in the cold afternoon at the market, hot burgers clutched in our hands.

"Have you ever thought about posting your art online?" I ask. "Like, sharing it? You could start a Redbubble account and get people to buy your artwork on stuff."

Clover snorts. "No one would want to buy my art."

"*I* would! I'd love a notebook or a mug with your art on it! And I bet there are loads of other people who would. You should give it a try."

For a moment, Clover continues to chew her bottom lip while she looks down at a watercolour piece of Victor and Yuri from *Yuri on Ice*, ice-skating on a frozen lake under a sky full of stars.

Then she closes the book.

"If you love cosplay so much," she says, "why haven't you tried it?"

Um... sorry...? But what does that have to do with anything? And what was with the accusing tone in Clover's voice just now? Even though her hands are in her lap, it's like she just pointed a finger at me.

I push away the instinct to bite back and reply, "There's never been an opportunity for me to."

"That's not true. You live in *London*. Do you know how many cosplay groups there are in London? How many social groups there are for otaku there? How many comic cons happen there every year?"

My stomach drops with the same force as if I'd stepped off a cliff. The moment of suspension lasts for a few moments. Then I hit the bottom and my face grows hot. What is with this sudden attitude? Why is Clover turning this back on me? I was just trying to help her.

"Look," I say, sitting back, "you told me you wanted to get to know other people who like anime and manga. And since you're stuck in the middle of nowhere, the only way to do that is to connect with people online. I only suggested posting your art on the internet because it's good. Like, *really* good, and putting it out there would help you talk to the people you're so desperate to." I stand up. "I'm going to get a drink."

I try not to storm through to the kitchen, but I hit the ground hard with every step. I fill a glass at the tap, gulp it down in one, and then slam it down onto the kitchen counter. I wince at the loud bang it makes and immediately check for cracks. I breathe a sigh of relief when I find none.

I feel lighter. The moment of fury has passed, and now I'm just angry at myself for snapping at Clover. It's so frustrating to hear her complain about how lonely she is when she makes no effort to reach out to others. *But* she needs to get there in her own time, and snapping at her isn't going to help.

I take a deep breath and head back to the living room. Clover is sat on the sofa where I left her, holding her sketchbook, which is now closed. She's staring at the blank cover.

"I'm sorry," Clover says. "I'm not sure where that came from, but I... I hate that you're right. But I'm so nervous about putting myself out there for other people to tear apart."

"I'm sorry, too," I say. I sit beside her. "I shouldn't have snapped back at you like that."

Clover squeezes her hands together in her lap. "You were speaking the truth, though."

"So were you."

Silence stretches between us, and as it grows longer it starts to draw something out of me. Something I've wanted to share with Clover since Halloween when Leon lent me Genny's Sailor Moon outfit, but I've been keeping back out of fear. And if I don't share it now, I never will.

"So," I say, stretching out my legs, "about a year ago, I went to Camden on my own for a day. I wasn't really looking for anything - just went for a browse. I was walking past one of the stalls when I saw this dress… a Lolita dress, and I just had to try it on. I'd seen them online before and thought they were cute."

I find the photo on my phone - the one I took in the dressing room that I've never shown anyone else - and hold it up to Clover. I can hear my heartbeat in my ears as she looks at me in the pink and white frilly dress reflected in the dressing room mirror, pulling a peace sign.

There's a pause, which causes my nerves to start to unravel.

At last Clover says, "You look so cute. Did you buy it?"

I laugh with relief. "No," I say, pushing my glasses up my face. "I freaked, got changed and rushed out the shop. I found the dress online and have had it on a private Amazon list ever since. I keep thinking about buying it but… can't bring myself to do it."

"But why? You look adorable."

"Because I felt embarrassed for liking something like that." I press my sweating palms to my jeans. "I thought about buying it and then thought about what the shopkeeper would think about me as I went to pay for it, about the looks I would get carrying it back on the Tube, and then what I would have to say to my parents if they saw it. If my *friends* saw it." I shudder. "Like, I shouldn't like stuff like that - cute pink and lacy things, Victorian doll dresses and *Alice in Wonderland* stuff. They're for kids, and... like, the Lolita style is so problematic, but I do. I really love them." I sigh and slump back against the sofa. "I guess that's why I love shojo anime so much."

"You shouldn't be ashamed for what you like," Clover says.

"I know, but it's hard not to when people are always telling you what you like is weird. After Suzie got me into *Sailor Moon* and *Cardcaptor Sakura*, I showed a friend *Sailor Moon* because I thought she would love it as much as I did. After the first few minutes she said it was weird and asked if we could watch something else." I sink lower into the sofa. "I felt so embarrassed that I never mentioned *Sailor Moon* or *Cardcaptor Sakura* to any of my friends again."

"Last summer," Clover says, "Mum had to go on a week-long retreat for work, so Grandma had to pick me up and drop me off from the bus stop. I know," she adds, when she sees the look of horror on my face, "it was as bad as you're thinking it was. One afternoon when she was picking me up, this BBC programme came on about the anime industry. The presenter was talking to some white-collared dude who likely had never watched an anime in his life. He was going on about all the hentai stuff there is in the market, and making animanga out to be this awful thing that only produced pervy stuff. They didn't even mention series like *Naruto* or *Silver Spoon*, or *Bakuman*, or *Snow White with the Red Hair*, or any other manga that has an uplifting storyline that isn't just about a guy trying to get into a girl's pants. Gah!"

Clover punches a pillow.

"I hate," she says, punching the pillow at every other word, "how people look down their nose at animanga, without looking deeper into it to see how amazing and inspirational and life-changing the stories are. And I *know*, a lot of anime is full of crappy fan service, casual sexual harassment, and homophobic and transphobic jokes – which is so, so shit and awful – but it's like most people only want to show those parts to turn people against it before they've had a chance to try it themselves. And then those of us who like it get it in the neck."

Clover lets out a scream of frustration and goes to town on the pillow. I grab one for myself and hug it to my chest.

"Why," she demands, "couldn't I have liked something like *Love Island* instead? It would have made my life so much easier!"

"Yeah," I admit, "I guess it would have done, but that stuff is so heartless."

Clover sighs and lobs the pillow at the wall. "That's true. God. I feel like shit now. Fancy a tea?"

"Yes, please."

While Clover goes into the kitchen, I pick up my phone and start scrolling through Instagram. Rory's been trekking somewhere with his dad, who's in the TA. Henry's posting full-body selfies in his various suits, and Rachel's stretched out on a sofa with her guinea pigs. Ari, as ever, hasn't posted anything. Kai's doing paintballing with his brother. Jayden and Maryam are walking in some park. Zoe and Sienne are painting their toenails and watching *Bridesmaids*. When I've had enough of my feed, I start checking cosplayer pages. One of my favourite cosplayers has reposted an old photo she put up in October - she's dressed as Zelda from *Skyward Sword* and is standing underneath a banner outside a big building.

Just booked my tickets for @mcmcomiccon London May 2019! I'm so excited about attending my 7th con. Looking forward to seeing you all there! Now I just need to decide who I am going to go as!

I stare at the photo for a while, and at the banner in the background, and click on the photo's location tag of MCM London Comic Con. My heart skips a beat when I see the dozens of squares of cosplayers, the stalls of anime merch and manga, interview panels with manga publishers and anime streaming services, people posing with celebrities at meet and greets, and food stalls selling takoyaki, yakisoba, ramune and loads of other food I've only seen in anime.

Then it hits me.

It hits me so hard that I bolt upright from the sofa and propel myself into the kitchen. Clover is fussing Bonnie, waiting for the kettle to boil.

"Clover!" I shout just as the kettle finishes boiling.

"What?" she asks.

I turn my phone around and show her the photos. I look and sound manic, but I'm so excited that I can't keep it all in check. “We should go to comic con in May.”

“Comic con?”

“MCM Comic Con. At the ExCeL Centre. Look.” I hold my phone closer to her face to give her a good look at the photos as I scroll. I keep glancing at her face, watching her expression carefully. It doesn’t take long for her excitement to catch.

“We should go,” I whisper.

With her eyes still glued to the screen, Clover nods. Then she turns to me, a beaming smile on her face.

“Yes fucking please,” she says.

Chapter 29

Clover

“Go on.”

I inch my finger closer to the button, where it hovers, trembling while my heartbeat thumps in my ears.

“Just do it,” Leon urges from behind my shoulder. “One click and it’s done.”

I take a deep breath. He’s right. I should just press it, then my art blog will be live… for all the world to see.

HOLYCOWBALLSICAN’TPRESS IT!

“I can’t,” I whimper.

“Yes,” Rose says. “Yes, you can.”

“I can’t!”

“Then what was all that work for?” Leon points out.

"You've spent hours on that Wordpress site. If you don't make it live, you'll have wasted all that time."

I swivel around in my chair to tell Leon that outcome is completely fine with me, when another hand closes over mine and presses my finger down on the keyboard. Rose pulls away from mine, smiling at the screen.

"There," she says, "all done."

"Rose! What the hell?"

"Well, you wouldn't have done it otherwise. Go on. Check out the finished product."

I open my mouth to argue when I just... deflate. All the nerves and anger dissipate. I am relieved. It's done now. I click through to the front end of my new art blog. I must admit, the front page looks good, with a fancy header image, a couple of galleries to organise my artwork, and then a very short about page.

"Check all your social media links are working," Rose says.

As I go through them, Leon slumps on my bed.

"Genny and Page are besides themselves with excitement about your first con," he says.

"Are they going?" Rose asks.

"Of course," Leon says. "They go every year, twice a year. They sometimes even go to the Showmasters London Film and Comic Con in July, and to some of the regional MCMs. It used to be a networking thing for them for the company, but now they just go for fun."

"Have you ever been?"

"Nope, although Genny's tried to drag me there a few times."

"But you're coming with us in May?" I ask, giving him a stern look out the corner of my eye.

Leon pulls a face. "Going means dealing with the two things I hate the most – London and crowds – but," he adds when my frown deepens, "I'll think about it. Genny says the crowds aren't too bad on the Friday if you get there early. Saturday sounds like hell."

"If we went on Friday," I ask, "would you come with us?"

"What about school?" Rose asks.

"*Pfftt.*" I wave her meaningless worries away. "It'll be during study leave."

Rose adjusts her glasses. Bless her. She genuinely looks panicked about skipping school. "But what if we have exams?"

"We won't. It's the day before half-term. They won't be that cruel."

Rose raises her eyebrows. "Perhaps we should wait until the timetable comes out before we book our tickets. Just in case. But you should come with us, Leon."

"You can show off your awesome Goku cosplay," I add.

A smug smile tugs at the corners of Leon's mouth. "My Goku costume *is* pretty awesome."

I test the last social media link and find it all present and correct. I now have a Twitter and an Instagram account to manage. Rose made me post a load of stuff on there to "build a presence" before the blog launch – whatever that means. She was a little apprehensive at my choice of @otaku_trash02 as my handle, but it sums me up so perfectly that I refused to waver on it. I must admit, it's awesome having a place where I can freely retweet/like/

comment/share posts without fearing anyone I know – aside from Rose, Leon, Genny and Paige – knowing it's me doing it.

"Have you announced your new site is live?" Rose asks. I grimace. Rose points a finger at me. "Do it."

"That's such an anime pose."

Rose embellishes the pose by putting a hand on her hip and puffing out her chest. All she needs to do now is make her nostrils flare. "Do it."

I roll my eyes and reopen Twitter.

"What anime are you working through at the moment?" Leon asks, as I'm faffing around with the Instagram post. I hate cropping my artwork. It's a crime.

"We've just finished the first season of *The Morose Mononokean*," Rose says.

"It's the ideal time since season two has just started," I add.

"It's cool they're making more web comics into anime these days," Leon says.

"There!" I show Rose my Insta post on my phone and then the Twitter post on my laptop. "Happy now? Now it's your turn."

"Rose's turn to do what?" Leon asks.

"Start a new Insta and Twitter account for her otaku trash."

"Cool." Leon lies back on my bed, holding his phone above his head. "Tell me when they're live."

I close my laptop and swivel around. All the bravado has gone from Rose's face and she looks less sure than she did when she was issuing me commands.

"Have you thought of a handle?"

"Yeah," Rose says, touching the back of her head. "I have."

Then why does she look so embarrassed about it? I stare at her, waiting.

"So?" Leon asks. "What is it?"

"Gimme a minute." Rose bolts out my room. I hear her cross the landing and go into her room.

"What's with all the secrecy?" Leon whispers.

"Not sure," I reply. I push my chair back from my desk and glare at Rose's room. "She'd better not be chickening out from her end of the deal when she forced me to publish my site."

My phone pings. As I reach for it, Leon's phone pings.

A new Insta notification is on my lock screen: CardCaptor_Rose is now following you.

"That's such a cute handle!" I shout. I follow Rose back and then check who she's following. Leon and I are there, as well as Genny's and Paige's accounts, their gaming company, the official MCM account, and a load of cosplaying accounts.

Rose's face appears around the side of my bedroom door. "It's not too much, is it?" she asks.

"It's perfect," I assure her.

"You going to put your cosplay stuff on there?" Leon asks.

"Yeah. I might document the one I'm going to do for con in May."

"Any thoughts on who you're going to go as?"

Rose shakes her head. "Not yet. Maybe Sakura, but I'll

make another of her costumes."

"Start simple," I say. "Don't walk before you can run."

"Genny used to buy her cosplay stuff before she and Paige started making their own," Leon adds. "It's fine to start wearing shop bought before you start making your own – *if* you want to make your own."

"But it kind of feels like cheating," Rose says.

"Can you sew?" Rose shakes her head. Leon and I both sigh. "Then definitely start with the simple stuff. You going to cosplay, Clo?"

I puff out my cheeks. "Not sure. The idea doesn't make me comfortable. Not everyone goes in cosplay, do they?"

"No," Leon says. "Plenty of people don't."

"Alright. Perhaps next time." I glance at Rose, who is staring at a random spot on my floor with unfocused eyes. I can see the panic building behind them. "Are you sure you can make a costume by the end of May, Rose?"

"I'm going to have to keep it simple," Rose says, and she sounds sort of spaced out. "I'm losing a week in February half-term."

"Why?" Leon asks.

"I'm going to see my parents in Dubai, which I was really looking forward to, but now..." Rose drags a hand over her face. "No, no. I am still looking forward to going, but at the same time I really wish I had that week now to work on my cosplay."

"Well," Leon says, pulling himself up into a sitting position, "you'll have three months to complete it when you get back. And everyone knows all cosplays don't actually get finished until the night before con."

Chapter 30

Rose

"You're on mute." I point at my ear and shake my head. Clover rolls her eyes and then her voice comes through loud and clear.

"That's just embarrassing," she says.

"Happens to the best of us."

"Happens to those who are inept with using technology." She leans to the side, as though she's trying to see around me. "Is that your parents' Dubai house?"

"Well—" I lean to the side so Clover can see the room behind me, "—it's the one Dad's company are renting for him."

"Looks nice."

It is. It's a stone house plastered and painted peach. All four bedrooms have a balcony and Mum and Dad's room has a giant en suite - and I mean *giant*. Like large enough to hold a round sunken bath in the middle of the room that has jets like a hot tub.

"There's a pool out the back as well. Want to see?"

Clover pulls a face. "Nah. Pools aren't really my thing. Have you used it?"

"Yup. It was freezing!"

"But it's hot out there at the moment, isn't it?"

"Twenty-five degrees, but the pool doesn't warm up at all. It's fine after a few minutes, though."

Clover leans towards her laptop camera and puts her chin in her hands. "What else you been up to? I mean, I've seen your IG videos, but I'm not letting you get out of telling me about the experience."

I tell Clover about the shopping centres Mum took me to - to the one where each section had décor from a different part of the world, and another with a massive aquarium dominating the ground and middle floor. I tell her about the evening Dad left work early to meet Mum and me for dinner to watch the dancing fountains, and then the following day when all three of us went on a bus tour of the city and then went to the old souk market, crossing the Dubai Creek on an Abra ferry.

"Sounds nice," Clover says, although she would hate it in the heat and city. There are none of the rolling green fields out here that I've been used to for the past six months. Although I miss the endless green, I do not miss the mud, and going from minus figures into a twenty-five degree heat with sun was heavenly.

"How's the blog doing?" I ask.

Clover breaks out into a grin. "Really well. I've received so many lovely comments, and lots of people have been liking and sharing the stuff I post on social media."

"That's great. Have you been able to talk to any of them...?"

"Yeah," Clover says, although it is said with a hesitation that makes my heart sink. "I mean, I've talked to loads of other people about anime and manga, about our favourite scenes and characters."

I sense there is meant to be a "but" at the end of that sentence, but Clover doesn't offer up anything else. Hell. I was hoping that talking to people online would help, but maybe it hasn't in the way I wanted it to. I want to press Clover on the issue but now is not the time. Some conversations are best had face to face and I would prefer for Clover to talk to me when she is ready – I won't get anything out of her otherwise.

"Hey," I say in the brightest voice I can muster, "when I get back, fancy an anime day with Leon?"

Clover nods. "Sounds awesome."

"Alright. You'll have to decide what we watch."

"Already taken care of. Mum's got an Amazon Prime trial. So I want to watch *Wotakoi*. What you doing for your last two days?"

"Going out for dinner tonight. Dad knows this great spot out in the desert – there's an old fort out there that's been turned into a hotel. We're driving out there to watch the sunset."

"Watch out for any dungeons that spring up while you're out there."

"I mean, I don't think I'll be going into any if they do. Not without a Magi guide."

"And not without me."

I start thinking, and from the silence Clover falls into she's stuck in the same train of thought that I am. "If one did spring up, though," I say, "I would want it to be Baal's dungeon. Lightning would be such a cool element to be able to control, and his djinn equip is pretty awesome."

Clover wrinkles her nose. "Not sure I would be up for having a tail with my djinn equip. I'd rather have Alibaba's djinn – Amon? Fire all the way for me. Or Valefor." Clover rubs her thumbs and index fingers together over the top of her head. "I wouldn't mind having a pair of fluffy ears."

"I thought you said you didn't want a tail? Valefor's a nine tails – you'd have nine tails instead of one if you had him as your djinn."

"But they'd be fluffy tails, not scaly ones. It makes all the difference."

I grin. "You're such a furry."

Clover grins back at me. "And proud of it."

We catch up on a few other things – apparently Grandma visited the day after I left and was very disappointed that I wasn't around, although I'm relieved to have missed her – and then we wave goodbye.

As the connection fades, I hear Dad come in through the front door and the sound of him throwing his keys in the bowl by the door.

"I'm home!" he calls.

"Hello!" Mum calls from the living room.

"Hello!" I shout from my room upstairs.

"Everyone ready to leave in twenty minutes?"

"Yup!"

"Yup!"

"Good!"

Mum and Dad say the hotel isn't anything fancy, but I change into the nicest dress I brought with me. We set off in Dad's four-by-four across the desert. It's still light when we leave the house, but Dad wants to allow plenty of time to get there for the sunset.

When we arrive, we're shown upstairs onto the ramparts that overlook the swimming pool. The desert stretches out before us, vast and flat. Looking out at it, I can imagine a dungeon erupting out of the sand, ready to be conquered like in *Magi: The Labyrinth of Magic*. Eugh. Is this what anime has reduced me to?

"Strawberry beer?" Dad asks as we look at the menus.

"Am I allowed?" I ask.

"It's alcohol free – like most drinks out here."

"Alright."

The waiter brings our drinks, already poured out. Mum holds hers out. "Cheers!" We knock our glasses together.

"So," Dad says, "what's the plan with your university application? Which open days do you want to go to?"

"I'm not sure yet," I say.

"Have you decided what you're going to study?" Mum asks.

"I want to study law," I say, pushing my glasses up my face, but as I say the words a strange taste fills my mouth.

"Alright," Dad says, "that's easy then. I would highly

recommend Warwick as a place to look at."

Mum scoffs. "Don't be ridiculous. Westminster is the place Rose should go to if she wants to study law."

Dad makes a dismissive sound, which makes Mum's gaze narrow. Dad nudges me with his elbow. "Don't go to Westminster unless you want a second-class degree. You'll never learn what it's really like to be a lawyer unless you go somewhere that will give you *experience*."

"What about Oxbridge?" Mum says. "I think they both do law undergraduate courses. That's if you *want* to go to Oxford or Cambridge."

"I'm not sure where I want to go," I say, even though I had decided. A few weeks ago if you had asked me, I would have told you UCL was my first choice. But now, I'm not sure where I want to go next year.

And Dear Universe. I'm not even sure anymore that I want to study law. Every time I say that I want to become a lawyer the words feel less and less right. Now I'm starting to wonder if they ever felt right. Like, I only chose law because I didn't know what else to do and everyone's always said that I should do a worthwhile job like my parents. Now I'm hurtling down a course I'll never be able to turn back from. And as much as I should say something, I feel like it's too late to change direction and I don't know where I would go if I did.

Chapter 31

Clover

I'm going to have an admin morning.

Pfftt. I know, right? It surprised me as well, but I've posted a few new art pieces this month and am aware I have COMMENTS on my blog I need to go through. Like, real people are commenting on my artwork. OK, some of them are spam comments from people who are trying to sell me something, but some of them are GENUINE people saying how much they like my artwork. My Elric brothers piece is receiving all the love. Maybe I should do a few more *Fullmetal* posts.

I disappear down a bit of a rabbit hole of liking and replying. One of the people who regularly likes and comments on my posts runs their own anime- and manga-dedicated blog, called bokutoland. I scroll through a couple of posts, skim reading their spoiler-free anime and manga reviews, posts that are comments on anime news, trips to comic book shops and Japanese restaurants, and their posts about their trip to Japan last year. That last one leaves me green with envy.

Just as I'm about to pull myself out of the doom scroll, the title of the next post catches my eye: Secretive Otaku – When to reveal your true self.

I take a deep breath and read. By the time I get to the end, I have tears in my eyes. Turns out the author of bokutoland had their very own Natasha when they were at school. They did stop watching anime, and only got back into it when they went to uni. But they didn't tell anyone at uni that they liked watching anime until they met someone who started talking about anime in the middle of the refectory and most of the people they were sitting with joined in. It took for someone to ask bokutoland if they watched anime for them to join in the conversation.

They said it was like a muzzle had been removed.

Five years after finishing uni they're still friends with that group and hang out with them often to game, binge anime or go to the cinema. At the end of the post there's a picture of the group, dressed as various *Haikyu!!* characters outside one of the northern MCM Comic Cons.

It's taken me years to finally admit to someone that I like what I like. But I still don't do it to everyone. At my first place of work after uni, I told them I was going to comic con and got some strange looks and comments from some of the older people there. One woman said, "I'm not into that weird shit."

OK, hun. You do you, because I'm not expecting you to be into the same stuff as me. I'm not into water sports and hockey, but I don't make comments about your hobbies that make you feel shit about yourself.

The place I work at now, I was there for a year before I told them I was going to con during my time off. Most of the team gave me blank looks, or said they didn't know what that was, but one of the managers was like, "Oh, is that where they dress up as characters? I'd love to do that one day."

I don't want to compare coming out as an otaku to coming out as part of the LBGT community - because we haven't faced hundreds of years of persecution for being who we are and aren't always fighting for our rights - but I only ever tell others that I watch anime when I feel safe. When I've gotten to know the people I'm talking to and I know that they won't start making comments behind my back.

If you are comfortable telling everyone you meet that you like watching anime and reading manga, go for it! But if you, like me, have had some shit in the past and don't feel comfortable going around in an Akatsuki hoodie, then don't. But remember the online otaku community is here for you to ensure you are not alone.

There are dozens - perhaps hundreds - of comments on the post. I skim them. Someone points out that if more people admitted that they liked animanga, there probably wouldn't be such a stigma around it. Someone comments on that comment pointing out how much manga sales have risen in the West over the last year, showing that more people are reading it. Someone else says that the people who bullied bokutoland were likely doing it because they wanted to make themselves feel better about their empty existence. I think of Natasha and her posse when I read that comment and snort.

The blog post leaves me hopeful. It's true as well that if people did start admitting that they liked animanga, it would be so much easier for us to find each other. Is there anyone else in my year who is an otaku? But the prospect of talking about animanga at school makes a cold sickly feeling hit my stomach.

OK, perhaps I'm not there yet.

I'm aware it's getting close to the time Mum and I need to take Bonnie for a walk before we go to MK, but I've got enough time to sort out all the Instagram and Twitter notifications I've been getting. Honestly, I've woken up most mornings to find them stacked on top of one another. I never have the energy to look at them, so I just swipe them away and ignore the little numbers next to the icons. I'm more energetic today, so I load up Twitter... and then Instagram.

At first I wonder if it's a prank.

I mean, how – HOW?! – could I have 300 new Twitter followers and 500 – I REPEAT, 500!! – new Instagram followers. In one night.

When I shut my eyes last night I had a comfortable 200 on each platform, now I have more than double that number on each. DURING THE COURSE OF ONE NIGHT! And even as I'm sat here, scrolling through the endless likes/retweets/comments/follows more are joining the top of the queue.

What is going on?!

I hear the front door open and close downstairs. Rose is back from her run. I throw on my dressing gown and slippers and rush downstairs. Rose is easing off her running shoes, which are covered in mud.

"Damn this mud," she says, wiping her fingers on her leggings, which are just as splattered with mud as her shoes. I don't know why she tries to keep it off her. I learnt long ago just to accept it.

"Rose!" I shove my phone in her face. "Look! Look at my followers!"

"Back off a bit. Hold it up for me – I can't touch your phone unless you want mud all over it." My heart pounds while she squints at the screen. "Did you always have that many followers?"

"I got three hundred new Twitter followers last night, and *five hundred* new Insta followers last night. Yes, you heard me," I add when Rose's eyes grow wide.

"Someone with a big following must have shared your artwork. Have you worked out who it was?"

"How do I?"

"Scroll down to the end of the notifications, and find the first one you received. It's likely them."

It's a manga bookstagram account. I've been following them since the beginning, but they've just noticed me. And shared one of my posts with their 4,000 followers both on Twitter and on Instagram.

Holy cow balls.

"Great," Rose says when I relay my findings, "I'm really pleased for you, but can I go take a shower now?"

As Rose heads upstairs, Mum comes downstairs in her walking gear and they do an awkward passing thing on the stairs. Mum raises her eyebrows when she sees my PJs.

"You still want to take Bonnie out before we go to MK?" she asks.

I've been obsessing over my phone all morning. I've completely lost track of time.

"Gimme a sec," I say and rush upstairs.

As I'm changing, a Facebook message pops up on the screen. It's Fran again. I skim read the first lines of the message as they are displayed on the screen and then dismiss the message. I don't understand why she keeps messaging me. I keep noticing her glancing at me at school, often taking the seat next to me in the common room. It's like she's waiting to talk to me. I wish she wouldn't. I don't know what I would say back to her if she did.

When I come downstairs, Mum's on the phone. So much for getting me to hurry out the door. I'm about to chastise her when I hear her say, "... yeah, Mum. Yeah, alright. I'll see you then. Bye, Mum. Bye."

Her mouth is set tight when she puts the phone down.

"Did she apologise this time?" I ask.

"No," Mum says. "Of course not."

"Fuck her," I say, which makes Mum smile. "Why is she so awful?"

Mum sighs. "She's an old lady."

"That's not an excuse. You're never too old to change."

I take the squeeze on the shoulder that Mum gives me as a sign that she agrees but is too tired to do anything about it. And as much as I want to do something about it, as soon as that old woman fixes me with her eagle eyes I'll turn into a tongue-tied coward.

The early March wind is bitter and by the time we get back from walking Bonnie the backs of my thighs are ice cold, and the skin on my cheeks feels like someone's taken a grater to it. But while we were walking, we saw the daffodils starting to poke their heads above the dirt, fields that the farmers had raked ready for planting, and a field of sheep with coloured spots on their wool. I guess it can't be too many weeks until we'll have lambs kicking their heels up in the fields and wheat poking its head up through the ground. As much as I hate the hot weather of summer, I love seeing the first bursts of colour and life that spring brings. I really wish the world could just skip over summer and go straight to autumn. Hot chocolate, blankets, pumpkins, spending hours inside in front of a roaring fire because the weather is awful out. Bring it on.

Mum and I take turns showering, then the three of us – Mum, Rose and me – pile into her car and set off for MK to buy Rose's cosplaying supplies.

"Have you made up your mind about who you are going to cosplay as?" I ask as we spin around one of Milton Keynes's many roundabouts.

"So," Rose says, "I had a good think about what you and Leon said about not making things too complicated for myself."

"Yeah?"

"And—" she clenches her hands, "—I've decided to completely disregard your advice."

I smirk. "Fair, but on your head be it. I thought it might have been a great excuse for you to buy and wear that Lolita dress you've had your eye on."

"I did think about that, but... I'm not ready to go in Lolita clothing... yet. Perhaps next year, but this year I want to go as a character."

"Who?"

"I was thinking Akko from *Little Witch Academia*. I don't think their school outfits will be too difficult to make."

"Oooh, OK. I like it. That shouldn't be too hard... right?"

Rose and I exchange a look. I must admit her idea sounds fun, but my gut tells me - as someone who has never made a piece of clothing before - that it might not be as simple as it looks.

Once we've parked and are inside the centre, Mum gives us some money each.

"For lunch," she says, "and anything else you fancy if there's anything left over. Give me a ring when you've finished. I'll just be browsing around - feel like I deserve a day of R&R since I have a PCC meeting this evening."

First stop on the list is John Lewis. We find the fabric section, where we get lost in looking at different rolls of fabric and patterns for skirts and waistcoats.

"I can use one of my old school shirts," Rose says. She turns a pattern packet over and looks at the back. "Then I'll just need to make or find the split tie thing, and also a red belt. Think I can get away with not making a cloak?"

"Genny says it always gets hot in the ExCel Centre, so I wouldn't bother." I search for *Little Witch Academia* and scroll through some images. "What about a hat? You have to have a hat even if you're not going to have a cloak. And a wand. You'll only be half a witch if you don't have a hat and wand."

"Only if I have time. I might buy the wand, though..."

"What about a broom?"

"I'll buy one."

"You can borrow mine if you want – I'm sure Kiki won't mind." She pauses. "Couldn't you buy a waistcoat and a skirt?"

"I'm worried the colour won't match if I do that." As Rose stares down at the packet her eyes grow large and distant. Oh, shit. She's spacing out. "Am I a fool?" she whispers. "How can I get this all done in three months, while also studying for exams and taking driving lessons? What makes me think I can do this?"

"Listen," I say, taking the packet out of her hand, "if all goes to shit and you don't find the time, you can always buy some stuff off Amazon. I know you think it's cheating, but it's better than going half-dressed, or working yourself into the grave trying to get it all done."

"Thanks," Rose mutters, and I can almost see her soul trying to escape her body.

I look down at my phone again. "What are you going to do about the boots?"

Rose winces. "I haven't thought about it yet."

She finally chooses a skirt and waistcoat pattern. Then we move onto the fabric and get very distracted looking at all the different patterns and varieties, which are totally useless for Rose's cosplay. At last, Rose finds a couple of choices in the colour she wants, and then starts panicking about which type to buy. I have no idea, and Google offers no solid advice. I read something about buying certain fabrics for certain types of clothes to ensure the cuts falls right...?! I consider calling Mum for her advice when a shop assistant comes over to check we're OK. It takes one look at our faces to show that we are very far from it.

Once she sees the patterns we're buying, she tells us which one would work best and how much we'd need.

"Have you thought about buttons for the waistcoat?" she asks.

Rose's eyes take on a panicky shine. "No," she says.

"Well, we've got a nice selection over there if you want to have a look."

"OK." Rose hangs her head as she shuffles over to the buttons display. I follow her and help her choose a set.

"What are you making these clothes for?" the lady asks as she's sorting everything out at the till. I avoid looking at the price as it climbs higher and higher with each scan. THIS is another reason for me to not get into cosplay.

"Err, em..." Rose adjusts her glasses as she stumbles over her words. "It's for... a, erm, a Halloween costume."

I turn around so the lady can't see the laugh straining to get out.

"Oh, you're very prepared," the lady says.

"Erm, yes, I guess I am."

As the lady bags the last item, I finally look at the price and my jaw drops. Rose hands over a card without flinching. But as we leave the shop, she says, "There goes my birthday money."

"But you've got everything you need?"

"I hope so. Where do you want to go next?"

I grin. "My haven."

Half an hour later I'm leaving the art shop, my backpack stuffed with supplies for my coursework. Rose left the shop after a few minutes and I find her sitting on a bench outside, scrolling through her phone.

"Got everything?" she asks.

"Yup. Lunchtime?"

"Yup."

We have lunch at Itsu. While we're at the table, Rose snaps a photo of the contents of her shopping bag.

"For the Gram," she says. I check her account when she pops to the loo. She's made her third post on her CardCaptor_Rose account showing the materials she bought with a caption about how excited and nervous she is about starting her first project. She's got a couple of likes on the post from fellow cosplayers. I feel a thrill of excitement for her. While she's gone, I snap a photo of the art supplies I've bought and upload it as a story.

Full of food, we wander down to Waterstones and we pass a bubble tea stand. I nudge Rose as it comes into sight.

"Want some?" I ask.

"Always."

We wander slowly the rest of the way, sipping and chewing our tapioca pearls. I've got a brown sugar tea, and Rose has a strawberry fruit tea with popping pearls.

"Any new followers?" Rose asks.

I check my phone and the sight kicks my stomach. “Twenty more.”

“Wow. That’s amazing.”

“Yeah,” I say and take a long drink of my tea.

A silence stretches between us. Rose is waiting for me to say more, but... I don’t know what to say. Yeah. I guess it’s great, but... if it’s so great, then why is my stomach so tight?

By the time we’ve reached Waterstones and thrown our drained bubble tea cups in the recycling, I still haven’t been able to get the words out to sum up how I’m feeling.

How do I explain to Rose after all the support she’s given me to get the blog live that it’s not filling the hole inside me that I wanted it to? That I become lonelier the higher the numbers climb?

I just hope that con is able to satisfy the empty space inside me.

Chapter 32

Rose

There's something going on in Clover's head that she's not telling me. There's a focus in her eyes and a tension in her shoulders that wasn't there before. She looks like she might tell me what is going on, but as we make our way through the shopping centre, she stays quiet as she sips her bubble tea.

Dear Universe. Don't suppose you want to give me the power to be able to read her mind for a moment, just so I know what's going on? No? OK, then. Guess it was a bit too much to ask.

Clover doesn't say a word to me as we head into Waterstones.

Right. If she's not going to tell me what's going on, then I'll just have to distract her from whatever it is. Taking a breath, I grab her arm.

"Come on," I say and pull her around the shop until we find the manga section. It's smaller than I hoped it might be – just two small shelves in a whole store of books – but Clover's eyes still light up at the sight of it.

We start pulling books down from the shelves for a browse. At first Clover just reads and flicks through volumes quietly, then she starts showing stuff to me – volumes of *Death Note* and *Fullmetal Alchemist*, which she says we need to watch the anime of soon, an omnibus of *Wotakoi*, which we haven't had a chance to watch since I came back from Dubai, and a manga called *Golden Kamuy*, which she says Leon and her binge-watched the first season of in a day. I pull down a couple of series that look of interest and Clover reads them over my shoulder. Soon we're laughing and whispering like normal.

"I'm going to go look at the art books," Clover says after a while.

"Alright." I slide the volume of *Snow White with the Red Hair* back onto the shelf. "I'll stay down here."

No longer worried, I browse the shelves and pull out the second volume of *Yona of the Dawn*. I've read the first volume Genny and Paige gave to me in my Shojo Starter Pack and really loved it – and also developed a massive crush on Hak and his smirk – so pick up the second and start reading. A few pages in I decide I'm going to buy it. Although I have just spent far too much on cosplay materials. Perhaps I should—

"Rose!"

Ari's walking towards me, a grin on his face.

My face starts to break into a smile, but then I remember the manga volume in my hands.

And my stomach drops out from underneath me.

My grip on the book grows slack as I watch Ari walk closer towards me. I'm only half aware of it falling, but then Ari catches it before it hits the floor and reality snaps back into focus.

"Careful," he says, laughing, "if you damage it, you have to buy it."

My mouth is dry. My heart is kicking against the inside of my chest.

I should say something. Just a simple "Hello" would be fine, but all my mind is full of right now is: Shit shit shit shit shit shit shit shit shit shit shit shit shit shit shit shit shit shit!!!!

He saw me.

Ari saw me reading a manga volume. I can't even pass it off as something else, or stuff it back into the shelves to hide it. Because he's got the damn thing in his hands!!

Dear Universe. What do I do?! He can't know. He can't know that I like manga, because if he does, he'll tell someone at school, then EVERYONE will know.

And they'll call me weird, and they'll do to me what they did to Clover.

I can't live with that. I can't. I just can't.

"Rose?" Ari's looking at me with this concerned look. "What's the matter?" He glances behind him at the shop entrance. "Are we being filmed or something?"

"No!" I say, so loudly that a couple of other shoppers

turn around to stare at us.

Pull yourself together, Rose!

"No," I say, softer this time. "I was... just surprised to see you here. Sorry... I... I need to go. See you at school."

This is one of those fight or flight situations, and it looks like I'm choosing to fly. As I climb the stairs, I'm aware of Ari calling my name behind me, but I start taking the stairs two at a time. I move around the first floor as quickly as I can without running, hunting out Clover. I find her flicking through a photography book on Harajuku fashion.

I grab her arm, making her jump. She yanks her arm out of my grip, and her eyes blaze with anger as she turns to me.

"What the fu—" She relaxes when she sees it's me. "Oh, it's—"

"We need to go," I say. "Now."

She frowns. "Why? What's hap—"

I want to shake her. *We don't have time for this!* "I saw Ari downstairs," I hiss.

"Who?"

"From school! He saw me in the manga section. Come on. We need to go."

I give Clover time to slot the book back on the shelf then drag her down the other staircase and out of the shop. Thankfully we don't see Ari on our way out.

Chapter 33

Clover

I mean, it wasn't that big of a deal, was it?

Surely she could have just passed it off as something else. Like, she was there picking up a friend's birthday present, or just having a browse... because she was JUST BROWSING?

But Rose is panicking – the anxious energy radiates off her as we're sitting together in the back of Mum's car – so I guess it must be that big of a deal. She hasn't said a word since we fled Waterstones, apart from suggesting that we phone Mum to say we're ready to go home, and then telling Mum in a falsely cheery voice that we had a nice day.

When we get home, Rose goes to her room. Knowing she needs some space, I go into mine and unpack my new art supplies. I turn on my laptop and check the stats on my blog. As I suspected, they've skyrocketed along with the number of comments I've got to go through and approve. And my Twitter and Insta followers just keep climbing.

I flick between the three of them, half marvelling and half freaking out at how things exploded overnight. All those hundreds of people who are liking, sharing, criticising and commenting on my crappy artwork.

Gaaaahhhh!

I slam my laptop lid closed and throw myself down on the bed.

I shouldn't have started that shitty blog. I was expecting just a few people to look at it – like a handful of people who would never leave a comment or like a post. Perhaps one person who would share it on their social media without any sort of comment, just sharing it with their followers because they liked it, the sort of person who shared dozens of similar posts every day.

BUT NOT THIS!!

I put a pillow over my head and breathe in the scent of washing powder. In the dark I wait for my thoughts to flatline, so I can make them focus on something else. Unfortunately, that something else is the events of this afternoon.

Did something happen that Rose isn't telling me? Did Ari say something to her when I was upstairs?

It takes another couple of seconds of staring at the ceiling for me to say "Screw this" and storm across the landing into Rose's room. She's sitting at her desk, her homework spread out in front of her. But she's scrolling through her phone instead.

"What's the matter?" I ask her.

"Nothing's the matter," she says without looking up.

I suppress the urge to roll my eyes. I mean, the girl looks like she has a sour plum in her mouth and she rushed me out of Waterstones without giving me a chance to buy anything. So there is *clearly* something the matter that she doesn't want to talk about. And as much as I want to badger her until she tells me what it is, I need to give her some space.

"OK," I say, "but remember that you can talk to me whenever you want."

I start to head back to my room, when Rose blurts out, "Ari saw me in Waterstones."

I pause. "Huh?" I mean, she told me that she saw Ari in the bookshop. But if Rose remembers she doesn't show it. The same look of panic she had on her face in the shop is back.

"Ari! From school?" Her hands shake as they push up her glasses. "He saw me browsing the manga section."

"So?" She's definitely already told me this. Why's it such a big deal if Ari saw her?

"SO!" Rose's eyes widen. "He saw me looking at manga. Now he knows that I like manga and he's going to tell someone at school that he saw me there and that I'm into manga and anime and then everyone's going to think I'm..." She puts her head in her hands and rests her elbows on the table.

"Really?" I snort. "Is that all? Life isn't going to end

because people at school find out you like animanga."

"How can you say that after what you went through," Rose mutters into her palms. "How can you say that after Natasha made your life hell after she found out you like anime?"

"It didn't end my life. I'm still here. And still a proud otaku."

"But," Rose says, "people will think I'm *weird*."

A bolt of anger jolts through me, tightening my jaw.

"Well," I say with venom, "maybe people wouldn't see it that way if more people admitted that they liked it. Like, maybe if you were willing to post about it on your social media and talk about it at school, then arseholes like Natasha would realise that there are more of us than they think."

Rose's head snaps up. "That's rich coming from you."

I cross my arms and raise my chin. I hear the cartilage in my shoulders crack as I force them back. "What the hell does that mean?"

"You can't ask someone else to do something that you're not willing to do yourself. And all those self-deprecating comments you keep making about being trash? It's like you want to hate yourself for liking what you like."

Roses's comment stings the back of my neck. I don't do that, do I? "I don't hate myself..." I say.

"Well, you hardly shout your love from the rooftops. You wouldn't even let me see inside your room for the first few months. Hell, you barely talked to me because you were so scared of me finding out what you liked!"

"If anyone asked me if I was an otaku, then I would

say I was. But there's no way you would ever admit to it if someone asked you."

Rose's fingers dig into her thighs, creasing her jeans. "I would if it meant protecting myself from ending up alone."

"But you wouldn't end up alone," I mutter.

"What?" Rose's eyes meet mine and some of the tension defuses from the air. Perhaps there might be a way to salvage this situation. But then I go and open my big mouth.

"There's no way anyone would bully you for liking animanga," I say, "not when you fit in so well with everyone else. Natasha had already picked me out as being different before she stole that notebook from my bag. People like you. There's no way—"

"Fit in?" Rose snorts as she looks down at her hands, making me suddenly very aware of the differences in our skin tone in a way I haven't been before. "You really think I fit in around here."

The back of my throat burns as my stomach lurches. "I... I didn't mean... I'm sor—"

"You see," Rose says, very loudly. "This is why I can't let other people know what I'm into. It's not worth the risk."

Sickness has now gone. Anger is back and bubbling hot inside me. "Because you're afraid you'll end up like me?" I ask. Rose's silence is all I need to confirm what I think. "So those people in London aren't really your friends?" I snort. "If you're afraid of telling them that you like what you like because you're worried that they'll blank you, then perhaps they aren't really—"

"They *are* my friends," Rose snaps. "Your friends don't have to like all the same things you do." She meets my eye. "Perhaps you wouldn't feel so lonely if you didn't judge people before you got to know them."

My jaw clicks. "You have to have something in common to talk to your friends about, otherwise what's the point? And if someone isn't into animanga, then what can I talk to them about?"

"No wonder you're so lonely if that's your attitude."

"No wonder you're afraid of admitting what you like if you're so afraid your fake friends will turn their backs on you!"

"They're not fake!" Rose shouts, but I'm already storming out. I slam my bedroom door behind it so hard it rattles on the hinges.

Then I crawl under my covers and cry.

Chapter 34

Rose

There's this awful tension in the house.

The air is Arctic cold and I find myself walking around hunched, like there's a target on my back. The temperature drops several degrees whenever Clover and I are in the same room. When we're sitting in the car on the way to or from the bus stop, I can almost hear the air cracking under pressure.

If Helen notices she doesn't say anything, but she talks less at dinner and when we're in the car. Sometimes she glances between the two of us, trying to work out what has happened.

I bury myself in revision, essays and French listening

exercises, trying to forget about our fight, and the bag of fabric, buttons and patterns that is sitting under my bed where I kicked it after our argument. I haven't updated my cosplay Instagram account since buying the stuff. I checked in a few days afterwards to see if it would motivate me into starting the project, but it just made me sad so I logged out. So much for feeling excited. Since Clover and I are no longer talking to each other, I can't see us going.

The first day back at school after our shopping trip, I'm too busy shitting myself with worry that Ari's told people what he saw at the weekend to notice the tension in the car. Clover's sitting in the front seat, something she hasn't done since after October half-term, earbuds in and music blasting. She doesn't look at me as she walks onto the bus and sits in her usual seat. I take mine and jiggle my leg all the way to Ari's stop.

But he doesn't get on.

At first I was relieved, because perhaps he's off school today. But the relief doesn't last long and the weight resettles back in my stomach as we draw nearer to school. I'm going to have to speak to Ari at some point – and I have no idea what to say to him when I do see him.

As I step off the bus, my heart starts to go crazy in my chest. My shoulders go back up around my ears and I look at the ground as I make my way to the sixth-form common room, too afraid to look up for fear of seeing someone I know.

But when I reach the common room I have no option but to look up as I step into the room. I feel sick as I push the doors open and every muscle tenses, waiting for the onslaught.

"Rose!" Henry smiles and waves at me. Rachel and Rory are sitting on either side of him. Rachel – as always – is tapping away at her phone and Rory is reading. With my heart in my mouth, I walk over to their group of chairs. "How was your weekend?"

"Good," I say. "I didn't see Ari on the bus this morning."

Rachel glances up from her phone. "He passed his test on Saturday, so he's likely driving in. Lucky bastard."

"He won't get a parking space if he leaves it too late," Henry says.

"This is the only time in my life that I've cursed that my birthday is in August," Rory says.

"Oh, speak of the devil."

Spinning his car key around his finger, Ari saunters across the room.

"What's up, pedestrians?" he says, throwing himself into the chair next to me. My stomach twists. What will he say? Will it all come out now? Oh, Dear Universe. Please be kind to me and I promise I'll give vegetarianism another serious think.

But then Ari catches my eye and gives me one of his charming smiles.

What the hell does that mean?

Is that meant to be reassuring? Because it's having the opposite effect.

My thigh muscles tense under my hands, ready to propel me out the door if he so much as mentions our encounter the other weekend.

"OK, Mr September Birthday," Rory says. "You don't have to be so smug."

"Oh." Ari stretches out his legs and crosses them at the ankles. "I do, because I know you're all itching with jealousy."

"We won't be itching when you have to fill up the car with petrol for the first time," Rachel says.

Ari shrugs. "A small price to pay for freedom. You know this weekend I'm thinking about..."

They keep talking but I don't hear them. The anxious thoughts spiral out of control, filling every part of my head. I'm waiting for Ari to mention driving to MK and seeing me in Waterstones reading manga. Then his words will make everyone stare at me and I'll run out the door. Because there's no way I can save face when they find out.

Perhaps I should just leave now.

Would Helen come pick me up from school if I got the office to phone her and say I was ill? No, I can't make her take time off work for a fake illness. But going home would be so much easier than staying here while my stomach ties itself into knots waiting for Ari to say something.

"... won't you, Rose?"

Shit. Someone just said my name.

I look up. Ari is staring at me with his head tilted to one side, a lopsided grin on his face.

"Won't I what?" I ask. My hands are itching to touch my glasses, but my body has frozen.

"Miss me on the bus," Ari says, "now that I'm driving in every day."

We stare at each other for a few seconds, and in those few seconds I know from the look in his eyes that he isn't going to say anything about our encounter in Waterstones.

I lean back in my chair, letting my held breath escape. Then I snort and kick his legs away from mine. "I'll have more room for my feet without you."

Rachel snorts and then holds up her hand for a high five, which I slap with great satisfaction.

One week after the fight, I'm lying on my bed with my bedroom door closed staring at the ceiling, when my phone buzzes.

```
Maryam
Free for a call?
```

I call her.

"I can't remember the last time I wasn't the one to call you," she says as she picks up. "What's up?"

"Nothing's up," I mutter, rolling over onto my side.

There's a pause on the other end of the phone. "OK," Maryam says slowly. "Then why are you pouting?"

"I'm not pouting."

"You are."

"How can you tell if I don't have the video on?"

"Because we've known each other since we were seven years old and I know your tones of voice, therefore I can tell right now that you are pouting." I bring my knees up to my chin. "You also haven't messaged me all week *and* you haven't joined in with any of the group chats, so there's that."

There's a long pause.

"Clover and I had a fight," I say. "We said some horrid things to each other and I don't want to talk about it."

"Oh, Rose." Maryam's sympathetic tones make me pull myself into a tighter ball. "That's... that's not like you."

"I know."

There's another long pause and I can sense Maryam thinking on the other end of the phone. A small part of me wants to tell her what happened – about all the things we hurled at each other and the seams we tried to pick apart – but if I start talking about it I will cry. It's all too raw at the moment.

"Well," Maryam says at last, "when you're ready to talk about it, you know where to find me."

"Thanks," I say.

"So, Jayden and I have decided to break up at the end of next year."

"Wait! What?!" I sit upright. "What happened? Are you OK?"

Maryam laughs. My stomach drops. Is she joking in a sick attempt to shock me out of my misery? It's a cruel joke, but there's no way Maryam and Jayden could break up. They've been going out for five years. They're like two sides of the same coin, so at ease with one another and the perfect balance for each other.

"Jayden's going to Edinburgh for uni." Maryam's voice is very calm. She must have been holding this back a long time if she can speak about it with so little emotion. "And I'm staying here, you know, so I can look after Mum. We had a talk the other day and both of us are worried about maintaining the long-distance relationship. I know he wouldn't cheat on me, or I on him, but... it's going to be hard, so we decided that it would be best to break it off once school ends and have three years away from each other to meet other people and see whether we miss each other. And if we do, then we'll work out what to do next."

They will. They will miss each other. But if I was in their position, I would also want to break it off instead of keeping up the long distance. Despite the jealousy I've sometimes felt seeing couples at school, I'm glad now that I didn't find anyone I wanted to date. It's one less thing to stress about.

"I'm so sorry, Mar," I say. "But I know you and Jayden will have thought about this a lot and will have made the right decision for the both of you."

"Yeah. It wasn't easy. We looked at the ways we could see each other, but... it's like seventy pounds for a return train ticket to Edinburgh. There's no way I could afford to do that often, and it would mean leaving Dad alone to look after Mum. It just... it just wasn't practical. Although, I would have loved to have visited Edinburgh. It sounds like such a cool city."

"Perhaps we can go one day," I say. "Once things have settled down. Go for a long weekend or something?"

I hear Maryam's smile on the other end of the phone – she's not the only one who knows their friend's facial expressions from the tone of their voice. "That would be awesome. You might have to wait a while for me to get a decent enough job to save up."

"No rush. Edinburgh's not going anywhere."

"And, anyway, once you're a lawyer you'll be rolling in money, so you can just pay for me to go."

Maryam says it like a joke, but I don't laugh. Instead a familiar weight settles into my stomach.

"Rose?" Maryam says, once the silence stretches on for a little too long.

The words are stuck in my throat, glued there by fear, and once they get free they're soft and small. "What if I don't want to become a lawyer?"

And then I burst into tears.

"Hey."

The tap on my shoulder makes me pull my headphones off. Ari is standing behind me, coat on and bag over his shoulder.

"We need to head," he says. I look behind him to the clock on the wall and almost have a heart attack at the time.

"Sorry!" Paper crinkles and tears as I shove everything into my bag. "*Tess of the D'Urbervilles* had my full attention."

"Lucky her," Ari says.

We leave the science block. The school grounds are quiet with all the other classes still on-going. We don't have the same class - he's got business studies and I have history - but our classrooms are next door to each other in the house. This is the first time we've been alone together since that weekend I ran away from him in Waterstones nearly two weeks ago.

I don't find my voice until we reach the stables.

"I'm sorry for the way I acted the other weekend... When you talked to me in Waterstones. I was... surprised to see you."

Ari laughs and the sound dispels all my fears. "You shouldn't be surprised that I go to bookshops." He wiggles his eyebrows at me. "Believe it or not, I do read. Mostly fantasy, sci-fi and a bit of horror, yes, but I have been known to push the boat out and read crime or literary. Or even manga and comics if the mood takes me."

I frown. "You like manga?"

"Yeah. Dark and gritty stuff like *Tokyo Ghoul* and *Golden Kamuy*, and also Junji Ito. The dark and heavy stuff."

"I didn't peg you for a manga reader."

Ari laughs again and thumps the fence post as we pass the changing rooms. "What does someone who reads manga look like?"

I stop walking.

That GIF of the man in the black turtleneck making the mind-blown action? Yeah. That's me right now.

Because I'm thinking about Clover and her whacky hair, strolling through the mud in her waterproofs and wellies. Leon and his man bun, checked shirt, muddy jeans and puffer jacket. Genny and her gothic make-up and clothes. Paige and her short hair and poncho. Ari and his well-fitting suit that makes him look like he belongs in a City firm.

"Rose?" Ari asks.

"I'm not sure," I reply.

"Of what?"

"Of what a manga reader looks like."

"There you go, then." We start walking again. "I

guessed your preferred genre of manga correctly. I knew you were a shojo fan."

"I've watched some shonen and seinen anime!"

Ari holds his hands up. "OK. OK. No judgement here."

A warmth fills my chest. All the way through history I'm buzzing with excitement to see Clover again, but as Mrs Lanlard is telling us about Gladstone's mission to pacify Ireland, I remember all the awful things we said to each other and know it will be a while yet before either of us will be ready to talk to each other.

Chapter 35

Clover

Watching anime alone never used to bother me. I mean, I always did it for hours on end on my own, but now... it's weird. Walking Bonnie feels the same. I used to love walking alone, music blasting in my ears, or just listening to the sounds of the countryside and letting my thoughts spiral out of control thinking about animanga.

It's not as fun without Rose.

When she first arrived, I couldn't wait for her to leave, but in the two weeks we haven't spoken to each other I've missed her like Haru misses the water. And over the past few weeks, it's like an icy Barrier has slammed down between us.

Leon texts me on a drizzly Saturday afternoon as I'm re-watching *Silver Spoon* for the God-only-knows-th-time. It's my comfort blanket when I'm at the bottom of the pit.

Lee-kun
You know I don't like to pry but this has been worrying me for the past fortnight because normally I'm muting my phone notifications from how much you two are spamming the group chat but it's been dead all this time so I need to say something...
Has something happened between you and Rose?

Ko-chan
Yes

Lee-kun
Want to talk about it?

Ko-chan
Not really

Although I want to. I really, *really* want to, but I would start crying if I did. And I'm determined not to cry about it anymore.

Because every time I think about it, about Rose telling me that I'll end up alone because I prejudge people, and that I'm closed minded – those words get stuck in a loop in my head. And beat me down further with every replay.

And it's not true.

It's not.

Isn't it?

I don't prejudge people, and I'm not closed minded.

There's no point wasting my time on people who don't have the same interests as me.

I know who my squad are. I've just got to find them. And they're not at school.

So far Mum's just Mum about the whole icy silence between Rose and I, but I can tell she knows there's something going on. On the same day Leon texts me, it's mine and Mum's turn to wash up. I'm scrubbing away at the lumps of dried mashed potato on the bottom of the saucepan when Mum finally breaks her silence.

"What's going on between you and Rose?"

You know when you just get a feeling that a taboo subject is about to be broached? I knew from the moment Rose left the room that this conversation was coming, so I've been turning over what I would say to Mum when she asked me.

And I arrived at the conclusion that the best thing to do would be to remain silent.

Because I've finally arrived at the numb stage of this whole fiasco, which is a much better stage to be at than the constant crying stage.

"You know," Mum says, as she picks up a colander, "not talking after you've had a fight with someone isn't worth it. If Claire or I had put aside our pride after we had our fight, then we could have avoided the thirteen years of silence."

My ears prick up.

Even though Mum is doing this as some sort of parable, I don't care as long as I get to find out what the big thing was that kept her and Rose's mum apart for all those years.

"Yeah?" I say, hoping that my voice doesn't sound too hopeful.

Mum puts the colander down and picks up a wooden spoon. "Yeah. I always resented Claire for being perfect - for having top grades and the career goals that made her the apple of our mother's eye. Everything was so much harder for me - I wasn't good at school and... well, my mum's opinion of me hasn't changed much over the past three decades. All that anger and resentment bubbled inside me for years, and it just got worse after Claire kept hitting all these milestones before me and Mum kept rubbing her success in my face.

"All that resentment... just sort of exploded when we had a meal one day together. We said some really nasty things to each other and I stormed out, instead of apologising like I should have done. Then when your dad died, Claire reached out and asked if I wanted help - even though I wanted nothing more, I felt too proud to accept her help and slapped it back in her face."

Mum has stopped drying. I glance at the drying rack and find it empty. I've been scrubbing at the same saucepan for the whole time she's been talking. I rinse it and put it on the rack.

"After Claire and I reconnected," Mum continues, "she told me she resented me for how chill I was when she always felt under pressure to always be the best - to always push herself to achieve more." Mum laughs. "She said being a lawyer didn't make it any easier. Our stupid pride lost thirteen years we could have been together. I regret losing those thirteen years more than anything else."

I nod, but the pressure builds behind my eyes and I get that awful pain in my nose that signals I'm about to start crying. Then Mum is pulling me into her chest and there are tears and soap bubbles everywhere.

When I've stopped sobbing, Mum kisses the top of my head and says, "Just talk to her, Clo."

I sniff back a lump of snot and pull away so I can wipe my face on my sleeve.

"Alright," I say.

We stand there for a while, Mum with her arms around me while I press my face into her shoulder, waiting for the tears to stop. She smells like candle wax and incense.

"Anything else bothering you?" Mum asks. I nod into her shoulder. "Do you want to talk about it?" I nod again.

She waits while I summon my courage.

"I'm worried about what's going to happen at the end of next year," I say at last.

"The school year?"

"Yeah. Everyone keeps talking about what they want to do at uni, or after uni, but... I don't know what I want to do or where I want to go."

Mum rubs my back. "I felt like that at your age, and I often still feel like that."

"Does anything help?"

"Talking through your problems with someone else."

"Then why won't you let me talk to you about it?" I sniff again and rub my face with my other sleeve. "Every time I try to talk to you, you pull away."

Mum sighs. "I'm such a rubbish mum, aren't I? Sorry,

I've made another mess, but I was worried about dictating your life the way that my mum tried to dictate mine. Telling me what I should be doing and not allowing me to do what I wanted to do. I was hoping that you would work out for yourself what you wanted to do. But it sounds like I should have been more open. Sorry, Clo. Sounds like we need a mother-daughter day. I promise I'll block off a weekend soon and we can take ourselves out."

"Yes, please," I say.

By the time we finish the washing up, my shoulders feel lighter, but the overwhelming pressure is still there. Mum heads into the living room to watch some housing programme and I head upstairs and stand outside Rose's closed bedroom door. Ever since our argument, she's been keeping it shut, when she always used to stand it open.

Come on, Clover. It's now or never.

Don't let your pride get in the way.

I stand at the bottom of her bedroom steps for a few seconds. Then I break through the ice that's enveloped my body and lunge for Rose's door. I knock three times and then step back. Rose's face looks unsurprised when she sees me standing outside. I'm also relieved that she doesn't look pissed off. In fact, she looks more embarrassed than anything else.

"Hi," we say at the same time.

The moment that word is in the air, the first crack start to form in The Barrier.

"You OK?" Rose asks, adjusting her glasses.

"Yeah," I say. I rub at the dried tears on my cheeks. My eyes feel puffy. I bet they're bloodshot. "Yeah," I say again, "Mum and I were just having a moment."

"Alright."

"Look," I say and then I want to stare at my feet, but I force myself to keep my eyes on Rose's, "I'm sorry. For all those awful things I said. I... I shouldn't have said them. I didn't think about... everything from your point of view. You shouldn't have to let everyone know if you like animanga. You should do what is best for you. I only pushed you because I read this blog post and it got me fired up. I'm also sorry for what I said about you fitting in... It was awful of me. I hadn't thought about what it must be like for you living out here, going to our school."

"I'm sorry too." Rose swallows. There's regret in her expression. "I shouldn't have laid into you like that. You shouldn't have to make friends with people if you don't want to."

"But I do want to!" I cry, so loudly that Rose flinches. "Sorry, but—" I pinch my leg but the tears start to rise again, "—I thought the blog would make me happy. And it does, sort of. I've received so many lovely comments from people who love my art, and I've read posts by people who love animanga as much as I do, but... then they start talking about all the cool things they've been doing with their friends in real life and it makes me feel like crap. The feeling of connection I get from talking to someone on social media just doesn't last - it's just not the same as when you, Leon and I hang out together. Both of you are worth more than my hundreds of followers."

"Some people would kill to have the amount of followers you do."

I shudder. "To be honest, it's like I have hundreds of eyes staring at me all the time. Those numbers are meaningless."

Rose laughs and lifts her glasses off her face so she can brush the heel of her hand under her eye.

"I want to make friends," I admit. "I don't want to be lonely at school, but I've pushed everyone away for so long it's too late to make an effort."

Rose sniffs. "You know," she says, "there's a girl at school who asked me if you were OK. If you wanted to approach someone at school, I think she's interested in getting to know you more."

"Who was it?"

"I... I don't know. She had her hair in bunches."

"That sounds like Fran..." That must be why she's messaged me so many times. And why she keeps looking like she wants to talk to me at school.

"You should try talking to her," Rose suggests.

I swallow. "OK," I say, "I'll try."

Rose looks relieved.

"What was the blog post that got you so fired up?" she asks.

"Oh." I shrug. "Someone who likes my stuff a lot wrote a post on how they started admitting to people that they're an otaku. A lot of what they said resonated with me. Someone commented saying that if more people admitted to liking animanga then we probably wouldn't have to hide it."

"You know," she says, "I had a chat with Ari the other week and it turns out he's also into anime and manga."

"Really?" Rose smiles at the high pitch my voice has taken. "I mean, he doesn't look like—" I stop myself right there, because I should know by now that just because someone looks and dresses in the opposite way to how I do, doesn't mean they can't be into the same things as me.

"Yeah," Rose says, "I was shocked as well. I guess there are more of us otaku around than we thought. And... it's a shame we don't know who each other are because we don't talk about what we like so openly. Because we're too afraid of what small-minded people like Natasha would say if we started talking about what we liked."

It doesn't sound like a promise, but it's a start.

There's a pause, but it isn't one of the heavy pauses that have been between us for the past few weeks. Something's changed. I hold out my arms. "Hug?"

Rose nods. The hug is a little awkward and stiff, but in that moment The Barrier comes crashing down around our feet.

"Hey," I say, as we break apart, "I know the reason why our mums didn't talk for thirteen years."

Rose raises her eyebrows. "Really?"

I wiggle my eyebrows. "Really, really. Turns out..." I glance at the stairs, to where Mum is in the living room. Rose pulls me into her room and shuts the door behind us. Rose sits on her bed and I take her desk chair and tell her what Mum told me.

"I was expecting something more dramatic," Rose says.

"Me too. But... I can't imagine Mum being involved in anything too dramatic."

"I don't think my mum has the time to be involved in anything dramatic."

"I can't believe they didn't talk to each other for

thirteen years just because of... that..."

"Well, I mean, we didn't talk to each other for thirteen days."

"There is a difference between days and years. But... yeah, OK, point taken."

There's a pause, and then Rose says, "You know, I've missed watching *Mob Psycho*... Want to watch an episode or two tonight?"

I break out into a grin. "Nothing would make me happier."

Chapter 36

Rose

"This stuff sounds so dry." Clover flips onto the next prompt card and pulls a face. "I'm so glad I'm not doing history."

"Just think of them as anime characters." I break off another piece of chocolate from my Easter egg. "Gladstone would be all stiff and straight, but Disraeli would be the flamboyant playboy type who flirts with everyone."

"I ship it," Clover whispers.

"Oh for the love of—" I hold my head in my hands. "I won't be able to get that image out of my head now."

Clover laughs so hard that Leon looks up from the other side of the coffee table where he's got his headphones in, scribbling away on a piece of paper.

"You should write your essay on how Queen Victoria was a fujoshi and was secretly shipping them."

"I don't think there's any evidence for that, and I really don't want to throw my exam."

There's a knock on the living room door. Helen comes in holding a tray heavy with steaming mugs of tea and plates of biscuits.

"How's it going?" she asks, setting the tray down on the table amongst the Easter egg wrappers, empty mugs and revision notes.

"Bricking it," I say.

"You're going to be fine," Clover says. "You've got weeks until your exams and you know most if it already."

"How you doing, Leon?" Helen asks, loud enough for Leon to hear through his headphones.

Leon takes them off and says in a deadpan voice, "I think I'm fucked." Helen laughs so hard tea sloshes out of the mug she's placing on the table.

"You're not fucked," Clover says.

"Well," I say, "if you do fail everything, at least the farm's there ready and waiting for you."

"Yeah," Leon says, "but my parents won't let me take it over without going to agriculture college. They would make me retake everything until I got what I need to get in." Leon sighs, puts his headphones back in and returns to scribbling.

"Clo," Helen says, "how you feeling?"

"Fine," Clover says, waving a dismissive hand. "It'll be fine."

"I wish I was as relaxed as you," I say.

Clover helps me run through the last of my history key cards. She looks at her own textbooks and sighs.

"Think I'll go do some art as a break," she says, standing. "Although it's not really a break."

I glance at my English literature revision notes. "I'll come with you," I say. "I could use a break to work on my cosplay."

We leave Leon in the zone and relocate to the kitchen. Clover sets up her easel, canvas and paints by the window, while I pull Helen's sewing machine up onto the table. I'm finally at the stage where I'm sewing all the parts of my waistcoat together, but it took a few lessons from Helen for both of us to be happy with me using the sewing machine. I snap a photo of the machine on the table with my half-finished cosplay beside it and upload it to Instagram with an update. It's procrastination from actually doing the project, but I'll be glad I've done it when I look back.

"Any requests?" Clover asks, shaking her phone at me with Spotify already loaded onto the screen.

"Instrumental would be nice. A soundtrack."

"I have just the thing." Clover presses play and sets her phone down on the table. I lean forward. She selected the *Made in Abyss* soundtrack. Clover suggested we watch the anime, but after I watched the trailer on YouTube I decided it wasn't for me. The soundtrack is really something special, though. Instead, we've worked our way through the Studio Ghibli collection since the start of the Easter holidays, and Clover is planning an anime day the weekend before we go back to school, to watch *Snow White with the Red Hair*. I've had to reorganise my revision timetable a dozen times with all the anime days Clover's sprang on me over the course of our three-week break.

Clover pulls her purple hair up into a ponytail and gets out her paints while I continue tacking the pieces of my waistcoat together. Soon the air smells of oil paint and turpentine. We fall into a rhythm that has become familiar since the Easter holidays, just the two of us being in the same room together working on our own separate things, whether it's revising, coursework, making cosplay or reading. I've grown to really love these moments. It's comforting being in the same room with someone, listening to the same music, while you work on separate things that you both enjoy.

I'm inspecting my work and worrying whether I've made the seam too small – I'm not sure I would survive a costume malfunction during my first comic con – when my phone buzzes.

Maryam
Soooo... Kai and Sienne kissed at the weekend

I scream and drop my waistcoat so I can pick up my phone with both hands.

"What is it?" Clover yells.

"Kai and Sienne finally kissed!"

My fingers have never moved so fast when typing a reply.

"Who?" Clover demands.

Rose

OMG FINALLY!!
TELL ME THE DETAILS!!

Maryam
Sam had a house party at the weekend
Zoe and Sienne were dancing in the basement when Kai and George came down to dance with them
Zoe said she turned around one moment to talk to George and then turned back around to Sienne and found her and Kai pressed up against the wall going at it

Rose
OMG what?

Maryam
I know

Rose
What was the trigger? What made them go from 0 to 100?

Maryam
I don't think kissing equals 100
But Sienne told Zoe that something just clicked
Not sure what that means

Rose
I hope it wasn't just the alcohol...
Heard anything from Kai?

Maryam

I've got Jayden on the case but I think he's following some sort of secret boy code where he won't tell me anything Kai told him

Rose
Well I hope they work it out
I can't believe it's taken them this long to see what the rest of us have known for years
How are you and Jayden doing?

Maryam
We're OK
Something's changed since we decided to break up but we're OK

Rose
I'm so sorry Mar
Here if you want to talk xxx

Maryam
Thank you xxx
What's going on with you?

Rose
We're having a revision day

Maryam
Great revision game atm

Rose
Hush
We're having a break
I'm

I glance down at my cosplay. My fingers hover over the buttons, twitching to type out the truth that might change everything or nothing. It's Maryam, for God's sake. If there's one person on this earth I can tell about my cosplay without fear of rejection, it should be her. But I chicken out.

drinking coffee and eating biscuits while
Clover works on her art coursework
Leon's the only one doing revision right now

Maryam
I'm glad the two of you are talking again

Rose
So am I

"How's it going?" There's a rush of cold air as Helen comes in from the garden, peeling off her gardening gloves.

"Good," Clover says. "How's the rhubarb?"

"Almost ready. Better than the tulips, which the deer's chewed again. Can I put in a request for rhubarb and custard slices?"

Clover throws back her head and presses her hand to her forehead, flicking paint across her canvas. "I'll have to see what my inner artist says."

"Well, your inner artist better let me know by Tuesday because I need to go shopping." Helen stops her journey across the room and peers at my waistcoat. "Looking good."

I pull a face as I put my phone down. "I'm never going to get it done in time. We've only got a month and I haven't finished the waistcoat yet."

"I'm here for help if you want it," Helen says. "Unless you want to do it all yourself, then that's cool."

"I'm going to give it a go. Even if it kills me, I'll get it done in time."

"OK, but please don't kill yourself. Claire will never forgive me."

My head starts to pound from concentrating so much. I'm on the verge of wanting to tear the whole thing up and start again, when I decide maybe I need a break.

I look up and watch Clover paint her landscape for a while. It's so calming I zone out.

"Have you ever thought about doing art at uni?" I ask.

Clover doesn't answer and keeps brushing paint into her canvas. Did she not hear me? Or did I say something I shouldn't have? Then she says, "I don't know. I don't know if I even want to go to uni. But trying to get a job without a uni degree is really hard, and I don't even know what I want to do as a *career*. Art's all I'm good at but everyone's always going on about how studying it at uni is a massive waste of time and..." Clover sighs. "Never mind."

I wait for Clover to say more, but she focuses on her canvas and I know she is not going to tell me anymore. Should I pressure her? No. She will tell me when she is ready.

Chapter 37

Clover

The day's so much brighter when I step out of the gym. It was sunny when I stepped inside the exam hall, but now I'm looking up at the sky without any weight on my shoulders it looks so open and blue.

All coursework handed in? Check.

Last exam taken? Check.

I stretch up my arms and manage to hold myself back from screaming "I'm free!" into the deep blue. I hurry back to the common room to grab my phone.

Ko-chan
I'M FREEEEE!!!!
It's all done

I'm so relieved

Lee-kun
At least until this time next year

Ko-chan
Why did you have to go there?!?!
You've ruined my mood

Rose
Exams never really finish

Ko-chan
They can if you choose not to do anything that involves exams
Have you finished your theory @Rose?

Rose
Yeah I'm all done
It was fine
I think…
I might have botched the hazard test
Never sure if I've clicked too many times or too little

Lee-kun
Got your practical booked in?

Rose
At the start of June
When this whole exam/con madness is over

Ko-chan
ONLY TWO WEEKS TO GO!!

I'M SO EXCITED!!

Rose
I'm going to be finishing the skirt on the train at this rate

Lee-kun
Genny does that every year

"Clover?"

The sudden sound of the voice behind me brings me out of my phone daydream. I look back and find Fran standing there. She's smiling but looks less and less sure of herself with every second I stare at her.

"Hi?" I say.

"Hi," Fran says.

There's another pause, in which I start to feel really uncomfortable, then Fran's eyes flick to my hand. "I... like your phone case," she says.

My phone case is light blue with an illustration of Tetsuya 2 from *Kuroko's Basketball* on the back. It breaks all the rules of not bringing animanga-related stuff to school, but after Rose and I made up, I've started to give less of a crap about those self-made rules. I slide my phone back into my bag, wondering where this is going.

"He looks like my Reg – he's an Alaskan Klee Kai."

If I was an anime character right now, my ears would have doubled in size. Is this some sort of elaborate plan on Fran's part to get some dirt on me to then take to Natasha? But I've never seen her talk to Natasha and Rose did say that she might be interested in getting to know me more... And if someone wants to talk about dogs I'm more than happy to oblige.

"I didn't know you had a dog," I say.

Fran laughs. "He's the best boy. Look." She takes out her phone and shows me photos of a dog that I have to admit looks very much like a grown-up version of Tetsuya 2. The smile on my face grows wider with every photo Fran shows me.

"He's so cute," I say as Fran pauses on a photo of Reg jumping over a bar on an obstacle course. "How did you teach him to do that? I can never get Bonnie to complete any obstacles on the courses. She just stares at them, like 'What do you expect me to do with this?'"

"Oh," Fran says, "I just followed some tutorial videos online. Reg's one of those dogs that needs to be worked – he's really intelligent and gets bored easily. Is Bonnie your dog?"

"Yeah. She's a chocolate lab. Here." I get my phone back out and show Fran my Bonnie album. Fran coos over all my photos of her, and laughs at the videos I took on the snow day when we went sledging.

"She's adorable. Did you say her name was Bonnie?"

"Yeah. Named after the Bournville chocolate bar. We just call her Bonnie all the time, though."

"OMG. That's hilarious. Who's the other dog in that video?"

"Alexander. He's my friend's dog."

"Do you know what breed he is?"

"A huntaway, I think. They're from New Zealand."

"He's so cute. Eugh. I just love dogs. They're the best."

"Agreed. Have you always had dogs?"

"Yeah. My uncle competes in Crufts every year."

"Really?"

"Really, really. He's never won anything, but, look." She scrolls through her phone and finds a photo of a smiling man who looks like an estate agent, holding the lead of an Afghan hound while they stand in a very recognisable green arena.

Fran goes onto her uncle's Facebook page and shows me all the backstage Crufts photos, the photos of all the dogs he takes to the show, and some interior shots of his house which is filled with dog grooming stuff, special bathrooms the dogs use and massive plush dog beds. Seriously, those things look comfier than my bed. His dogs look like the most pampered dogs in the world.

"What exam did you just have?" Fran asks.

"Religious studies," I reply.

"Nice. Last one?"

"Yup. Do you have an exam today, since you're here?"

"No. I'm rubbish at studying at home, so I come in everyday to make myself do it." She gives me a nervous smile. Am I really that scary to talk to? I hope not, because I want to talk to her more.

Behind Fran, the clock on the wall ticks over to twelve o'clock. A couple of people in the common room start to leave, pulling on their jackets, which we still have to wear in the lunch room even though it's boiling outside. I rock back and forth a little. This is an opportunity I shouldn't pass up, but there's a massive ball of anxiety blocking my throat, stopping any words from escaping. Ever since Rose told me about Fran, I've been thinking about ways to talk to her. I've tried a few times to send her a message, but it felt too awkward to reply to the ones she sent me months ago, and too random to send her one out of the blue – I wouldn't know what to say to her anyway. What do I say to someone who isn't into anime? But here we are, having a conversation. Perhaps Rose is right – perhaps I can get along with someone who isn't into animanga.

"Want to grab lunch together?" I ask, but it all comes out in a bit of a tumbled rush. A small frown line appears between Fran's eyebrows. I clear my throat and ask again. This time she smiles and this one is bigger and brighter than the first.

"Sure."

As we walk out of the sixth-form common room and down the stairs of the science block, Natasha comes up the stairs. Like usual, my heart starts to pound in my chest whenever I get anywhere close to her. But just as we're a few paces apart, instead of looking down at my feet as I always do when we pass each other, I raise my head. Natasha senses my stare and looks up. I expect her to smirk at me, to ask me what the hell I'm looking at, to make me feel as small as I was at eleven years old when she stood up on that bench in the changing rooms. Instead, she just stares blankly at me. She stinks of cigarette smoke, and despite the make-up she's wearing there are faint lines underneath her eyes. She looks tired and sad.

So I give her a smile.

We stay in each other's line of sight long enough for me to register the surprise on her face as Fran and I pass her. Walking the rest of the way to the dining room, I feel the lightest on school grounds that I ever have.

Chapter 38

Rose

When I wake up, I'm not in my bed. There's a hard surface under my head and I'm staring at a pile of navy cloth. It takes a minute of blinking at the pile of cloth and needles, pins and thread scattered all over my desk to realise what I've done.

When I do I sit upright so quickly my neck clicks.

Shit. What time is it?

7.29.

Double shit.

I fell asleep at my desk. Working on my cosplay, which I didn't finish.

And we leave for London in seven hours, and I have a

driving lesson this morning.

Triple shit.

There's a double knock on my bedroom door. Clover flings it open. She's holding her self-made countdown calendar. Beaming, she rips off the top sheet revealing a 1 underneath the 2.

"Con tomorrow!" she sings in a warbling operatic. She grins at me. "Oh, good. You're already up and dressed."

I groan and drag my hands over my face. I reach for my glasses. "I haven't been to bed yet. I fell asleep at my desk."

Clover eyes the pile of cloth. "Did you finish the skirt?"

"All the machine work is done. I've just got to finish the hand stitching."

"That's good, though."

"It should have been finished days ago. Ugghh." I lay back down on the desk. "Why did I think making my own cosplay from scratch would be a good idea? How am I meant to get it finished before we leave?"

"There's still time tonight and on the train. And tomorrow morning if needed. It's basically done and it looks amazing!"

"Thanks." I take a deep breath and pull myself up. "Right. I need to shower."

"Rose," Clover whispers.

I give her a look and for the first time notice how wide her grin is. It really is stretching from ear to ear, and her eyes are bright.

"Comic con tomorrow," she whispers.

Her excitement is infectious and I find myself

mirroring her expression.

"Yeah," I say. "Tomorrow."

Clover makes a high-pitched noise I bet has Bonnie pricking her ears up in the kitchen and spins out my room.

I shower, get changed and have just managed to finish breakfast when Helen comes in, twirling her car keys around her finger.

"Ready?" she asks.

I drive us into town, to the pub where my driving instructor is waiting for me. Helen collects me from the lesson with a boot full of food shopping. She asks if I want to drive back, but I'm so exhausted I pass. There follows a few frantic hours of sewing, packing, lunching and trying to calm Clover down as she races around the house shouting, "Cooooon!"

Then before I know it, it's quarter to three and Leon is here with his bag, *and I still haven't finished my frigging cosplay!* So I pack it in my rucksack with my purse, house keys – which I have checked half a dozen times to ensure I have packed – and other items I need to hand.

Helen drives us all to the train station.

"Have fun," Helen says and she hugs Clover to her. "Text me when you're on the train home on Saturday." She gives me and Leon a hug as well.

The train arrives on time and since it's the middle of a working day, it's very quiet. The moment we sit down at a table, I pull out my skirt and start stitching.

For the whole half-an-hour journey to Euston, Clover jabbers on non-stop. She's almost bouncing in her seat, speculating about what we might see tomorrow, what cosplays everyone will be wearing, what she's planning on buying, what she's planning on eating. Her excitement is contagious, and soon all three of us are talking way too loudly. I end up not getting as much of my skirt done as I planned to. As we pull into Euston, I snap a quick photo of my skirt and sewing in my bag and upload it to Instagram with lots of crying emojis.

We bundle off the train at Euston and head to the Underground. It's a tricky manoeuvre on the Northern Line, then a walk to an overground station, and then another change onto the correct overground line to get to my house. While we're on the Underground my latest posts gets a couple of likes and comments from fellow panicking cosplayers about how I'm not alone in the last-minute rush.

When the train pulls into Chingford station, my heart squeezes. The sight is all so familiar, and yet alien at the same time. Half of me feels like this is any other day and that I never left London, and yet I'm very aware of Leon and Clover piling off the train behind me.

The first sight of my house in eight months hits me like a punch to the gut.

I half expected it to have changed, but it looks the same as ever. Although something feels different. The road looks smaller. The whole neighbourhood, which I used to think was spacious, is claustrophobic and greyer. There's little of the colour and space here that Harboury has, and all trace of the sound of mooing cows, squawking pheasants and roaring tractor engines has disappeared. Instead, I hear cars driving too quickly, people laughing and shouting, dogs barking, and the beep of pedestrian crossings.

I've still missed it, though, with all my heart.

I'm home.

As we're crossing the street to my house, I'm aware of someone calling my name. When we're across the other side of the pavement, I turn to where the sound is coming from. Maryam runs down the road towards me, grinning and waving.

My stomach drops.

"Oh my gosh, hello!" She envelops me in a back-crushing hug. I hug her back with as much ferocity.

"Hello," I say.

Maryam puts her hands on my shoulders and holds me out at arm's length. "You didn't tell me you were coming back!"

"Only for a day and two nights. And we've got a full schedule."

Maryam notices Clover and Leon behind me, and gives them a wave.

"Clover and Leon?" she asks.

"That's us," Leon says, while Clover looks wary.

"Nice to meet you."

"Nice to meet you...?"

"Maryam." Maryam gives me a side look that makes me feel two feet tall. "Has Rose not mentioned me?"

"Oh," Clover says. "You're the one who burst their yogurt all over the school ceiling."

I wince as Maryam turns her blazing eyes on me.

"Yes," she says. "Yes, I was. What a thing to be known for."

"It's memorable," I say.

"It certainly is," Leon adds.

"So what are you here in London for?" Maryam asks. "Is Rose showing you the sights?"

Leon opens his mouth to say something, but Clover puts her hand on his arm. She meets my eyes and I swallow.

It's now or never, Rose.

If you pass up this opportunity, you might not get another.

My hand tightens around my suitcase handle as the words rise to the surface.

"We're going to MCM Comic Con, at the ExCeL Centre tomorrow."

The pause only lasts for a second, but it's a painful second as I wait for Maryam's face to arrange itself into an expression I can read.

Then her eyebrows raise and her mouth makes a small O. Then she laughs.

"Oh, wow. That is not what I was expecting you to be into after coming back from the countryside. I thought you'd be going to Farm Festival or something."

"Hey," Leon objects. "Farm Festival is a great weekend."

"Sorry," Maryam says, "I'm sure it is. But Comic Con sounds more exciting." She catches my eye and grins. "Have fun and I can't wait to see the pics on Insta." She pulls me into another hug. "Can't wait to see you soon."

"Not long now," I say and hold her close while my heartbeat pounds in my ears. I told her. I can't believe I just told her, and Maryam hasn't wanted to distance herself from me. Even after not telling her I wouldn't be here this weekend... "Even if I can't drag everyone else to Harboury in the summer, I'm going to do my best to get you there."

Maryam laughs and squeezes me extra tight.

Then we're waving goodbye and the three of us are entering the house. I give Leon and Clover a quick tour and show them the rooms they'll be sleeping in, and give them covers to make their beds. While they're occupied, I sink down onto my bed and pull out my phone.

Rose
Sorry I didn't tell you I was coming down this weekend
It's not that I didn't want to see you
xxx

The minute it takes Maryam to reply is the longest minute of my life.

Maryam
It's fine
I can see you're busy
Xxx

But I need to give her a better explanation. It was really shitty of me to not mention to her that I was coming down this weekend. I should have done it, but... well...

Rose
I was afraid of what you would say if you found out I was going to comic con

That you might think I was weird for liking that stuff

I press my forehead to my phone and breathe deep while I wait for Maryam to reply.

Maryam
You're a massive idiot
You know that right?
I mean I'm surprised that you're going because you never showed any hint of liking that stuff
But why would I give a fig if you're going to comic con?
I mean have you MET Jayden?
You should know I don't care if my friends like old men who cast spells and white people with pointy ears

That one makes me snort.

Rose
I know but one of my friends made me feel bad once for liking what I like
And it made me feel like shit and afraid to tell anyone else

Maryam
Then that person wasn't really your friend
Want me to find them and sort them out?

She adds a GIF of some tough-looking guy cracking his knuckles.

Rose
Have I ever told you how lucky I am to have you as a friend?

Maryam
Not often enough
Love you xxx

Rose
Love you too xxx

I breathe out one final sigh of relief, and stand up and start making my own bed.

"What do you want to do about dinner?" I ask, when we're gathered in the living room.

Leon and Clover exchange a look and I have a feeling they've talked about this already.

"Can we get a takeaway?" Clover asks, with a reverent whisper. "Like Deliveroo or something?"

I smile at the excitement in their eyes. "Sure."

I download the Deliveroo app onto my phone - I deleted it the day I arrived in Harboury and saw that the village was far outside their delivery zone - and hand it to Clover and Leon to pick what they want. It's like handing babies a new toy for the first time. I bite back a laugh at the amazement in their eyes. It's kind of adorable.

"There's so much to choose from," Clover whispers.

In the end they order from The Jade Dragon, a Chinese restaurant which is a family favourite. We order way too much food and then scroll through Netflix trying to agree on a film to watch. By the time the food has arrived, we've settled on *Scott Pilgrim.*

By the end of the film, my stomach is fit to burst, and I've done the final stitches on my skirt.

"It's done," I proclaim, holding it up.

"Well done," Leon says. "Paige texted to say she's just finished their cosplay for tomorrow."

I take out my phone and snap a photo of my finished skirt. "What are they coming as?"

Leon taps the side of his nose. "It's a secret, apparently."

"Guys," Clover whispers, a hand on her stomach. "I'm so excited I think I might be sick."

"Please don't be," Leon says.

We get Clover to bed with a big glass of water and bowl – just in case – and it's not until I'm lying in bed that the bundle of excitement and nerves hits me like an oncoming train. Worries about tomorrow spiral through my head.

What if I say something wrong? Or do something wrong?

What if someone says my cosplay is shit? What if my cosplay falls apart in front of everyone?

What if I get run out of the convention for being a fraud?

When sleep finally finds me, it's far from restful.

Chapter 39

Clover

I don't sleep.

The combination of bubbling excitement in my stomach and the constant light and noise of London - people talking, cars roaring by outside the window, cats fighting, and dogs and foxes barking - means the moment I feel like I've closed my eyes my alarm starts blaring.

I stare at the ceiling, drained. God, the last thing I wanted was to attend my first con as a zombie.

I'm still staring at the ceiling, trying to urge my dead limbs back to life, when my bedroom door cracks open and Rose's and Leon's grinning faces appear.

"Comic con," they whisper together and then slowly

slide out of sight, shutting the door behind them. I smile as I hear them giggling in the hallway like five-year-olds.

"Come on, Clover!" Rose shouts at last. "Leon's made pancakes for breakfast."

"Coming!" I shout. I count down from three and then roll out of bed.

There's a pile of pancakes waiting for me on the dining table and a selection of sauces. We had to bring all the food we needed with us, as Rose's parents cleaned the house out before they left for Dubai. I drown my stack in chocolate sauce and scatter over some chopped strawberries. Rose and Leon are already halfway through their stacks, chatting about their cosplay plans – Leon's already styled his hair but is going to change with Rose when we get to the centre. Looks like I'll be hanging around for a while when we get there before we go into the hall.

Listening to them talk, my stomach sinks a little. I haven't made a mistake to not cosplay – I need to experience this as myself for the first time, with as little add-ons as possible to ensure I'm comfortable – but hearing them talk about their costumes, and seeing the journey Rose has gone through to make hers, I feel like I'm missing out on something.

We wash up slowly and get ready at our own pace – Rose doesn't want to leave so early we get caught up in the work rush hour, and the con doesn't allow normal ticket holders into the centre until midday. When it's time to leave, we grab our stuff and hustle out the door. I always thought travelling around London was super easy – that all the Tube lines connected to each other and stretched all over the city – but Rose leads us on a series of complex hops between trains that means we end up changing four times before we're finally on the last line to the ExCeL. Leon and I follow Rose, who weaves through crowds of people, up and down escalators and through tunnels onto different platforms as easily as if she's walking around her own house. Londoners are scary people.

A lethal cocktail of nervousness and stress have been shaking up in my stomach during the journey. Combined with the coffee I had at breakfast and how tired I am, I really do not feel good. But when we emerge onto the platform at Channing Town, my nausea disappears and the excitement that flooded my body last night comes rushing back.

Because the platform is full of cosplayers.

The sight of it shocks me so much, I grab hold of Leon's arm. At the same time Rose grabs hold of my other arm. The three of us stand frozen at the side of the platform staring at the sea of costumes, wigs, and cardboard and plastic weapons.

"Oh. My. God," I whisper. "Am I dreaming? Pinch me. Please. Pinch me and prove that this is real."

"Pinch yourself, you masochist," Leon says.

"I spot Usagi," Rose whispers. I follow her line of sight to a girl dressed as the main character from *Sailor Moon* snapping a selfie.

"I see an Edward Elric," Leon says.

"Is that MikaYuu?" A terrible high-pitched squeal comes out when I get a clearer look at two cosplayers, one dressed in black and green, and the other dressed in white and black. "It is!"

Leon laughs but starts to peel my fingers off his arm, which I'm gripping too tightly again.

While we wait for the train to pull up, we play spot the cosplayer, guessing who each of them is. I snap a candid photo of the crowd and upload it to my Insta stories, tagging the location and MCM. Then I snap a photo of the three of us, grinning like Cheshire Cats into the camera. I'm about to upload it to my stories when I remember Rose won't want it on my account in case anyone she knows sees it. And I don't know if I want to upload it onto mine in case someone from school sees it, even if there's very little chance of someone finding it.

I'm about to close the app when Rose says, "It's fine." I glance at her and she nods at the photo on my phone screen. "You can upload it. I don't mind."

At that moment the train appears and everyone starts to shift, so I only have time to upload it and not time to think about the significance of what she just allowed me to do. Or the fact that I just did it and no longer care if someone from school does see it. The train pulls into Custom House and everyone gets off.

"Don't forget to swipe your card," Rose reminds us, pointing to the Oyster card stand as we make our way out of the station.

The crowd surges along a wide flight of stairs up to the centre. We're shepherded around the side of the building and into a huge room that looks like a lorry loading bay. Then we arrive at the start of a maze of barriers placed in a zigzag. The queue isn't too long and moves quickly, but looking at how large the snake barrier is made to be I can imagine how crowded it can get at the peak times. I'm so glad we came today and not tomorrow.

As we stand in line, I take a look at the queue of cosplayers winding around the room. There are obvious groups of people clustered together, and talking and posing for photos, and solitary figures tapping away on their phones or reading a book as they take slow steps forward. There are a couple of families, and, although I'm really not a fan of kids, the sight of them dressed in their mini cosplays outfits makes something melt in my chest.

Everyone has the same wide smiles on their faces and excited shine in their eyes. No one is giving anyone else strange looks for what they're wearing, or for displaying so loudly what they like. Everyone looks like me.

Everyone here is just like me.

Emotion wells up inside me, tightening my throat and making my eyes damp. It's so intense, I grab one of Rose's hands and one of Leon's.

"I can't believe we're here," I whisper.

Both of them squeeze back.

"It really is something special," Rose says.

Once we're through ticket inspections and have been given our wristbands, we follow the signs to the toilets and cloakroom. Leon disappears into the men's while Rose and I head to the ladies. The toilets are filled with people putting the finishing touches to their cosplay, leaning over the basins to use the mirrors. Rose and I glance at each other and communicate silently that we'll see each other outside.

When I've relieved myself, I head back outside to the bottom of the stairwell and press myself into a corner. I jump back on Instagram and search the MCM Comic Con London location tag. There's loads of posts from companies who have set up stalls in the hall – my heart skips a beat at the shots of tables filled with manga volumes – as well as artists in the comic village, and cosplayers posing outside and in the queue. I'm still scrolling and liking, waiting for Leon and Rose to appear, when a notification appears.

Genny's replied to my Insta story.

gothandnerdy
Welcome home
Paige and I are going through the barriers
See you soon

otaku_trash02
OMG!!!!
I feel sick with excitement
We're in the cloakroom
Waiting for Rose and Leon to get changed...

"Hey." Leon slides along the wall next to me. He's changed into the orange and blue jumpsuit and he's also touched up his hair.

"Genny and Paige are almost in," I say.

"Cool. Oh, there's Rose. Wow. Did she really make all that herself?"

"Yup," I say, grinning at her as she walks over to us. I have no idea why she looks so nervous, because she really does look awesome. The navy waistcoat and pleated skirt turned out really well, and you really can't tell that the knee-high boots are spray painted to match her clothes.

Rose tugs on the sleeves of her white school shirt, which she's modified with matching navy buttons from her waistcoat, and adjusts the wide red belt around her middle. Her usual glasses are gone, replaced with contacts, and she's holding a plastic Shiny Rod she bought online. She worried about not having a hat or a broom, but she doesn't need them. The outfit looks complete without them.

"Does it look shit?" she asks, straightening her split necktie.

"Don't," I say, waggling a finger at her. "You look A-MAZE-ZING. Seriously. Like really good."

"But everyone else's cosplays are so much better." Rose's eyes are wide with wonder as she watches a group of *One Piece* cosplayers walk up the steps. "I'm so worried someone's going to point out all the flaws in my costume."

"If they do," I say, "I'll punch them. Come on." I grab their arms and pull them towards the cloakroom. "I want to start exploring!"

Rose and Leon check in their extra bags and then we head back upstairs, where we find Genny and Page waiting for us. I squeal at their cosplays.

"You're Melie and Seth!" I cry and get enveloped into a Genny and Paige sandwich. I get a photo with them, my face squidged between theirs. Then I get another with all five of us crowded into the frame. My arm's not long enough, so Leon ends up holding the camera.

"You look amazing, Rose," Paige says.

"Yes," I say, loudly, before Rose can say anything, "she does, doesn't she?"

Rose gives me a withering look, but then smiles.

"Thank you, Paige. Your costumes are amazing, though. What are they from?"

"An anime called *Radiant* – I'm surprised Clover hasn't shown it to you yet."

"We'll get there," I promise.

Genny loops her arm through Paige's. "We'll leave the three of you to explore on your own. Enjoy! We'll catch you later. If you need us, we'll likely be in the gaming section."

Paige blows us a kiss then the two of them get lost in the crowd.

"OK," Rose says. "Shall we head inside?"

"Yes," Leon says. "Let's."

I nod. "I'm ready."

The centre's split into two halves, with a wide corridor running down the middle. There are maps up at a couple of points down the corridor, but we breeze past them into the first part of the exhibition hall.

A sea of stalls greets us. Huge banners hang from the ceiling advertise upcoming Western and anime films. We pass stalls selling anime DVDs, Funko figures, cosplay items, CDs by Japanese artists, geeky bath bombs, anime fan art, body pillows, a massive stall full of Pusheen merchandise, nerdy clothing, pottery printed with witchy designs, a small section dedicated to steampunk clothing and cosplay items, and so much that makes my eyes grow wider and wider.

Stunned by the amount of stuff, we wander between the stalls, just gazing at the items on display. I want to stop and have a closer look, but I'm so overwhelmed I just allow my feet to keep walking. And there's another whole side of the con we haven't explored. By the time we get to the other side of the hall, an hour has passed and I'm a little light-headed. I glance at Leon and Rose. They look just as dazed as I do.

"Shall we have some lunch first?" Rose suggests.

Leon nods. "Good idea."

"I saw some food stalls over there." We follow Rose's guidance and move to the other side of the hall. We ignore the generic food trucks selling hot dogs, burgers and all that stuff, and get in line for the independent traders selling katsudon, yakisoba, gyoza and so much other food that makes my mouth water. Once again I'm paralysed by the choice. Could I eat it all? Do I have enough money to eat it all? Is my stomach big enough to eat it all? If not, what do I choose?

"I'm going to have yakisoba," Leon says, and with the determination of someone who is trying not to change their mind, strides towards the end of the queue for the stall he wants.

"Yakitori for me," Rose says. "What about you, Clo?"

"I can't make up my mind," I say. And then someone walks past me holding a tray of takoyaki. My heart skips a beat. Where did they get those from? Then I see the stall selling them tucked around the side of another. "Scrap that. I'm getting takoyaki. Meet you back here?"

Rose nods and we go our separate ways.

The three of us find a quiet space to eat. There's an area with chairs and tables, but it's packed. We follow the example of a lot of other people and take a spot on the floor. The takoyaki is hot and soft, doughy, chewy and fishy. It's amazing. We agree we could all do with something to drink and spot a bubble tea stall.

"We need a plan of attack," Rose says, as we amble along, taking big sips of our drinks. "Otherwise I we're just going to wander around aimlessly all day."

"Shall we head over the road?" Leon suggests. "Take our time over there and then come back here again? There were some stalls I spotted I want to take another look at, but I want to *do* something first."

"Like what?" I ask.

"Genny says you can try out some of the stuff in the gaming section - like new games."

"Let's go there next then."

We cross the corridor onto the other side of the convention centre, which looks and feels a lot less crowded. There's more space between the stalls and less people. The sight of the open space makes something in my chest loosen. It's easier to breathe and my head is clearer.

It's obvious which side is the gaming section. There are banners for upcoming games hanging from the ceiling over stalls sporting the big console branding. There are also stalls selling D&D dice and merch, and a playing area for *Magic: The Gathering.*

We jump onto the end of the line to try PlayStation VR. I've never played on VR before and leave the demo with my head spinning a bit, but grinning. Rose looks a little sick from the experience. Leon and I drag Rose around the rest of the gaming section, stopping to play on the portable consoles and browse the tables of video and board games on offer. Leon is the first of us to make a purchase, buying an indie game which looks pretty cool.

There are more stalls on this side selling nerdy stuff.

We take our time browsing these ones, pointing stuff out to each other. I send a photo of a Tetsuya 2 plushie to Fran, who replies with lots of heart eyes emojis and an invitation for me to come to hers to meet Reg. I reply with the thrashing Kermit GIF and a message filled with lots of exclamation marks accepting her invitation.

We've stopped in front of a stall selling some cute LBGT+ badges, t-shirts and other items, when someone says, "Excuse me."

We all turn around and there's a girl dressed in Lolita clothes, holding a closed frilly umbrella and her phone. She's looking at Rose, who is blinking at her in surprise.

"Would it be OK if I take a photo of you?" she asks.

Rose blinks a few more times. "Of course," she says.

The girl smiles. "Thank you. Your cosplay's amazing. I love *Little Witch Academia*."

"Thank you," Rose says. "I love it too. Well, obviously I do otherwise I wouldn't be cosplaying as one of the characters."

The girl laughs and then gets her compact DSLR camera out her bag. Rose poses in the middle of the corridor between the stalls and the girl snaps the photo. Rose asks if she can take a photo of the girl in return, which she agrees to. As they exchange social media handles, the smile on Rose's face makes my heart soar.

"See," I tell her, bumping her hip with mine, "your cosplay's great."

The more we wander, the more people ask to take photos with Rose – at one point a woman with a big video camera asks to take some shots of her in the aisle and Rose almost self-combusts with excitement. Leon gets his photo taken with a couple of groups of *Dragon Ball* cosplayers. He takes it gracefully, but I can tell he's not too bothered about it. But Rose's smile grows brighter with every photo she is asked to pose for and every social media handle she notes into her phone. I couldn't be prouder of my little protégé than right now. Look at how much she's grown.

When I'm waiting for Rose to have her photo taken again, I'm aware that a person with short brown hair wearing a non-binary flag pin walking past me has paused. I meet their eye. They're glancing at my t-shirt. It's one that I bought on Redbubble – it's light blue and has a dolphin, a shark, a butterfly, a penguin and a killer whale on it. To the everyday person, that's all the design is, but to an otaku it means so much more.

As they meet my eye, I can see that they get it.

"Is your t-shirt a *Free!* reference?" they ask.

I grin. "It sure is."

"It's so awesome," they say. "Have you seen *50% Off*?" I nod, probably far too enthusiastically. "I saw someone cosplaying as Thugisa a few minutes ago."

My heartbeat actually quickens. "Oh my god. I need to go find them."

They smile and say they hope I enjoy the rest of con. They leave me grinning like a fool. I can't believe I just spoke to someone who got my *Free!* t-shirt and also knew who Thugisa is. Holy cow balls. Is this what other people feel like every day? Because it's fucking awesome.

On the same side of the gaming section is a collection of stalls promoting movie stuff. Most of them are the big studios, apart from one stall which is a licenser of anime films and shows. At the back of that bit is a very spacious section with a couple of tables and crowd barriers. On the map it's marked as the autograph area. To the right, at the far end of the hall, is an area that's been curtained off. There's a sign on the curtain that reads, "Main stage".

We check out who's in the signing area and what talks are on the main stage, but decide we're not bothered about stopping. We cross back over the first side of the hall we tried to tackle and start afresh. I stop at a stall selling art tablets and make Leon and Rose wait for me for ages while I try out a couple of items. Of course I end up falling in love with the most expensive option, but isn't that just typical? I make a note of the product but it will take me forever to save up to buy one.

We find the Comic Village, which we must have completely skipped. We wander through the stalls selling independent comics. I buy a couple of volumes that look interesting and end up gushing to the vendors about our favourite manga series. I spend fifteen minutes talking with one about art styles and only drag myself away when Leon gives me a little tug on the arm to urge me on. I move away, grinning and dizzy with happiness at the moment of intense connection.

We come across the bookseller stalls selling English licensed manga and split up. Leon just buys volume one of *Devilman*, whereas Rose and I walk away with our bags bulging with books and our purses significantly lighter. And they keep getting lighter as we take a second turn of the stalls.

"I need a sit down," Rose says when we've finished our circulation of that side of the hall.

"I wouldn't say no to a quiet moment," Leon says.

I nod, although I don't really want to stop. I want to keep walking around until I turn into a skeleton and then crumble into dust. I want my ashes to be laid to rest in this hall, so I can haunt this place for eternity, attending every con that takes place here.

But when we find a quiet space on the floor near the comic village to have a rest, a wave of exhaustion hits me as I sit down. Rose takes out the snacks she bought at the sweet stall and hands them around. I suck on the hard sweets as I stare into the hall, grateful for the sugar. The person who complemented my *Free!* t-shirt is behind one of the comic stalls with a Filipino woman with green-tinted black hair. Their stall is piled with comic books that look to be part of the same series. There's a big banner behind them that says "Mizu no Sekai: It's so aqua punk!". They have cardboard cut-outs of some of their characters behind their stall. They look kinda cool - a teen girl with half a shaved head with webbed hands holding a trident, a short girl with a beaming smile, a teen boy with a fin-like Mohawk and webbed hands, and a dog with a wide Y-shaped tail like a whale's.

"Hey there!"

Paige and Genny join our floor circle, groaning as they sit down.

"I always forget about the con fatigue," Genny says, rubbing her feet. "How have you enjoyed your first con?"

"I don't want it to end," I say.

"Where can we apply to live here?" Rose asks.

"Well, it doesn't end until they shut the doors," Paige says. "You've still got plenty of time. By the way, Clo, I've been keeping up with your art blog. It's amazing. I love your style."

This praise, coming from Paige, who is one of the best artists I know, gives me such a rush.

"Thank you."

"Genny and I were wondering if you would be interested in doing some work for us at some point?"

"We think your style would really fit our next project," Genny adds.

Everyone stares at me. They're all waiting for me to say something, but all I can do is blink.

Did they just say what I think they said?

Is this real?

"Clo?" Paige asks, her forehead furrowed in concern.

At last I blurt out, "That would be so cool."

Genny laughs. "Great. We can get you started over the summer, if you want? Then you can do some more after your A levels if you're still interested."

I shrug. "I can keep going over the school year. I can fit it in."

"Let's see how it goes," Paige says. "We don't want your mum to exorcise us if you fail your exams."

"How's the current game coming along?" Leon asks, popping another sweet into his mouth.

Genny and Paige grin at each other.

"It's almost done," Genny says. "Aaaand, last year we met someone at a gaming convention. They got excited about the concept so we showed it to them."

"And they're going to publish it!" Paige cries, throwing her hands up in the air. "They're going to bring out physical copies of it on the Switch! They're going to throw *marketing* money at us."

Genny wipes away an imaginary tear. "I can't believe we're finally marketable."

"That's amazing!" I cry.

"Congrats," Rose says, grinning.

"That's huge," Leon says, holding up his hand. "Congrats, sis." Genny high fives him.

"It's the step up we really needed," Genny says, "and if it all succeeds then we can do so much more with the company." The married couple exchange another look – it's the sort of look that makes my stomach flip. Something's up.

"Do you want to tell them?" Paige asks.

"Tell us what?" Leon asks.

"So," Genny says, "you know that old barn that Dad's been umming and ahhing forever about converting into something?"

"Yeah," Leon says slowly.

"We're going to rent it off him and turn it into a studio office and apartment."

"Oh," Leon says, but his brow remains furrowed.

"You're moving back to Harboury?" I ask.

"We're fed up of living in London," Paige says. "The future is all home working anyway."

Genny wraps an arm around Leon's neck and pulls him to her. "What's the matter, little bro? You not pleased that your big sis is moving back home?"

"No," Leon says, although he's pouting and his eyes are downcast. "It's just that... Dad didn't consult me about this."

"You're seventeen." Genny pokes him in the ribs. "The farm's not yours yet."

"I know. I know it's just that..."

The look on Leon's face makes my heart clench. He looks afraid, and I don't understand why until Genny says in a low voice, "Don't worry. I won't be laying a finger on it," that I understand. As Leon's expression relaxes the excitement wells up inside me.

"I'm so happy!" I squeal. "We're going to be all together! It'll be like Christmas Eve every single day!"

"We can finally settle that score," Paige says.

"Damn right," I say, and our hands clasp with a satisfying *slap!*

"Oh god." Genny sighs. "I should have put this in the cons column when we were weighing up whether to move."

"What was at the top of the pros column?" Rose asks.

"Clover's baking," Paige and Genny say together.

"I can confirm that it's worth moving from London for," Rose says.

My head is in danger of splitting from how wide I'm smiling right now.

Chapter 40

Rose

Half an hour before closing time finds us all sitting in a corner of the hall, drinking ramune. The energy we had at the start of the day has drained away and I feel if I stop consuming sugar I'm going to melt. I can't count how many times we've toured the halls, wandering up and down the stall aisles. I know the ExCeL Centre as well as I do my own house.

"I'm ready to leave now," Leon says.

I've also been thinking that for a little while now. My feet ache and I've got the beginnings of a headache behind my eyes, but I've been holding back saying it because even though my body is telling me it's time to go, my heart doesn't want to leave.

Although the thought of collapsing into bed right now is a welcome one. What time is it anyway?

"When did it get to be half past six?" I ask, looking down at my phone.

Genny laughs. "Con tends to do that to you. I think I'm just about beat."

"Me too." Paige yawns.

"But I don't want to leave," Clover cries.

"You've only got half an hour until they close," Genny says. "Make the most of it."

But even Clover's body has given up, because as much as I can see she wants to run around the centre for the last few minutes, she slumps back against the wall instead.

Leon collects our empty ramune bottles and throws them in the recycling bins.

"Come on," he says and holds a hand out to Clover. He hauls her to her feet as the rest of us stand up.

"But I don't want to leave," Clover says as we make our way towards the toilets to get changed. Back in our street clothes on the DLR train, Clover keeps her face turned towards the window and keeps wiping her eyes. Leon puts an arm around her shoulders and allows her to lean on him. My throat tightens as we watch Custom House station with the cosplayers standing on the platform shrink into the distance.

"There's always next year," Leon tells Clover.

"Or October if you're desperate," Paige adds.

"I think I might be," Clover says.

We say goodbye to Paige and Genny at Poplar station. Genny whispers something in Clover's ear that makes her smile and laugh, and then we're waving to them as the train pulls out of the platform. When we get back to my house, we drink tea together in the living room, too exhausted to talk.

"Anyone hungry?" I ask. Both Leon and Clover shake their heads. I'm not either, but I just wanted to check. Can't believe how much we ate throughout the day.

"Guys," Clover says, as we climb the stairs to our bedrooms, "that was the best day of my life. And it was even more special because I got to share it with you." She opens up her arms. "Group hug?"

Leon and I crush her between us without hesitation.

When I crawl into my bed, my body is so heavy with sleep I start to drift off in seconds. Then I remember I have to take out my contacts. Once that's done, my head hits the pillow and I'm out.

I'm glad we didn't book onto a train for the return back to Bucks, because getting out the house the next day is a chore.

I lie in bed for ages, listening to the sounds of the neighbourhood waking up on a Saturday morning. My limbs ache with the same intensity as if I've been for a long run. Then I hear either Clover or Leon use the bathroom. It's time to get up.

I open my door at the same time as Leon opens his. Residue of whatever product he used yesterday is still in his hair. Half of it lies flat against his head from sleeping on it, while the other half stands on end. We blink at each other. He looks as tired as I am.

"Morning," I say.

"Morning," he grunts.

When Clover emerges from the bathroom, she looks like she's still asleep.

"I had a dream about comic con last night," she says.

"Oh no," Leon says.

"They decided to make it a permanent thing, so we all moved there and lived in houses that overlooked the hall – like a massive market square. It was so beautiful."

"It wouldn't be so special if it was always there," I say.

Clover nods and slumps back to her room.

We have breakfast, wash up, pack up and clean up, and then head to Euston.

Once we've settled on the train, Clover finally gets over her heartbreak and starts recounting everything that happened yesterday. I must admit that I'm only half listening. I'm so listless. Exhausted. All the excitement that has building up for the past four months has drained out of me. Exams are done. Con's done.

Now I'm ready to sleep for the whole of the summer.

My phone buzzes in my pocket. It's a Facebook message from Ari.

```
Ari
Is this you at 1:04?
```

Then he shares the link to a Facebook video.

What the hell is this? Confused, I click on the link. Then my stomach drops when the link takes me to the MCM Comic Con Facebook page. The sound plays on low as the video starts. It's a montage video from yesterday, which starts with the doors of the ExCeL Centre opening and allowing the first flood of people to come inside. There are shots of the stalls, the food, the banners and the gaming section, the comic village and then the cosplayers.

Then, at 1:04, a girl dressed in a white shirt, navy waistcoat and skirt comes on screen. She's got the brightest smile on her face as she twirls around, showing off her cosplay, and then starts pointing her wand at the camera.

Holy shit, that's me.

I stare at the video, watching it play over and over. With each replay, my heart beats faster and my stomach rolls higher.

How did Ari see this video? What if someone else sees it?

By the time Ari's second message pings up on screen my hands are shaking.

Ari
If it is you look awesome
Did you make your cosplay yourself?

A second message snaps me out of my panic mode and as I stare at it, a sense of calm washes over me.

I look awesome?

The comment takes me by surprise. I mean, I *know* I look awesome, but I didn't think anyone else would think that.

My phone is heavy in my hands as I pause with my thumbs hanging above the keyboard, thinking through my reply.

At last a single thought pushes its way through the others: *Fuck it.*

My thumbs fly across the keys as I type my response.

Rose
Yup that's me
Was at Con yesterday
Heading back from London now
And yes made the whole costume myself - apart from the shirt

Not giving Ari a chance to reply, I go back to the video and hit the share button. I post it on my timeline with the message:

Amazing time at @LondonComicCon yesterday. Wish I had booked to go for the whole weekend rather than just yesterday. My first cosplay also made it into the below video. Check me out at 1:04.

I hit post and immediately check into my Amazon account, go to my wish list and hit the "Add to basket" button next to the Lolita dress. A few more taps on my phone and the dress is ordered. The big knot of anxiety in my chest unravels all at once and I sit back with a sigh. Leon and Clover are staring at me with concern. I must have looked pretty intense just then.

"You aright?" Leon asks.

I grin. "Of course. Never better."

Leon's dad picks us up at the station in a battered four-by-four truck thing that looks out of place in the town. Bonnie and Alexander are in the back and greet Clover and Leon with as much excitement as they greet them.

"Bonnie's been helping me out on the farm while your mum's at work," Leon's dad explains. "Alexander's been showing her the ropes."

"Is that right?" Clover coos and rubs Bonnie's side as the brown Labrador pants and wags her tail enthusiastically.

Leon's dad drops us off at Clover's front door. Clover and Leon knock their forearms together. I wave goodbye to Leon. Clover and I go indoors with Bonnie. We drop our bags in the hallway and head straight to the kitchen to put the kettle on. Without the need to communicate to each other how we feel, we sit down at the kitchen table and drink our tea in a comfortable exhausted silence.

All my thoughts are occupied by a playback of yesterday's events, and if I know my cousin - which I do by this point - she's also replaying the whole day.

"I saw the video you shared on your timeline," Clover says, breaking the silence. "It's so cool you made it into the official video. Although—" she takes a sip of her tea, "—I was surprised you shared it."

I wrap my hands around my mug.

"Ari sent the video to me," I say. "I must admit, it freaked me out at first, but then he said I looked awesome and asked me questions about my cosplay, and then I started thinking about how Maryam reacted when we told her we were going to con. And I started thinking about everyone we saw yesterday - everyone dressed in their cosplay on the Tube, all the stall owners and the organisers of the event who made it all possible. All of them hold the same love for nerdy stuff that we do. And... I guess it made me realise that I'm not ashamed of what I like anymore."

Clover nods. "Being there yesterday made me feel the same – seeing how many other people are into animanga. It made me so proud to be part of the same community." She smiles. "I don't feel like trash anymore, or that I'm the only person in the world who likes what I like. I feel like..."

"Gold?"

Clover's eyes light up. "Yeah. Gold." She smiles as she pulls out her phone. "I like that." She taps away on her phone for a bit, and then my own phone buzzes on the table.

@otaku_gold02 has sent you a message.

otaku_gold02 Let's go to Comic Con again in October :)

"That handle suits you a lot more," I say. "Although you realise you'll have to relink everything on your blog now."

"Ugh," Clover groans. "I didn't think about that. What a pain." She puts her phone down on the table. "I also had a revelation yesterday about what I want to do at university..." She struggles to get the words out, so I stay quiet while she turns them over. At last she says, "I want to do art, or animation. So I can work at Paige's and Genny's gaming company, or one like it, or do something in the gaming or animation industry. I want a life where I always feel like I'm at comic con."

"That would be a good choice for you." I take a long drink from my tea and when I put the mug down, I end up speaking to my reflection rather than Clover. "I've been having second thoughts about what I want to do at uni. I thought I wanted to be a lawyer, but now after making my cosplay, and speaking to everyone yesterday about their cosplays... it's made me think that maybe I want to do something different." I take a deep breath. "The idea of spending my life doing law makes me so sad."

Clover smiles at me over the top of her mug. "I wholeheartedly support your decision. But what would you study instead?"

"I'm not sure yet. I might take a year out and work. Take a look at all the world can offer me."

"Wow. OK. That's a plan, then. Although, poor Grandma is gonna be so pissed."

I meet Clover's eyes and the two of us burst into laughter.

About the author

Adelaide Newton is an author based in Bristol, UK. They are a Bath Spa Creative Writing BA graduate. At the crack of dawn and at the weekend, you can find them typing away at their WIP. By day, they work in marketing. You can find them online at www.adelaidenewton.co.uk. You can connect with Adelaide on Twitter, Instagram, and TikTok at @bookworm_scribe. Or you can drop them an email at adelaide.newton@hotmail.co.uk. And although they use Adelaide on their covers, they much prefer being called Addy.

Enjoyed this book?

As a self-published author, I don't have the powerful machine of a publishing company behind me to generate a buzz around my books - a buzz that will put my book into the hands of more readers. Therefore, if you enjoyed this book, I would be very grateful if you could spend a couple of minutes leaving a review on the Amazon page. This will help bring the book to the attention of future readers. Thank you.

Printed in Great Britain
by Amazon